When
the Warrior
Returns

When the Warrior Returns

Making the Transition at Home

Edited by Nathan D. Ainspan and Walter E. Penk
Foreword by Patty Shinseki

NAVAL INSTITUTE PRESS | ANNAPOLIS, MARYLAND

This book has been brought to publication with the
generous assistance of Marguerite and Gerry Lenfest.

Naval Institute Press
291 Wood Road
Annapolis, MD 21402

Library of Congress Cataloging-in-Publication Data
When the warrior returns : making the transition at home / edited by Nathan D. Ainspan
and Walter E. Penk.
    p. cm.
  Includes bibliographical references and index.
  ISBN 978-1-61251-090-3 (pbk. : alk. paper) — ISBN 978-1-61251-091-0 (e-book)
1. Veterans' families—United States—Handbooks, manuals, etc. 2. Veterans—United
States—Handbooks, manuals, etc. 3. Families of military personnel—Handbooks,
manuals, etc. 4. Families of military personnel—Services for—United States. 5. Soldiers—
Family relationships—United States—Handbooks, manuals, etc. 6. Veterans—United
States—Psychology. 7. Veterans—Services for—United States. I. Ainspan, Nathan D.
(Nathan David), 1966- II. Penk, Walter.
  UB403.W52 2012
  362.860973—dc23
                              2012018293

∞ This paper meets the requirements of ANSI/NISO z39.48-1992 (Permanence of Paper).
Printed in the United States of America.

20 19 18 17 16 15 14 13 12   9 8 7 6 5 4 3 2 1
First printing

The views expressed in this book do not reflect the opinions of the Department of Veterans Affairs,
National Defense University, Uniformed Services University, United States Air Force, United States
Army, United States Navy, United States Marines Corps, the Office of the Secretary of Defense, or the
Department of Defense. Government agencies, military branches, and universities are listed for affilia-
tion purposes only.

In Memoriam
David Elliot Cabrera
Lieutenant Colonel
United States Army

The Cabrera family: Corbin, Roanin, August, Maxwell, David, and Gillian

Perhaps it reinforces the need for a book like this that we dedicate it to Lt. Col. David Cabrera (the lead author of the first chapter) and to his family. While the editors were completing the final edits to his chapter he was killed in Kabul, Afghanistan, on 29 October 2011 by a vehicle-borne suicide attack on his convoy. This was his third deployment. David is survived by his wife (August), their two sons, Maxwell and Roanin, and David's older son and daughter, Corbin and Gillian.

David was from Florida and graduated from Texas A&M University with a degree in psychology in 1992. He earned a master's degree in social work from the University of Texas at Arlington, and in 2006 completed his PhD in social work at the Catholic University of America in Washington, D.C. He joined the U.S. Army in 1996 as a social work officer in the Medical Service Corps. He served in assignments in Germany, Washington, D.C., Fort Lewis, and Bethesda, Maryland, where he was the director of social work and assistant professor in the Department of Family Medicine at the Uniformed Services University of Health Sciences, at the time of his last deployment. David was deployed in Hungary, Croatia, and Bosnia as part of Operation Joint Endeavor/Guard in the mid-1990s, and his second deployment was with the 3/2 Stryker Brigade in northern Iraq in 2006.

Much can be (and has been) said about David as a great husband, father, friend, and adventurer. However, given our focus on the dedication required of service members and their families, perhaps the best tribute to David came from Col. Derrick Arincorayan, the Army's chief social work officer, in an e-mail to the Army's social work officers on 31 October 2011:

> I want you all to know that early this year LTC Cabrera called me and asked me if I needed someone to deploy and requested that I consider him for future deployments. . . . I thanked him for stepping forward and informed him to standby as I was processing the tasker. David was on his 2nd Combat Tour and in country for less than 30 days. . . . Since April 2010 when I took the job of the Social Work Consultant, I have received deployment taskers almost monthly and sometimes weekly depending on the OPTEMPO and time of year. These deployment taskers weigh heavy on my heart especially when I have to task officers who have served on multiple combat tours. What has been very difficult for me to bear is that David was a part of a rare group of social work officers who were willing to go back to combat without any prompt from me or the Army. It takes a special breed of soldier and officer to do this knowing the risk that lies ahead each and every time he or she deploys. I will be forever indebted to David for making the ultimate sacrifice.
>
> I will end here with this final note. Each time I hear [of] the death of a U.S. Soldier killed in action I feel farther away from home. Today I feel even further away from home because we lost one of our brothers, a Social Work Officer. David died serving his country and his fellow soldiers in a role that only few are called to do and have the art or skill to execute. Please keep David and his Family in your prayers.
>
> David, until we meet again!! I will see you on the high ground!! *Imua Lahui Kekoa Laau* (Forward moves the Healing Warrior!!!).

David is not the only one who gave his life for the country. His wife August and their children—like so many others touched by the losses and tragedies of this and other wars—have and will continue to give their lives for their country as they face the years ahead without their husband and father. We give to them our deepest and most heartfelt thanks and sympathies, and we dedicate this book to them and to the memory of their loved one, Lt. Col. David Cabrera.

Until we meet again, my brother,

COL. ANTHONY COX
United States Army

This book is dedicated to my son,
Isaac Mark Doyle Ainspan,
three years old at the time of this book's release.
My feelings for him—and his relationship with everyone in my family—
helped me gain a personal understanding of what
our warrior families are experiencing and
the necessity for a book like this.

With all the love that a proud father can offer,
NATHAN D. AINSPAN, PhD

For Dolores Krajicek Little Penk,
her children, Judith, John, George, and Thomas, and
her grandchildren, Babette, Rochelle, and Matthew

WALTER PENK, PhD, ABPP

Contents

Illustrations and Tables

Foreword

"The equipment won't always be perfect, my orders won't always be perfect, and the organization we create won't always be perfect. What has to be perfect is that trust with the families."

GENERAL MARTY DEMPSEY,
CHAIRMAN, JOINT CHIEFS OF STAFF

More than a decade of conflict has revealed how deeply the effects of war have tested the endurance of today's families and shaped their thoughts about war and service in the military itself. Military families serve and sacrifice right along with the men and women in uniform who serve our nation. They demonstrate extraordinary courage, and provide unwavering love and support without fanfare. Such remarkable strength and resilience deserve our deepest gratitude, and my respect for them will be forever unchanged. The military family support environment has evolved since 1965 when I began my journey as an Army wife. Central to that change was the military's growing recognition of the military family's value and importance to mission readiness. My own early encounters with military life were less affirming.

Thanksgiving 1965: The 25th Infantry Division, based at Schofield barracks, Hawaii, had been secretly alerted for combat duty in Vietnam. All preparations were done in secret, oblivious to this new science teacher at a local high school who awaited the arrival of her husband from Airborne and Ranger training in Georgia. The stark reality that we were going to war greeted us in mid-December when we were reunited, and Ric reported in to his first duty station at Schofield Barracks. With a mere two weeks before deployment . . . long hours readying equipment; eleven immunizations in one day with understandable after-effects; preparing uniforms and supplies; steeling ourselves mentally and emotionally; no time for Christmas, except for a small tree . . . it was frenetic, intense, a blur.

New Year's 1966: The continuous, deep rumble of heavy military equipment shook the ground, seeming to settle uneasily on my chest. The incessant drone of engines filled the quiet Wahiawa, Hawaii, neighborhood. Needing company, I went to spend the night with my sister in Honolulu. Driving past Honolulu Harbor, I was caught completely off guard by the sight of massive transport ships assembled there. Intense spotlights illuminated equipment and personnel of the 25th Infantry Division being loaded on board those vessels. My husband was one of those Soldiers boarding the USS *General Walker* that night, a new Army second lieutenant, barely seven months since commissioning at West Point and our wedding. Those bewildering sounds and images are etched in my memory, along with the emptiness, fear of the unknown, and feeling of total unpreparedness for what was to come. Thus, began my journey as a military spouse, young, naïve, alone, and frightened . . . which would in time grow into a life's calling.

We all grew up quickly. Our husbands lost their youth in Vietnam and returned from combat changed in many ways. There were no family support mechanisms in place; communications and notifications were slow and spotty, at best. We did not know to expect otherwise and did not know to ask. Most spouses went home to live with their families for the duration. Families were not a priority in the draft military, with most married within the officer and senior non-commissioned officer ranks. In contrast, today's smaller, professional volunteer force, comprised of the Active component, National Guard, and Reserves, is 54 percent married, and families are considered an integral part of mission readiness, with family support services organized to enhance well-being.

Summer 1971: For us, two combat tours in Vietnam appeared to be carbon copy chapters . . . two children, each born during my husband's deployments; two serious injuries followed by long convalescences; uncertainty and adjustments were the norm. Our future was not promising! The permanent injuries put us on a track headed out of the Army, despite a request for a waiver to remain on active duty. We were surprised and relieved when word arrived that a few amputees were being allowed to remain in uniform, Ric being one of them. The news triggered a reversal in plans for our family. Often, I believe we are forced to become masters at adaptability out of necessity. For our family, it was a welcomed blessing. The rest is history.

Wounded warriors currently have a first option to remain in uniform, if they choose to and are physically able to meet the standard. Still the process of recovery is long, the effects of emotional injuries are complex, and the forever impact upon the family and children can be overwhelming. Each injury is personal, each recovery unique, and each family approaches its challenges in its own way to care for their loved one. Our own adult children still remember the impact of their dad's injuries and recovery. They and other children of combat veterans experience the impacts of war even long after the service member returns. Children are often innocent participants to changes in the home, and they deserve nurturing, relevant, and timely responses to foster resilience and offer hope.

Military spouses learn from those who precede us, modeling lessons learned at each posting, including the development of fundamental leadership skills. Close friendships become stand-in families for those serving far from home, especially overseas. Volunteer networks, driven by necessity, augment the military support systems, which in time become absorbed into the institutional systems themselves, as resources are allocated toward supporting the families. Military spouse volunteers take on leadership responsibilities, serving as ambassadors, as personal witnesses, and as stewards to the needs of growing numbers of serving families, while often managing careers, households, and raising the families alone.

November 9, 1989: The end of the Cold War brought large reductions in force structure but an increase in military operations stressing downsizing systems and the people in them. Training requirements meant multiple absences, and numerous military operations, including the Gulf War and the Balkans, conveyed a sense of perpetual turbulence. Spouse leaders learn life lessons that often far exceed their ages or levels of experience. They serve as confidants and are the likely conduits to the professionals and programs necessary to address the complex issues shared in private. They voluntarily assume positions of responsibility, not wearing the uniform or rank that denotes authority. Yet, they succeed, knowing that they are able to contribute by helping to affect an environment in which people are inspired to operate as a team. Fostering a sense of community, they eagerly reach out to support one another in the good times and in moments of greatest need.

September 11, 2001: We all know where we were and how we reacted to the events that day. Personal connections to dear ones who perished, the severely injured, traumatized, and the gripping emotional aftermath will be forever with us. Amid the devastation, fear, and uncertainty, we saw firsthand the courage and compassion of people. They put aside their own needs; they revealed an indomitable human spirit that offered a flicker of hope to those suffering unspeakable loss during one of the darkest times in our recent history. Once more, marshaling strength and resolve, they began their preparations for what was likely to be the next war.

June 11, 2003: We had begun our military journey in Vietnam; we had come full circle to retire in the midst of Afghanistan and Iraq. For thirty-eight years and thirty-one changes of address, the undeniable dedication and determination of those who choose to serve inspired and motivated us, and instilled a pride that binds and endures. Just as bonds of trust are developed among service members, spouses and family members also cultivate strong connections, embracing the values of service to something greater than self. Through these associations, strong ties are created that last a lifetime and remain long after uniforms are shed. Our children, whose transitions through eight and nine different schools respectively, feel that Army life broadened their horizons and instilled a curiosity about a world they now describe to our seven grandchildren with color and vibrancy.

The greatest gift was being called to serve. The challenges accompanying such service are best accommodated through supportive loved ones, caring communities, and compassionate responses that can result in positive outcomes. We are blessed in so many ways . . . so many people have touched our lives and enriched our experiences with purpose and meaning. We are truly grateful, especially for our good fortune to be called to continue to serve. I think of the thousands of military spouses, children, and families who await the safe return of their loved ones still, and those whose loved ones did not return.

The distinguished editors and authors of *When the Warrior Returns: Making the Transition at Home* bring to life all that a military family experiences and more. They present an important and comprehensive discussion about the courageous men and women who serve our nation today and their families and children, the consequences of deployment, and the issues that await them on the home front. Dealing with the intricacies of reintegration following long absences can be complex, involving the sensitivities of restoring a sense of balance within the family. The chapters address the many facets of military and family life, the diversity of the force, and the complexities of current issues facing them. Any transition presents its challenges, and a transition from the uniform to the civilian workforce or higher education is especially so, often requiring delicate navigation through a maze of choices.

How I wish a resource such as this existed during my time. It is personal for me to note the viable solutions and tools they provide as key to ensuring smooth transitions, enhancing personal relationships, and strengthening family function. The authors have a familiarity with the issues, and offer realistic and practical discussions that reflect the depth of their understanding and a dedication to their work. This book provides considerations for further study, partnership, and collaboration for helping healthy systems and people to grow, respond, and adapt to changing circumstances. Its guidance will be a valuable tool for all who seek answers for personal or professional use . . . and gives hope and promise to all who are *making a transition.*

Patty Shinseki, Board Member,
The Military Child Education Coalition

Acknowledgments

One idea that we emphasize throughout this book is the necessity of teamwork to meet the challenges of transition out of the military. This book is also the product of teamwork. You will see the editors' names on the cover of this book and the names of the fifty contributors in the list of contributors in the back of the book. But there are other members of the team that put this book together who deserve to be mentioned

This book would not have been possible—or even exist—without our editor, Adam Kane, at Naval Institute Press. It was Adam who first approached us with the initial idea for a book for family members, guided it through the acquisition process at NIP, and served as an invaluable resource, a great sounding board, and indispensable source of support during the two years this book was in progress.

We are also grateful to our copy editor, Jehanne Moharram, who reviewed our work with her careful eyes, caught many things that escaped our review, responded to our questions, and accepted our revisions, the revisions of revisions, and, "Oh, just one last tiny revision." For all of that, we thank her.

We both want to thank our wives—Debbie Ann Doyle Ainspan, PhD, and Dolores Krajicek Little Penk, PhD, for their support throughout this whole process.

And finally, but especially, we express our gratitude to the readers of this book—the men and women of our armed forces and their families who stand by them and together help keep our families safe and secure.

Thank you all.

Nathan D. Ainspan, PhD, and Walter E. Penk, PhD

Acknowledgments for Chapter 7

We would like to thank the following for their contribution to this book chapter: Judi Dekle, Senior Program Analyst, Department of Defense, Office of Family Policy, Children and Youth; Ryan Yarnell, Financial Readiness Specialist, Fort

Meade, Maryland; Lee Acker, Financial Specialist, Fleet and Family Support Center, Naval Support Activity (NSA), Bethesda, Maryland; Yuko Whitestone; Julie Yates, Life Skills Family Employment Program Manager, Fort Meade; Catherine F. Ferran, Chief, Army Community Service, Fort Meade; MA1 Brian Necaise, Security Officer, Uniformed Services University of the Health Sciences (USUHS), Bethesda; and Lt. Col. Curtis Strader, United States Marine Corps Headquarters, Combat and Operational Stress Control. Portions of this chapter were presented at the 2011 Department of Defense/U.S. Department of Agriculture Family Resilience Conference: Forging the Partnership, on 27 April 2011 in Chicago.

Introduction

To the military families reading this book: We offer our respect and gratitude for your family's dedication and commitment to our nation. We do not have to tell you what deployment feels like—you have experienced it, and probably more than just once. You understand perfectly the old line about the family serving and sacrificing just as much (and sometimes even more so) than the family member in uniform.

You have learned what to expect with each deployment and by now the whole process has become second nature to your family. But while your family may be old hands at deployment, the reintegration process—particularly if your service member is leaving the armed forces for good to transition into civilian life—may be a completely new experience for you. The whole experience of returning and reintegrating into civilian life in America may be more foreign to you and your service member than the conditions were in Iraq or Afghanistan, or wherever your family member may have served.

Your family is probably asking some of these questions:

- After months or even years apart how can I reconnect with my husband?
- How can my wife describe what she did over there to our young kids?
- My son has been in the Army his whole life and is only thirty. Now that he is leaving the Army where can he get a job?
- My daughter has heard about the GI Bill. How can she use it to go to college?

Your service member may have been injured or wounded while in uniform and now, in addition to the questions listed above, your family has additional concerns:

- My partner has been acting strange lately. Is this a case of post-traumatic stress disorder (PTSD) or a traumatic brain injury (TBI)? What can I do to help?
- My boyfriend was injured and lost a leg. Since I am not his wife, what rights do I have to see and help him?

- My husband has severe injuries from an improvised explosive device and uses a wheelchair. Can he still get a job doing something he loves? Can he go to school with these injuries?

Suicide among returning service members has also increased dramatically: We are now seeing more service members die by their own hands than those who were killed in combat. Illegal drug use, abuse of legal drugs, and reckless behaviors (like driving dangerously) are also rampant among returning service members. Your family member may be displaying some of these behaviors and you may be concerned if they are indicative of more serious problems.

We assembled fifty authors to write this book to provide you with answers to these questions and many more. We realized that, while you have access to many books and other sources of information during your family member's deployment, it is hard to find this kind of information to help guide you through the reintegration process and help you understand and cope with what comes next. Our authors come from every branch of the military (including many who were deployed during the current conflicts), the Department of Veterans Affairs, family members of deployed service members, and from leaders of organizations dedicated to helping families like yours. Those who wrote came together out of their concern and desire to provide assistance for the military, veterans, and their families. We address different aspects of reintegration from the logistical (i.e., getting a job) to the emotional (how to cope with new feelings about returning home). We also offer suggestions on how you and your family can improve your resiliency so that you will be better equipped to take on these challenges and struggles, as well as the joys that you can share being together as a family.

Our objective in this book echoes the words of the Constitution your service member defended and protected in uniform: We hope this book will help you achieve life, liberty, and the pursuit of happiness that is the center of our citizenship together. We understand that your family member has been through difficult and dangerous times. While the reintegration and the next steps your family faces may be difficult, they will not be as difficult or dangerous as your time supporting your family member in service and in deployment. In addition you will be together and can draw on each other for support now. This book will show you how to do this.

Tens of thousands of service members were injured or disabled during their deployment, and because of this we also have chapters on how this will impact your family and how caring for a wounded warrior will impact the rest of the family. In other chapters we take on the difficult topics of suicide, drug abuse, personal relationships, and even your post-deployment sex life. Your children will also be impacted by your service member's reintegration, so three chapters are dedicated to helping them through their concerns. The military has changed in composition so that our current fighting force is different than it has been in the past. The final chapters of the book look at some of the new types of military families that have not been addressed in the past—the families of female warriors, the families of the National Guard and Reserves, and the families of unmarried and blended-family warriors. We hope to address the homecoming needs of all military and veterans who, with their families, are returning from war to times of peace.

The material presented in the following chapters covers a lot of ground and is quite thorough. We want to be completely honest and present the resources in these chapters with a message to you: The Web sites, hot lines, and organizations described and recommended in these chapters are overwhelmed with the sheer volume of service members reintegrating back home and the number and range of problems they are having. While the federal government and its agencies have created most of these resources, many may not be sufficiently funded to handle the intense demand, others may seem overly bureaucratic and difficult to deal with, and some may not as yet operate as efficiently as they should be operating. The two editors of this book work for federal agencies focused on service members and veterans (Nathan works as a civilian for the Army and Walter has spent five decades in the VA), and we both freely admit that it is hard for agencies to fully provide the resources your family desperately needs at times when wars are ending and civilian needs are increasing. For one example, many of the authors in this book recommend the Military OneSource as a comprehensive location of helpful information for anyone in uniform. We have it listed as the first source in our Appendix, but if you talk to some military families you may find some who have not had good experiences with it.

Therefore we present the material in this book with a caveat. The information contained in these resources may be helpful to your family but none of it is likely to be completely sufficient. You will need to reach out to multiple places many times to obtain the full range of services you deserve and to get answers to your questions. Do not hesitate to demand the resources and benefits you are owed. Keep track of all of your records. Proceed on the possibility that extra copies of your records are needed, just in case your contacts cannot find them when they are needed. If one individual turns you down do not hesitate to appeal and keep pushing until you get what you need. You need to be active, not passive, to seek out and to manage your family's benefits. Do not be shy about asking (or demanding) things that your family needs. You are your family's own advocate and prime fighter to get the resources and benefits you deserve and have earned. While deployed your service member had to learn to thrive in the field with access to limited information and resources and probably had to frequently go out and advocate and argue to get the materials and resources needed to fight the enemy over there. Your warrior learned to draw on each team member, and it took teamwork to win. This battle for resources will continue back home, and your family will need to continue to challenge, argue, and demand resources and benefits as a cohesive team. In many cases, if the government cannot provide you with something (like a doctor's appointment for a disability evaluation), go seek out the service from another provider (such as a private doctor). The reality is that services will not fall upon you all like showers of rain: Your family must seek the services. But now you are playing with the home team.

To help you with researching and obtaining benefits, we also suggest that you contact and join some of the veterans' service organizations (VSOs) listed in the Appendix. These groups can provide answers to your questions and guidance in ways to deal with the bureaucracy. Their members have gone through similar processes and dealt with the same problems, so many may be expert guides to your family. They are also effective at advocating for the needs of veterans and service members: Many maintain staff members in Washington and other places to make sure that your elected leaders remain aware of what military families are going through.

If you have trouble getting access to benefits and resources, you are not alone. Throughout American history the loyalty and dedication of service members and their families have frequently been repaid by being ignored or having benefits denied to them at the same time that the country's leaders and politicians sang the praises of the brave members of the armed forces. Only after concerted efforts by the service members and their families brought national attention to these issues (and sometimes shame to the leadership) have benefits been introduced or re-instated. Some examples: In 1924 Congress passed the World War Adjusted Act to provide bonuses to veterans of World War I, but payments greater than $50 were not paid to the veterans for twenty years. It took 40,000 veterans marching across the country to Washington, D.C., in the "Bonus Marches" of 1932 to force Congress to authorize the payments of the bonuses. In another example, in 1946 the director of VA Medicine, General Omar Bradley, reported that the VA had ninety-seven hospitals with a total bed capacity of 82,241 patients with facilities for another 13,594 beds under construction. But because of the conclusion of World War II, the nation had more than 15 million veterans on its rolls with all hospitals filled to capacity and with long waiting lists of veterans waiting to get in for treatment. The U.S. federal government rushed to meet the rising needs then, just as it must do now.

These examples from history suggest that, if you feel neglected and overwhelmed, you may need to assert yourself to get access to the services and resources that your family member earned in uniform. You are not alone; you are instead part of a long military tradition. You must assertively seek the services that have been earned. And many of the agencies and organizations described in this book are those resources designed and developed for you to get what you seek.

We offer these book chapters to help you and your family understand what is happening to you, with you, and for you. It is important to learn about the benefits and programs that are available for your family. It is important to comprehend the signs and symptoms of potential problems and understand how to address them so that much is gained before anything is lost. And it is essential to learn how to share these changes and these resources for your children, so that they receive investments in them from the sacrifices their parents undertook in serving the nation.

The following seventeen chapters in this book are organized in five sections: The first six chapters describe what military families are facing and how it may impact your family. The fourth chapter focuses on the additional needs of family members in a family with a disabled or wounded service member.

1. The Warrior's Family
2. The Immediate Post-Deployment Period: Deployments Are Hard, but Homecoming Can Be Even Harder
3. Life after Military Service: What You Need to Know and Do to Succeed as a Veteran Family
4. Family and Friends as Care Providers for Disabled Service Members
5. Emotions and Their Impact on Families
6. The Effects of Repeated Deployments on Warriors and Families

The next three chapters are more in a "how to" mode to address potential problems that could emerge from the deployment and tools you can use to recognize and address these issues:

7. Building Resilience in the Military Family during and following Deployment
8. Suicide and Suicide Prevention
9. Self-Medication and Drug Abuse

The next section, for families with children, describes how the deployment impacts children and teenagers, and offers suggestions on how to connect with them. Chapter 11 focuses on how your service member's injury might impact your children.

10. Got Kids? Parenting Tips for When Your Warrior Returns from Deployment
11. Children of Injured Military Parents
12. Children's Reactions to Deployment, Reintegration, and Injuries by Age Groups, with Recommendations on How to Help Them

The next section answers questions about what comes next in your life, with suggestions on looking for a job, going back to school, and reconnecting physically and emotionally after the deployment.

13. Family Assistance for Service Members Seeking Employment or Education

14. Sex and Intimacy after Combat

The final three chapters offer guidance for the families of unique populations of service members that have become more prevalent in the current conflict.

15. Female Warriors

16. Families of National Guard and Reserve Service Members

17. Unmarried Partners and Blended Families

The Appendix of this book is a listing of Web sites, organizations, books, and other resources that can provide further assistance and information to your family.

We hope that you will find the information in this book interesting and useful. On behalf of all the authors of this book we extend our respect and gratitude to your family and your service member. We will always remain indebted to your family for your service.

With our best wishes for a successful reintegration for your family,

Nathan D. Ainspan
Arlington, Virginia

Walter E. Penk
New Braunfels, Texas

Editors
February 2012

Ten Most Important Things to Do to Help
Improve Your Family's Reintegration

We asked the fifty contributors to this book to provide their three most important recommendations that can help you and your family member have a successful reintegration and can improve the transition process for your family. Here are their recommendations:

1. Do not be afraid to seek help if you need it for anyone in your family—all of you are going through the turmoil of this process.

2. Be patient and take it one day at a time. You are going through a marathon rather than a sprint.

3. Take time for yourself for the things that you enjoy. Keep active. Exercise regularly, read for pleasure, or take a long bath.

4. Understand that life progressed and people changed during the deployment. Your partner, your kids, and the rest of the family are not the same people you knew before the deployment.

5. Learn what resources and organizations are available and do not be shy in accessing and demanding what you need from them.

6. Keep the lines of communication open in your family and talk to your loved ones regularly (but choose the right time to talk).

7. Work to understand your loved one's perspective—your service member could be really hurting.

8. Be assertive and continuously advocate for your family's needs. Work with other military families and join veteran's service organizations to broaden your advocacy work.

9. Remain active in your community, your local organizations and religious groups, and continue your contacts with your friends. Let them know what you are going through and seek their support.

10. Speak with other military veterans going through the reintegration process so that you can learn from their experiences.

Abbreviations

AA	Alcoholics Anonymous
ACE	Ask, Care, Escort approach
APA	American Psychological Association
ASVAB	Armed Services Vocational Aptitude Battery
AUDIT-C	Alcohol Use Disorders Identification Test-Consumption
AUSA	Association of the United States Army
AVF	All-Volunteer Force
CAGE	cut down, annoyed when asked about drinking, guilty over drinking, eye-opener when awakening to manage self
CAI	Career Assessment Inventory
CAP	Computer/Electronic Accommodations Program
CEO	chief executive officer
CISS	Campbell Interest and Skills Survey
COM	chain of command
CONUS	continental United States
CRAFT	Community Reinforcement and Family Therapy
CSF	Comprehensive Soldier Fitness program
CSO	concerned significant other
CTE	chronic traumatic encephalopathy
CWT	Compensated Work Therapy
DANTES	Defense Activity for Non-Traditional Educational Support
DAV	Disabled American Veterans
DoD	Department of Defense
EMDR	Eye-Movement Desensitization and Reprocessing
ETS	Estimated Time of Separation

FAFSA	Free Application for Federal Student Aid
FOB	forward operating base
FOCUS	Families Overcoming Under Stress
FRG	Family Readiness Group
FUD	fear, uncertainty, and doubt
GAT	Global Assessment Tool
IAVA	Iraq and Afghanistan Veterans of America
IEDs	improvised explosive devices
IOP	Intensive Outpatient Program
IQ	intelligence quotient
IRA	Individual Retirement Account
JAG	Judge Advocate General Corps
JAN	Job Accommodation Network
MBTI	Myers-Briggs Type Indication
MET	Motivation Enhancement Therapy
MI	Motivational Interviewing
MIA	missing in action
MOAA	Military Officers Association of America
MOC	Military Occupational Classification
MOS	Military Occupational Specialty
mTBI	mild/minor traumatic brain injury
NA	Narcotics Anonymous
NIAAA	National Institute of Alcohol Abuse and Alcoholism
NSA	Naval Support Activity
OEF	Operation Enduring Freedom
OIF	Operation Iraqi Freedom
OND	Operation New Dawn
OPSEC	Operations Security
OPTEMPO	operating tempo
OSD	office for students with disabilities
PHQ	Patient Health Questionnaire
POW	prisoner of war
PTSD	post-traumatic stress disorder
PVA	Paralyzed Veterans of America

SAT	Standardized Admission Test
SBA	Small Business Administration
TAP	Transition Assistance Program
TBI	traumatic brain injury
TDY	temporary duty
TSP	Thrift Savings Plan
USDA	U.S. Department of Agriculture
USERRA	Uniformed Services Employment and Reemployment Act
USNI	United States Naval Institute
USO	United Service Organization
VA	U.S. Department of Veterans' Affairs
VBA	Veterans' Benefits Administration
VFW	Veterans of Foreign Wars
VSO	veterans' service organizations
WWP	Wounded Warrior Project

The Warrior's Family

David Cabrera, Charles Figley,
Jeffrey Yarvis, Anthony Cox

A decade of war has taken its toll on military service members and their families. Although there are approximately 815,000 active-duty military families, these service members and their 1.23 million family members compose only 0.7 percent of the American population. "We all serve" is a motto that resonates with military families. When a member of a family joins the military, everyone else in the family joins as well. This chapter will identify and explain some of the sacrifices made by families when their family member deploys to war, describe the consequences of these sacrifices, and list some of the resources available to gain support when needed. (See the appendix of this book for more resources.)

Warrior families may often be in the background of public discourse on the military, but they are critical to the success of each military mission. Although aspects of military life can be difficult for families, positive family functioning boosts each service member's morale, retention, and ability to carry out missions. It has been stated that both the military and the family are "greedy institutions" since they both seek exclusive and undivided loyalty from members. It is a healthy balance between these two greedy institutions that provides a protective barrier for each service member and his family. According to a military report, service members reported positive family relationships as a source of resilience, and problems at home as a source of stress and interference. A strong, effective, and sustainable military force is built of strong military families, and strong military families are built through service to each other and to the nation.

For more than ten years, military children and families have faced multiple challenges associated with the new reality of today's military: long and frequent deployments; shorter stays at home between deployments; and greater risks of death, injury, and psychological problems among service members. Deployments of twelve to fifteen months (occurring nearly every other year) as well as reduced dwell time have resulted in a perception among 70 percent of the active-duty spouses that service members are spending too much time away from home. Reserve spouses (32 percent) and National Guard spouses (23 percent) also feel that their service members are absent too much. Although most military children and families do rise to the occasion and do well, these challenges can take a toll on their health and well-being.

One of the best ways to prevent problems or to enhance resilience in military families is to identify what has proven effective and to use this as the basis of intervention. One of these approaches is the U.S. Army's Comprehensive Soldier Fitness (CSF) program, which extends the idea of "fitness" of soldiers beyond mere physical prowess to include psychosocial well-being. One key component of soldiers' psychological well-being is the well-being of their families. The U.S. Army is extending the CSF program directly to family members, so that family members can also be screened and trained in ways that improve their resilience. Information on the CSF program is at http://csf.army.mil. (For more information on how to build resilience in your family, see chapter 7.)

There are several million U.S. men and women in uniform today. In broad terms, this is a relatively young (50 percent of service members are below age twenty-five) and mostly male (85 percent) group, with individuals from rural, less affluent, and ethnic minority (African American and/or Latino) backgrounds over-represented. Almost all have a high school degree or equivalent, and 70 percent have at least some college credits. Just over half of them (56 percent) are married, with about 7 percent of the armed forces in dual-military marriages (i.e., married to another member of the military).

In contrast to the U.S. population as a whole, members of the military tend to marry earlier. Getting married at a younger age can be associated with more problems than marriage at an older age. Among married individuals in the armed forces, more than 70 percent have one or more children, and there are at least 1.85 million children with one or both parents in the military (44 percent of active-duty members have children and 43 percent of Reservists and National Guard members have children).

While most research and programs imply a narrow definition of what a family entails (usually a mother and a father—one of whom wears a uniform—and their biological children), this so-called nuclear family is not the only type that exists, especially in the contemporary United States. Single-parent families (currently over 5 percent of the active force) have also increased in recent decades, as well as blended families and intergenerational families. With the increase of women in the military, dual-career military families have increased (see chapters 15 and 17 for more information about these new types of families). In this book, the term "military family" is used to refer broadly to all individuals who are connected to the service member (both traditional and nontraditional families) and comprises people who share a common bond with the military and a future affected by it. They encompass an entire emotional system tied together by parents, siblings, extended family members, blended members, and in some case multiple military members. With the repeal of the "Don't Ask, Don't Tell" policy in 2011, gay and lesbian members are legally acknowledged throughout the military so military families are now even more diverse.

The Military Family during Peacetime

Even during peaceful times, military children and families face frequent military-induced family separations, frequent sudden moves, difficult reunions, long and often unpredictable duty hours, and the threat of injury or death of the military service member during routine training missions, and military confrontations short of war. On average, active-duty military families move every two to three years within the United States or overseas.

Secondary-school-age students in military families move three times more often than their civilian counterparts. These frequent relocations disrupt children's schoolwork, activities, and social networks, requiring ongoing adjustment to new schools and cultures. Children can grow up feeling rootless and may have difficulties building deeper relationships or maintaining long-term commitments. Especially during adolescence, interruption of peer relationships can be detrimental to a child's psychosocial development. Separation from a parent because of military assignments can also have negative impacts on a child's school performance and mental health. Frequent moves pose additional challenges for academic achievement and graduation due to differing school and state requirements. These problems are especially pronounced for students with special needs.

Nevertheless, the available evidence suggests that military children typically function as well as or even better than civilian children on most predictors of health, well-being, and academic achievement. They have similar or lower rates of childhood psychological problems, lower rates of juvenile delinquency, lower likelihood of alcohol or drug abuse, better grades, and higher median IQs than do their civilian counterparts. According to one large-scale survey of military adolescents, military children are generally healthy, have good peer relationships, are engaged in school and community, do well at school, and are satisfied with life. On average, military children report high optimism and positive self-images.

In modern warrior families, moving was less of a factor impacting psychological issues for military children (such as depression, anxiety, loneliness, self-esteem, peer relationships, etc.) than a child's perception of his relationship with his mother, the family's cohesiveness, and the child's mother's depression. In addition, compared to civilian children, military children have greater respect for authority and are more tolerant, resourceful, adaptable, responsible, and welcoming of challenges, and they have a greater likelihood of knowing and befriending someone who is "different." They also engage in fewer risky behaviors, exhibit greater self-control, show lower levels of impatience, aggression, and disobedience, and display higher levels of competitiveness. Most military children are happy to embrace the term "military brat" since it has come to mean "brave, resilient, adaptable, and trustworthy."

Difficult life events do not automatically lead to problems in children. In some cases, these challenges (like frequent moves or a deployed parent) provide children with an opportunity to grow. For instance, relocation can be a positive experience on children's academic achievement by using the move as an opportunity to change their behavior or to become more active in school. These military children and families have the opportunity to meet new people and make new friends, to visit different places, and to experience diverse cultures.

If families have positive attitudes toward relocation, social support, previous relocation experience, and active coping styles, they do better when they move. As stressful as parental separation can be, military children are afforded the opportunity to take on additional responsibilities and become more independent and mature. Although the inherent hierarchy and structure of military culture can produce resentment among some military children and decrease their independent thinking, it can also foster discipline. Furthermore, military values that emphasize service, sacrifice, honor, teamwork, loyalty, sense of purpose, sense of community, and pride can work as resilience factors to overcome the difficulties of military life.

The Military Family during War

The major challenge for military children and families during the current conflicts is a lengthy deployment of the military family member to a combat zone. Children not only miss the deployed parent but they also experience obvious uncertainty surrounding his safety, especially in single-parent or dual-military families. There are other issues as well.

Military children may be asked to take on greater responsibilities, and daily routines may change. Families may move to be closer to other relatives. Unlike relocation during times of peace, wartime relocation of families may require them to move off base into the civilian community where they lose the existing military support system. Nearly 900,000 U.S. children have had at least one of their parents deployed since 2001, and currently 73,000 children have one or both parents at war.

Long and frequent deployments of service members put military children and families at risk for psychosocial problems. According to U.S. Department of Defense data, between 2003 and 2008 the number of military children receiving outpatient mental health care doubled, and during that period inpatient visits by military children increased by 50 percent, with a 20 percent jump from 2007 to 2008 alone. This may indicate a cumulative toll of parental deployments on military children and an urgent need for increased mental health services for this group.

Several studies have looked at the impact of parental deployment on children during current wars. Although military children and families cope relatively well with shorter separations (less than six months), longer and multiple deployments create measurable distress.

The Impact of Parental Deployment

Parental deployments, especially among single parents, can affect the physical health, academic performance, behavior problems, depression, and anxiety of military children. Adolescent children of deployed parents show significantly higher levels of stress, systolic blood pressure, and heart rate than their civilian counterparts.

Children of deployed service members also show decreases in their academic performance, school engagement, and overall school adjustment. In one study, more than one third of school-age children showed high risk for psychosocial difficulties during parental deployment, 2.5 times the national norm. Children of deployed parents, especially older youth and girls, reported more problems with school, family, and mental health. The longer the parental deployment, the greater these problems can be—both during and after the parent's deployment.

Some other risk factors that can exacerbate the negative effects of deployment on military children and families include a history of family problems, younger parents, less educated families, foreign-born spouses, families with young children, those with lower pay grades or reduced income, those in the National Guard and Reserves, families with children who have disabilities, families with pregnancies, single-parent families, and families with mothers in the military. For spouses at home, a low perceived support from other unit spouses can also be a significant stressor.

A new challenge and big change for warrior families is the rapidity with which service members and their families can communicate these days. For the first time in history, warriors can phone, text, and e-mail their spouses and families instantly from the battlefield. Although the increased communication with family is generally a positive factor, unforeseen negative consequences can develop. One such negative consequence seen by the military was the way that deployed members of the military would notify spouses back home about killed and injured buddies long before the system could appropriately notify the family and provide them formal casualty assistance services. In some cases, the reports were erroneous and led to unnecessary emotional upheaval. To address this problem, some commands instituted communication "blackout" periods following a casualty in the unit—shutting down computer systems and ordering service members not to call home until the proper next of kin had been notified.

Another consequence of rapid communication is the continued presence of the warrior in the family's day-to-day life to the point that he or she was included in arguments over every purchase and every decision and had to explain where he or she was that afternoon. In World War II, when letters took three to six months to reach the front, service members and family members were circumspect in what they wrote to each other, knowing that the car would be fixed long before the letter reached him, and that the money she spent six months ago to get her hair fixed would be paid in full by the time his concern about spending it reached her. Today, one can eavesdrop in any overseas military base phone café and inevitably hear petty fights and arguments, as if the service members were in their living rooms and not a world apart.

The Vietnam War brought recent, relatively unfiltered media coverage from the warfront into the American living room on a nightly basis. The Persian Gulf War and the Cable News Network (CNN) made those reports live and continuous. The current conflicts—with cell and satellite phones, e-mail, chat, Twitter, and Skype—has personalized that level of involvement, bringing the service member's battlefield experiences to the family on a near real-time basis. This has created additional stress for spouses and children who are capable of witnessing or hearing unfiltered, firsthand accounts of the devastating trauma caused by or inflicted upon their spouse or parent.

Resilience in Families

Although military deployment poses risks, especially for some families, it is equally important to remember that many military children and families show resilience and growth. During the deployment of a family member, parents report that their children are closer to family and friends, and that they are more responsible, independent, and proud. As an example, in one study, 74 percent of the spouses of service members reported personal growth, despite also reporting increased loneliness, stress, and anxiety. Although service members as a population are highly vulnerable to experiencing adverse marital outcomes, no consistent evidence demonstrates that the normal, expected demands of military service will lead to higher rates of marital dissolution. This contradiction is likely attributed to the high availability of support for military families provided by the military. Since this kind of support can make such a difference, we strongly recommend that families make contact with the providers available in their communities (see the list in the appendix at the end of this book) and make use of these resources.

Resilience also plays an important role in all phases of deployment. Resilience mitigates stress and improves adjustment to deployment for children and families. Families that function most effectively are active, optimistic, self-reliant, and flexible, can find meaning in military life, and identify with the work of their uniformed family member. Family preparedness for deployment (as well as community and social support) leads to better adjustment. As an example, one study found that adolescents who adapted well during parental deployment showed the ability to put the situation in perspective, found positive uses for reframing problems, embraced change and adaptation as necessary, developed effective coping skills, and drew upon good relationships with family, friends, and neighbors. As one adolescent reported, "I have really good neighbors that understand the situation going on. And I'm always welcome at my neighbors'."

During deployment, the well-being of military children needs to be addressed, not just at the level of the individual child, but also in terms of larger social systems—the extended family, neighborhoods, schools, and communities. The community environment affects children's adjustment and resilience during wartime deployment, and parental stress strongly relates to a military child's psychosocial functioning during deployment. The challenges faced by military children can be exacerbated by a family's and a community's inability to recognize and provide proper support and assistance. If the family as a whole adjusts well to deployment, children can also adapt.

Most military families have done well and demonstrated resilience during peace and even war. Some problems do exist for some military families, but rarely to a greater extent than among civilian families. Contrast this conclusion with the notion of the "military family syndrome," which refers to a constellation of out-of-control offspring, authoritarian fathers, and depressed mothers. Even though this alleged problem has been refuted repeatedly by many studies, this myth continues to be as resilient as the healthy warrior families that the myth fails to acknowledge. The fact that military families overall have done well in the past deserves more recognition from the popular media and from the nation as a whole. If nothing else, the historical strength of the military family can serve as a source of pride and inspiration for the rest of the families in our nation.

Consequences of Deployment

The potential consequences of military service on a military family are great and varied. For the wounded warrior (who returns with physical or psychological injuries), for example, the physical and neurological impacts add to the psychosocial and emotional impact that naturally affects family life and relations after a deployment. How the warrior and military family deal with this issue is every bit as important as the injury itself. This statement bears equal truth if the injury is an amputation, traumatic brain injury, post-traumatic stress disorder (PTSD), or other injuries.

Combat changes everyone (including the warrior family) but not all change is negative. Warrior families need time to re-adjust to the new dynamics and can become stronger as a result. If difficulties persist or go beyond what is comfortable for the warrior or family, then they should immediately seek additional support. This support can come in many different varieties such as speaking with a chaplain, family support centers, behavioral health providers, medical providers, or other warrior families that have already experienced similar circumstances.

Warrior families need time to re-create the support systems that were in place before the deployment or before a move. A sense of isolation is very common for family members after moving and if a deployment is tied into that move, the bulk of the move and transition burden falls to the civilian or non-deployed spouse. Employment for military spouses can be difficult to maintain due to frequent moves. The "battle-hardened" warrior family learns to recognize and plan for sudden changes in moves, job shifts, new schools, and deployments as a normal part of military life. The injury or loss of a spouse can happen, and just as military planners pre-think and pre-plan for contingencies, warrior families should plan and prepare in advance for possible changes and losses.

Most warrior families will agree that it is a great honor to serve the country as part of the military, and these families share these values with their children, families, and friends through their actions. Indeed, the key to success as a warrior family is to see military service not as a job of one family member but as service to the country performed by the whole family. It is for this reason that warrior families need and deserve the benefits they receive.

Additional Strategies for Supporting Warrior Families

The debate surrounding successful transitions may be only a matter of perception. This perception of success may be skewed by some families who might be unwilling to seek help or who may be ignorant of the fact that assistance may be required. For those who seek psychotherapy for PTSD, for example, there are a number of evidence-based best practices including individual psychotherapies of exposure therapy (slow exposure to stressors to become acclimated to them), cognitive-behavioral therapy (redefine the way problems are seen), and Eye-Movement Desensitization and Reprocessing (EMDR—a therapy that helps the individual better process phobias and fears). There are family-informed therapies that include empowerment therapy, emotion-focused therapy, play therapy and filial therapy, structural-strategic therapy, and systemic therapy.

Military children and families often do well, but they are not invulnerable. Rather, they do well because they have compensating strengths and assets as a family. It is critical to identify what these may be, to enhance them, and to use what is learned to design interventions that maximize the strengths and assets to solve their problems.

A focus on what goes well does not mean that what goes poorly should be ignored. Indeed, strength-based interventions complement and extend problem-focused interventions. A comprehensive approach to the support of military families may be more effective than a problem-focused strategy, and it would certainly reduce the stigma that surrounds the seeking of "mental health" care. Programs and resources—formal and informal—already exist in both military and civilian sectors to support military children and families.

Targeted programs and services are helpful, but we need the further assistance, support, and engagement of the broader community. The National Center for Infants, Toddlers, and Families' Zero-to-Three has the "Coming Together around Military Families" initiative (http://www.zerotothree.org/about-us/funded-projects/military-families) that offers training resources for family members, academics, and clinical professionals. The Council on Social Work Education is also targeting the issues facing the warrior family and developing social work and marriage and family therapy curricula for graduate social work institutions training students interested in working with military and veteran families.

Conclusion

Throughout history, military children and families have shown great capacity to adapt to and grow from challenges, during both peace and war. With our involvement in the current wars, military families face multiple challenges that put them at high risk of distress and mental health problems. Their needs are greater than ever.

About one-third of America's population has a direct relationship with someone in the military, and virtually everyone has an indirect relationship. Military families live in our neighborhoods and their children go to our schools. Building and sustaining healthy, resilient, and thriving military children and families will bring benefits not just to them but ultimately to all Americans.

Ultimately, the effectiveness and retention of the warrior is directly tied to the warrior family. Family issues affect individual and unit readiness and function as a protective factor in preventing combat stress reactions. In this, the warrior family serves the nation and supports other warrior families. Reciprocally, the military and the nation must create and foster an environment where warrior families can function and thrive by creating and supporting family-friendly programs and policies.

A life in the military is one of sacrifice; little is written in stone, and the needs of the country often trump the needs of the individual or family. Nevertheless, for the warrior family, it is a good and honorable life.

References

Amato, P. R., A. Booth, D. R. Johnson, and S. J. Rogers. *Alone Together: How Marriage in America Is Changing.* Cambridge, MA: Harvard University Press, 2007.

American Psychological Association Presidential Task Force on Military Deployment Services for Youth, Families, and Service Members. *The Psychological Needs of U.S. Military Service Members and Their Families: A Preliminary Report.* Washington, DC: American Psychological Association, 2007.

Bank, S., and M. Kahn. *The Sibling Bond.* New York: Basic Books, 1982.

Barnes, V. A., H. Davis, and F. A. Treiber. "Perceived Stress, Heart Rate, and Blood Pressure among Adolescents with Family Members Deployed in Operation Iraqi Freedom." *Military Medicine* 172, no. 1 (2007): 40–43.

Black, W. G. "Military-induced Family Separation: A Stress Reduction Intervention." *Social Work* 38 (1993): 273–280.

Bowen, G. L., J. A. Mancini, J. A. Martin, W. B. Ware, and J. P. Nelson. "Promoting the Adaptation of Military Families: An Empirical Test of a Community Practice Model." *Family Relations* 52 (2003): 33–44.

Burrell, L., D. B. Durand, and J. Fortado. "Military Community Integration and Its Effect on Well-Being and Retention." *Armed Forces & Society* 30, no. 1 (2003): 7–24.

Butler, A. C., J. E. Chapman, E. M. Forman, and A. T. Beck. "The Empirical Status of Cognitive-Behavioral Therapy: A Review of Meta-Analyses." *Clinical Psychology Review* 26, no. 1 (January 2006): 17–31.

Carter, B., and M. McGoldrick, eds. *The Expanded Family Life Cycle: Individual, Family, and Social Perspective.* 3rd ed. Needham Heights, MA: Allyn and Bacon, 1999.

Chandra, A., R. M. Burns, T. Tanielian, L. H. Jaycox, and M. M. Scott. *Understanding the Impact of Deployment on Children and Families: Findings from a Pilot Study of Operation Purple Camp Participants.* Working paper. Santa Monica, CA: RAND Corporation, 2008.

Cornum, R., M. D. Matthews, and M. E. P. Seligman. "Comprehensive Soldier Fitness: Building Resilience in a Challenging Institutional Context." *American Psychologist* 66 (2011): 4–9.

Coulter, I., P. Lester, and J. S. Yarvis. "Social Fitness." Supplement 1, *Military Medicine* 175, no. 8 (2010): 88–96.

Council on Social Work Education (CSWE). *Advanced Social Work Practice in Military Social Work.* Alexandria, VA: CSWE, 2010.

Cozza, S. J., R. S. Chun, and J. A. Polo. "Military Families and Children during Operation Iraqi Freedom." *Psychiatric Quarterly* 76 (2005): 371–378.

Croan, G. M., C. T. Levine, and D. A. Blankinship. *Family Adjustment to Relocation (Technical Report No. 968).* Alexandria, VA: U.S. Army Research Institute, 1992.

Dekel, R., and H. Goldblatt. "Is There Intergenerational Transmission of Trauma? The Case of Combat Veterans' Children." *American Journal of Orthopsychiatry* 78, no. 3 (2008): 281–289.

Engel, R. C., L. B. Gallagher, and D. S. Lyle. "Military Deployments and Children's Academic Achievement: Evidence from Department of Defense Education Activity Schools." *Economics of Education Review* 29 (2010): 73–82.

Everson, R. B., and C. R. Figley, eds. *Families under Fire: Systemic Therapy with Military Families.* New York: Routledge, 2010.

Feldman, D. C., and H. B. Tompson. "Expatriation, Repatriation, and Domestic Geographical Relocation: An Empirical Investigation of Adjustment to New Job Assignments." *Journal of International Business Studies* 24 (1993): 507–529.

Flake, E. M., B. E. Davis, P. L. Johnson, and L. S. Middleton. "The Psychosocial Effects of Deployment on Military Children." *Journal of Developmental and Behavioral Pediatrics* 30 (2009): 271–278.

Frame, M. W., and C. Shehan. "Work and Well-being in the Two Person Career: Relocation Stress and Coping among Clergy Husbands and Wives." *Family Relations* 43 (1994): 169–205.

Gottman, J. M., J. S. Gottman, and C. Atkins. "The Comprehensive Soldier Fitness Program: Family Skills Component." *American Psychologist* 66 (2011): 52–57.

Hall, L. K. *Counseling Military Families: What Mental Health Professionals Need to Know.* New York: Routledge, 2008.

Hammer, L. B., J. C. Cullen, G. C. Marchand, and J. A. Dezsofi. "Reducing the Negative Impact of Work-Family Conflict on Military Personnel: Individual Coping Strategies and Multilevel Interventions." In *Military Life: The Psychology of Serving in Peace and Combat*, edited by C. A. Castro, A. B. Adler, and T. W. Britt, 220–242. Westport, CT: Praeger Security International, 2006.

Hays, J. C., D. T. Gold, and C. F. Pieper. "Sibling Bereavement in Late Life." *Omega: Journal of Death and Dying* 35 (1997): 25–42.

Hefling, K. "Siblings of Troops Often Are Forgotten Mourners." Associated Press, 24 September 2009. http://www.armytimes.com/news/2009/09/ap_military_grieving_siblings_092409/ (accessed 21 October 2009).

Huebner, A. J. "Impact of Deployment on Children and Families: Recent Research Updates." Presentation at the National Guard Professional Development Conference: Family Program Professional Development, Orlando, FL, January 2010.

Huebner, A. J., J. A. Mancini, G. L. Bowen, and D. K. Orthner. "Shadowed by War: Building Community Capacity to Support Military Families." *Family Relations* 58 (2009): 216–228.

Hutchinson, J. W. "Evaluating Risk-taking Behaviors of Youth in Military Families." *Journal of Adolescent Health* 39 (2006): 927–928.

Jeffreys, D. J., and J. D. Leitzel. "The Strengths and Vulnerabilities of Adolescents in Military Families." In *The Military Family: A Practice Guide for Human Service Providers*, edited by J. A. Martin, L. N. Rosen, and L. R. Sparacino, 225–240. Westport, CT: Praeger, 2000.

Jensen, P. S., G. A. Gordon, R. L. Lewis, and S. N. Xenakis. "The Military Family in Review: Context, Risk, and Prevention." *Journal of the American Academy of Child Psychiatry* 25 (1986): 225–234.

Jensen, P. S., D. Grogan, S. N. Xenakis, and M. W. Bain. "Father Absence: Effects on Child and Maternal Psychopathology." *Journal of the American Academy of Child and Adolescent Psychiatry* 28 (1989): 171–175.

Jensen, P. S., and J. A. Shaw. "The Effects of War and Parental Deployment upon Children and Adolescents." In *Emotional Aftermath of the Persian Gulf War: Veterans, Families, Communities, and Nations*, edited by R. J. Ursano and A. E. Norwood, 83–109. Washington, DC: American Psychiatric Press, 1996.

Karney, B. R., and J. S. Crown. *Families under Stress: An Assessment of Data, Theory, and Research on Marriage and Divorce in the Military*. Los Angeles, CA: National Defense Research Institute, RAND Corporation, 2007.

Kenny, J. A. "The Child in the Military Community." *Journal of the American Academy of Child Psychiatry* 6 (1967): 51–63.

Lagrone, D. M. "The Military Family Syndrome." *American Journal of Psychiatry* 135 (1978): 1040–1043.

Lester, P. B., S. McBride, P. D. Bliese, and A. B. Adler. "Bringing Science to Bear: An Empirical Assessment of the Comprehensive Soldier Fitness Program." *American Psychologist* 66 (2011): 77–81.

MacDermid, S. M. *Multiple Transitions of Deployment and Reunion for Military Families*. West Lafayette, IN: Military Family Research Institute, Purdue University, 2006. http://www.cfs.purdue.edu/mfri/DeployReunion.ppt.

Manning, D. T., P. M. Balson, and S. N. Xenakis. "Prevalence of Type A Behavior in American Combat Soldiers and Their Children." *Military Medicine* 153 (1988): 358–360.

Marchant, K. H., and F. J. Medway. "Adjustment and Achievement Associated with Mobility in Military Families." *Psychology in the Schools* 24 (1987): 289–294.

Mental Health Advisory Team 6. *Mental Health Advisory Team (MHAT) 6 Operation Enduring Freedom 2009 Afghanistan*. Report chartered by the Office of the Command Surgeon, U.S. Forces Afghanistan (USFOR-A) and Office of the Surgeon General, United States Army Medical Command, 6 November 2009. http://www.armymedicine.army.mil/reports/mhat/mhat_vi/MHAT_VI-OEF_Redacted.pdf.

Morrison, J. "Rethinking the Military Family Syndrome." *American Journal of Psychiatry* 138 (1981): 354–357.

Moss, M. S., S. Z. Moss, and R. O. Hansson. "Bereavement and Old Age." In *Handbook of Bereavement Research: Consequences, Coping, and Care*, edited by M. S. Stroebe, R. O. Hansson, W. Stroebe, and H. Schut, 241–260. Washington, DC: American Psychological Association, 2001.

Nansook, P. "Military Children and Families: Strengths and Challenges during Peace and War." *American Psychologist* 66, no. 1 (2011): 65–72.

O'Connell, P. V. "The Effect of Mobility on Selected Personality Characteristics of Ninth- and Twelfth-Grade Military Dependents." Unpublished PhD diss., University of Wisconsin-Milwaukee, 1981.

Paden, L. B., and L. J. Pezor. "Uniforms and Youth: The Military Child and His or Her Family." In *The Military Family in Peace and War*, edited by F. W. Kaslow, 3–24. New York: Springer, 1993.

Palmer, C. "A Theory of Risk and Resilience in Military Families." *Military Psychology* 20 (2008): 205–217.

Park, N., and C. Peterson. "Moral Competence and Character Strengths among Adolescents: The Development and Validation of the Values in Action Inventory of Strengths for Youth." *Journal of Adolescence* 29 (2006): 891–910.

———. "Positive Psychology and Character Strengths: Application to Strengths-Based School Counseling." *Professional School Counseling* 12 (2008): 85–92.

Park, N., C. Peterson, and S. M. Brunwasser. "Positive Psychology and Therapy." In *Cognitive and Behavioral Theories in Clinical Practice*, edited by N. Kazantzis, M. A. Reinecke, and A. Freeman, 278–306. New York: Guilford Press, 2009.

Peterson, A., E. B. Foa, and D. S. Riggs. "Prolonged Exposure Therapy." In *Treating PTSD in Military Personnel: A Clinical Handbook*, edited by B. Moore and W. E. Penk. New York: Guilford Press, 2009.

Peterson, C., and N. Park. "Positive Psychology as the Evenhanded Positive Psychologist Views It." *Psychological Inquiry* 14 (2003): 141–146.

Peterson, C., N. Park, and C. A. Castro. "Assessment for the U.S. Army Comprehensive Soldier Fitness Program: The Global Assessment Tool." *American Psychologist* 66 (2011): 10–18.

Pincus, S. H., R. House, J. Christensen, and L. E. Adler. "The Emotional Cycle of Deployment: A Military Family Perspective." *Journal of the Army Medical Department* 4/5/6 (2001): 615–623.

Rohall, D. E., M. W. Segal, and D. R. Segal. "Examining the Importance of Organizational Supports on Family Adjustment to Military Life in a Period of Increasing Separation." *Journal of Political and Military Psychology* 27 (1999): 49–65.

Rosen, L., and L. Moghadam. "Impact of Military Organization on Social Support Patterns of Army Wives." *Human Organization* 489 (1989): 1089–1095.

Russell, M. C. "Treating Combat-related Stress Disorders: A Multiple Case Study Utilizing Eye Movement Desensitization and Reprocessing (EMDR) with Battlefield Casualties from the Iraqi War." *Military Psychology* 18 (2006): 1–18.

Russell, M. C., H. Lipke, and C. R. Figley. "Eye Movement Desensitization and Reprocessing." In *Treating PTSD in Military Personnel: A Clinical Handbook*, edited by B. Moore and W. E. Penk, 74–89. New York: Guilford Press, 2011.

Schneider, R. J., and J. A. Martin. "Military Families and Combat Readiness." In *Military Psychiatry: Preparing in Peace for War*, edited by F. Jones, L. Sparacino, V. Wilcox, and J. Rothberg, 19–30. Washington, DC: Office of the Surgeon General, Department of the Army, 1994.

Segal, D. R., and M. W. Segal. "America's Military Population." *Population Bulletin* 59 (2004): 1–40.

Shaw, J. A. "Adolescents in the Mobile Military Community." In *Adolescent Psychiatry*, edited by D. X. Freedman et al., 7:191–198. Chicago, IL: University of Chicago Press, 1979.

Shinseki, E. K. *The Army Family*. White paper, Washington Headquarters Service, a DoD Field Activity, 2003. http://www.whs.mil/library/Dig/AR-M620U_20080912.pdf.

U.S. Army Research Institute for the Behavioral and Social Sciences. "Department of Defense Reaches Out to Children of Soldiers." *U.S. Medicine*, 22 October 2009. http://www.usmedicine.com/articles/Department-of-Defense-Reaches-Out-to-Children-of-Soldiers.html.

U.S. Department of Defense. "Demographics 2010: Profile of the Military Community." Washington, DC: Office of the Deputy Under Secretary of Defense (Military Community and Family Policy), 2011. http://www.militaryhomefront.dod.mil//12038/Project%20Documents/MilitaryHOMEFRONT/Reports/2010_Demographics_Report.pdf (accessed 2 December 2011).

U.S. Department of Defense, Defense Manpower Data Center. *The Changing Profile of the Army, 1985–2008*. Alexandria, VA: U.S. Department of Defense, 2008.

———. *Reserve Components: Noble Eagle/Enduring Freedom/Iraqi Freedom*. Alexandria, VA: U.S. Department of Defense, 2009.

———. *2008 Surveys of Military Spouses: Impact of Deployments on Spouses and Children*. Alexandria, VA: U.S. Department of Defense, 2009.

Watanabe, H. K. "A Survey of Adolescent Military Family Members' Self-image." *Journal of Youth and Adolescence* 14 (1985): 99–107.

Wertsch, M. E. *Military Brats: Legacies of Childhood inside the Fortress*. St. Louis, MO: Brightwell, 1991.

Westerink, J., and L. Giarratano. "The Impact of Post-Traumatic Stress Disorder on Partners and Children of Australian Vietnam Veterans." *Australian and New Zealand Journal of Psychiatry* 33 (1999): 841–847.

Wiens, T. W., and P. Boss. "Maintaining Family Resiliency before, during, and after Military Separation." In *Military Life: The Psychology of Serving in Peace and Combat*, edited by C. A. Castro, A. B. Adler, and T. W. Britt, 3:13–38. Westport, CT: Praeger Security International, 2006.

Yarvis, J. S. "When Trauma Comes Home: Reintegrating America's Returning Reservists to the Workplace and Their Families and the Subtleties of Reintegration." Presentation to the 15th International Conference on Violence, Abuse and Trauma, San Diego, CA, September 2010.

———. "Subthreshold PTSD in Veterans with Different Levels of Traumatic Stress: Implications for Prevention and Treatment with Populations with PTSD." Saarbrucken, Germany: VDM Verlag Dr. Muller Publishers.

Yarvis, J. S., P. Bordnick, C. Spivey, and D. Pedlar "Subthreshold PTSD: A Comparison of Depression, Alcohol, and Physical Health Problems in Canadian Peacekeepers with Different Levels of Traumatic Stress." *Stress, Trauma, & Crisis* 8, no. 203 (April 2005): 195–213.

Yarvis, J. S., and L. Schiess. "Subthreshold PTSD as a Predictor of Depression, Alcohol Use, and Health Problems in Soldiers." *Journal of Workplace Behavioral Health* 23, no. 4 (2008): 395–424.

Zero to Three, National Center for Infants, Toddlers, and Families. "Coming Together around Military Families." http://www.zerotothree.org/about-us/funded-projects/military-families/ (accessed 11 July 2011).

Zoroya, G. "Troops' Kids Feel War Toll." *USA Today*, 25 June 2009, http://www.usatoday.com/news/military/2009-06-24-military-kids_N.htm.

The Immediate Post-Deployment Period: **2**
Deployments Are Hard, but Homecoming Can Be Even Harder

Shirley M. Glynn

Warriors develop a number of strengths during deployments—they become sharper problem solvers, stronger leaders, and better team players. They build their capacities to trust and to think on their feet; they often become more certain of how important family and home are to them. Family members also develop strengths while their loved ones are on deployment—they often become more independent, more aware of their preferences and values, become more self-sufficient, and frequently develop stronger bonds with family and friends. But deployments also stretch warriors and their loved ones. Warriors typically face life threats, poor living conditions, and uncertainty about their own situations as well as concerns about how their families will manage while they are gone. Family members left at home worry about the danger their warrior loved ones face, and they confront their own challenges, including coping with the warrior's absence while taking on additional responsibilities to make up for his being away. In light of how stressful deployments can be, it is not surprising that homecomings are the stuff of legends—hundreds of books and movies have been written about the joys and challenges of families readjusting to the warriors' return and the struggles and achievements of warriors readjusting to their families and the larger society.

This chapter addresses how your family can increase the likelihood of things going well the first few months after your warrior's return. These are times of change and heightened emotions. Hopes run high but uncertainty is common. The material here is designed for your family and your warrior to stay steady in spite of all the changes. This chapter begins with a description of the typical cycle of family adjustment during deployment. While not all families go through these phases in exactly these ways, many do and the cycle presentation provides a good anchor point to begin the discussion on the immediate period after a deployment. Confusion, worries, and up-and-down emotions are all normal. The concept of resilience and how families can strengthen their resilience is then outlined. The military is working to shore up the resilience of warriors so they can function well even during periods of struggle and adversity; families often find they can grow and become stronger during difficult times as well. The immediate post-deployment adjustment period is then discussed. Tips and tools from other military families as well as from experts for managing the post-deployment adjustment period well are presented. This chapter is not long enough to cover all the issues that are important in this transition from warrior to home-based family member and every family experiences post-deployment adjustment a little differently. Nevertheless, it is hoped that this chapter will help families and warriors on their way to becoming even stronger after a deployment than they were before it.

It is important to remember that there are many types of families. According to a comprehensive Department of Defense report published in 2008, a little over half of active-duty military members are married, and one third of those couples have children. Thus, about half those returning from deployment are going home to partners and the other half to parents or other loved ones. Almost 6 percent of active-duty military members are single parents. These different types of family ties all influence expectations and experiences of homecoming. No one description fits all families, but there are a number of common challenges that many relatives and warriors face as they adjust in the first months after deployment.

The Cycle of Family Adjustment to Deployment

A number of researchers have studied how military families manage deployments, and they have identified stages of adjustment that many families go through as they deal with the wartime deployment experience. This cycle typically starts with *initial shock* at the deployment news, especially for deployments that occur early in a conflict and are particularly unexpected. For example, many of the warriors in the current conflicts actually enlisted during peacetime to serve their country and to get schooling or learn a trade, and neither they nor their families actually imagined they would be sent to battle. These individuals are especially likely to have a difficult time adjusting to the news of an impending deployment. Of course, family members frequently feel sad on *departure day*, but many others report feeling numb or cut-off. It is as if they are already preparing emotionally for the warrior being far away, so they are protecting themselves from being overwhelmed by painful feelings even as she is leaving. It is important to note that this numbing does not reflect a lack of caring, but really so much caring that it makes the grief of having to say goodbye almost unbearable.

Right after the departure, things often go pretty well for those left behind. Family members may go into "executive" mode and things often seem to be running more efficiently than anyone expected, especially if the family has had the opportunity to prepare well for the deployment. For some families, this period of good functioning continues. However, other families begin to wear down after a few weeks or months. The enormity of the change in the family—the warrior is gone and life is harder for the people left behind—becomes increasingly real. For these families, a period of off-and-on emotional chaos (e.g., emotional disorganization) begins. Family members may regret things they said or did not say at the time of departure and become superstitious about how their behavior may impact on their warrior loved one (e.g., "If I even let myself think my husband might be hurt, he will get hurt. I can't even let that thought come into my head"). Finances may be tight and childcare difficult to find. The partner in the United States may move to live with her parents or other family to get more support. Some families adjust a little better than others but it is not uncommon for this chaotic period to ebb and flow during the entire period of deployment, as things on the battlefront change (e.g., deaths of friends or fellow warriors, increase in conflicts or fighting, extended deployments) and there are more challenges at home (e.g., illness, financial pressures, single parenting).

Some families are able to achieve periods of *recovery and stabilization*. Family members still experience stress but they begin to adjust to "the new normal"— new routines take hold as family members make up for the absence of the warrior: mothers learn to do light plumbing, fathers learn to buy their daughters' clothes. Families become accustomed to the ways in which they can communicate with the warrior—when e-mail can be expected, when Skype or phone calls are likely— and develop routines to stay in touch.

Approximately six weeks before the end of the deployment, the *anticipation of homecoming* period begins. Plans are made for reunions, trips to meet the troops, family parties, and the like. Of course, the duration of the current conflicts has often meant that deployments are unexpectedly lengthened through policies such as stop-loss. Thus, even this anticipatory period can have some uncertainty. Nevertheless, for many families and warriors this is a more upbeat period as the end of the deployment is in sight and families anticipate being happily united with the warrior safely.

Finally, the *reunion* occurs. This is a period of high expectation and joy, which is sometimes followed by disappointment or anxiety. Both the warrior and loved ones have usually changed as a result of the deployment. Warriors may have been scarred by war, either physically or psychologically, while family members may interact in new and unexpected ways and have acquired skills that make the warrior feel replaceable—they have survived while the warrior is away, and even though the warrior is pleased about this, the happiness can be bittersweet. It can be a bit sad to learn that our loved ones can survive without us. Nevertheless, most families make a successful adjustment and are able to live together well again; some relationships are made even stronger because they have been challenged and prevailed. Our goal in this chapter is to help you navigate the waters to a successful readjustment.

Family Resilience

Mental health experts have long puzzled about how people cope with adversity and why some thrive while others deteriorate. For a long time, experts looking into this issue concentrated on the process of recovery. George Bonanno of Columbia University notes that the term "recovery" describes a process where, in response to loss, normal functioning gives way to at least mild levels of emotional problems (e.g., symptoms of depression or post-traumatic stress disorder, PTSD), usually for a period of at least several months, and then gradually returns to baseline levels. The conventional thinking is that people usually experience a dip in their functioning when faced with a loss like illness, death, or deployment, but most get back to how they felt before the traumatic event.

Bonanno thinks that we have actually missed understanding how many people deal more positively with adversity and loss. He describes resilience to loss and trauma as the ability of adults in normal circumstances who are exposed to an isolated traumatic event to maintain relatively stable, healthy levels of functioning. Resilient individuals may experience short upsets in their normal activities (e.g., several weeks of off-and-on worry or restless sleep) but generally exhibit a pattern of healthy functioning across time, as well as the capacity for taking on new challenges and experiencing positive emotions. They can still rely on their strengths to pull them through. (For more on resilience, see chapter 7.)

The military has embraced the concept of resilience, and has worked hard over the past ten years to help warriors develop resilience in the face of the stressors and losses they may encounter. More recently, the concept of resilience has been applied to military families. Cale Palmer at the University of Hawaii at Manoa has written about the deployment and post-deployment reunion periods being times of opportunity, in which resilience can be strengthened to help families continue functioning well and even grow from the challenges of the deployment and readjustment experience. The question becomes: What are the characteristics of resilient families and how can family members build resiliency during the post-deployment period?

Adrian DuPlessis van Breda, a military social worker in South Africa, has defined eight characteristics of military families that help make them resilient to the impact of wartime deployments. He identified these through a review of the scientific literature as well as based on his experience doing training for military families. The eight characteristics are listed below. Except for the last characteristic (which deals more with how the military can help families be more resilient), he has concentrated on identifying characteristics that families can strengthen and has offered tips on how to strengthen them to make deployments more manageable and less disruptive. These eight characteristics are:

- *Emotional Continuity*—the family's ability to manage the stressors of the deployment cycle without getting too high or too low at any given time.

- *Keeping Positive Perspectives on the Deployment*—the family's positive attitude toward deployments and the military.

- *Social Support System*—the family's capacity to use both the military support available to them (military leadership, family readiness groups, Yellow Ribbon programs) as well as informal support from extended family and friends, the community, and religious leaders.

- *Financial Preparation*—the family having adequate financial resources during separations, as well having paperwork in place prior to the deployment such as a will and power of attorney.

- *"Partner-Aware" Family Structure*—the capacity for the family to maintain a firm but flexible boundary around itself, permitting the smooth entry and exit of the deploying member, and to maintain an intact family structure during the separations. In short, this is a way of keeping the place of the deploying family member present in the family while he or she is gone.

- *Resilient Children*—the capacity of the family to keep the children "on an even keel" as much as possible through the deployment so that the parent remaining at home does not get overwhelmed.

- *Flexible Marriage*—a partnership where tasks are flexible enough that necessary duties are accomplished even when a family member is deployed. Even if members have typical "male" or "female" roles while both partners are present, the partner remaining home during deployment can either perform or oversee the other's typical responsibilities when the other partner is deployed so that things continue to run smoothly.

- *Family-Oriented Management*—a military setting that is sensitive to family needs, as reflected in policies such as providing sufficient lead time for deployments whenever possible, adequate periods home between deployments, and strong support for the family at home while the warrior is away.

Van Breda highlighted these particular characteristics because he also believes that they are resilience factors that can actually be improved with effort. Table 2.1

lists each of the characteristics and ways family members can work on them to get stronger. It can be useful for families to try to strengthen their capacities in each of these areas so they can increase the likelihood they will deal well with the initial post-deployment period and their life together after the service member returns home.

Table 2.1 Ways Families Can Improve Deployment Resilience

Resilience Characteristic	Description	Tips to Strengthen
Emotional Continuity	Manage deployment cycle ups and downs successfully	– Learn about the deployment cycle – Normalize changing reactions during the deployment – Notice if the warrior is feeling depressed and do something about it – Reach out for support – Be kind to family members
Positive Perspectives on the Deployment	Keep a positive attitude toward deployments and the military	– Identify the positive and negative aspects of deployment; concentrate on the positives – Learn techniques to counter negative thinking; get counseling if thinking stays negative – Learn the reasons behind the deployment from military leadership – Learn effective problem-solving skills
Social Support	Use formal and informal support systems, both in military and outside of the military	– Seek out friendships with military families – Develop relationships with neighbors, co-workers, extended family, and religious organizations – Use military support groups – Resolve conflicts with extended family before deployment – Develop a support system to address everyday living problems (car repairs, childcare, home maintenance) before the deployment – Foster spiritual and religious beliefs – Join Family Support/ Family Readiness Groups

Resilience Characteristic	Description	Tips to Strengthen
Financial Preparation	Have adequate financial resources during separations and paperwork in place prior to the deployment	– Discuss finances frequently and openly before the deployment; work to see the other's point of view if there is a difference of opinion – Live within your means – Have a minimum two weeks pay saved before deployment – Make plans for bill payment and credit access before deployment – Develop a will and power of attorney before deployment
"Partner-Aware" Family Structure	Make sure the deployed family member maintains a place in the family	– Keep regular contact with the warfighter while he is deployed – Keep pictures and reminders of the deployed family member around (e.g., his chair at the diner table) – Have the deploying family member leave tapes, audiobooks, etc. so he keeps a place in the family – Talk about role changes before the deployment and make plans to resume typical roles upon return
Resilient Children	Keep the children stable	– Educate the children about the deployment using maps, calendars, photos, or Google – Find ways the deployed parent can stay attached to the child—communicate, record audiobooks, and leave photos – Talk often about the child's feelings about deployment; normalize responses – Help the child use creative means of expression about feelings about the deployment—art, storytelling, etc.—and share with the deployed family member when possible – Avoid assigning older children roles as "protector" or "man of the house" but do give children age-appropriate tasks the deploying parent usually does *(continued on next page)*

Resilience Characteristic	Description	Tips to Strengthen
Resilient Children	Keep the children stable	– Warfighter can *individually* communicate with each child – As much as possible, keep family routines and rituals the same during deployment – The warfighter can rejoin the family gently, understanding the children's likely ambivalence about his return
Flexible Marriage	A secure marriage in which gender roles are flexible	– Non-deployed partners can develop skills to fulfill most family functions during the deployment – Deploying partners can recognize and praise the non-deployed partner's self-sufficiency and independence – Whenever possible, partners can make decisions together using available communication tools during the deployment – Partners can commit to sexual and emotional fidelity; if this is not agreed upon, then safe sex is imperative – Partners can recognize the post-deployment period can be a time of confusion and uncertainty as roles become readjusted; this is normal

Warriors in Transition: Families Thriving in the Immediate Post-Deployment Period

The immediate post-deployment period is usually a time of intense emotions. Both warriors and family members experience great joy and relief, but this can also be a time of worry and stress. *How will things have changed? How will the reunited family handle issues that were put off during the deployment? Will everybody get back to their old roles and behaviors? Should they? How will combat have changed my husband/wife/son/daughter/father/mother?* Sometimes the reunion is further complicated by issues of fidelity and trust that may have arisen in couples—either the deployed partner or the partner remaining at home may have strayed. (See chapter 14 about addressing problems of intimacy or cheating.) Given all this uncertainty, it is not surprising that reunions can be highly emotional times. Hopes and fears can both run high. This is normal and to be expected, and there are ways to organize the reunion and immediate post-deployment period to make it as positive as possible.

When mental health experts have studied the ways that families can best manage the immediate deployment period, it has become clear that *preparation* before and during the deployment as well as *specific action* during the reunion and the weeks after it can reduce stress and improve the likelihood that the family will grow positively during this whole process. Of course, the transition takes time, but many warriors report they have readjusted to their families and home lives within a month or two of their return.

Pre-deployment Preparation for a Successful Reunion

The seeds of a successful reunion usually are planted months before, when the family plans for the departure. Sometimes much about the reunion—even the likely date—is unknown, particularly when this is a first deployment. However, many families have dealt with multiple deployments and can identify several issues that must be successfully navigated during the deployment to promote a healthy transition back to the home front. The three big tasks during this pre-deployment preparation phase are: 1) keeping the lines of communication among family members open, 2) developing mutual agreements for decision-making while the warrior is gone, and 3) making plans for how things will get done when the warrior is not there. The overall goal here is to make plans to hold the place of the warrior in the family while still managing to function in his absence.

Most warriors provide both *instrumental* and *emotional* support to their family members. Instrumental support includes tasks like doing jobs around the house, bringing in an income, helping with homework, and the like. Emotional support involves showing love, encouragement, and support to members in the family. Families benefit when they plan in advance of the departure how their emotional and instrumental needs will be met. For instrumental tasks, the family can develop an agreed-upon list of resources to get them completed—trusted repair shops, handymen, friends who volunteer to help, and so forth. Emotional needs can be more difficult to fill—ongoing contact with your service member through Skype and e-mail, reaching out to other friends and family members, as well as using military resources such as family readiness or support groups, or the base chaplain, can be invaluable. If ongoing contact with the warrior will be possible through phone or Skype, then decisions to be made about the house and children can often be made together even during the deployment, but often how much access warriors will actually have to technology is not known in advance. Some families make agreements to not change the furniture in the house or the landscaping while the warrior is gone (or to send pictures and get input from the warrior if changes cannot be delayed until she returns). Not everything can be anticipated, but being thoughtful about what can be and planning for it gives most people a bit more sense of control and security.

The Homecoming

Homecomings often happen in stages. The warrior may be back in the United States for a few weeks doing post-deployment screenings (and perhaps completing discharge activities) before she actually comes home. This can be a time of great anticipation and relief for everyone in the family. The family knows that the warrior is safe and the warrior knows she will see the family soon. When the warrior finally does make it home, expectations often are very high: "Dad (or Mom) is finally home." "Things will get back to normal." "It will be like he never left." Families who have dealt with multiple deployments know that these high expectations can be a source of disappointment. Most families can readjust successfully, but this is a process that takes time, kindness, and understanding from everyone involved.

There are many challenges during the immediate post-discharge period. The warrior has to readjust to life in the United States. He will have spent months away from the people he loves, in a foreign land, in a completely different time zone, exposed to unusual sounds, languages, and smells, in difficult circumstances, often living with life threats and seeing death and wounding. To cope with the distance from the family and the death or injury they may see during the deployment, many warriors shut down emotionally. Even if fighting was sometimes exhilarating, much of the time "war is hell," and it takes time—often weeks or months—to get back into the rhythms of stateside life. This is normal and to be expected, but it can be hard for family members to cope when the warrior seems distant or preoccupied.

Meanwhile, the family has to readjust to the warrior's presence again. Even though the warrior was sorely missed, the family had to manage the tasks she was usually responsible for while she was gone, and it can be difficult to open up the family to include another decision-maker or disciplinarian again. Roles and expectations need to be renegotiated; children need to get used to another parent having more input into rules and decisions, and the partner or family member who remained home has to become re-accustomed to compromising with the warrior again. These compromises can be especially difficult if the warrior seems changed—more distant or unavailable or irritable. Things and routines that used to feel natural and everyday may feel awkward; it may take time to feel comfortable and easy together again.

Many families find there is an initial honeymoon period when the warrior comes home but then things get a bit rough. Many families have found that following some simple ground rules helped them get over this hump and get on with their lives. These include:

- *Keep expectations realistic.* Even when changes are positive, times of change can be stressful, and having high expectations of how terrific things will be often leads to a letdown. In the past, you may have had the experience of having gone through high school or college graduation, getting married, or starting a very desirable job. Even though these are all positive changes, they can also involve uncertainly, family conflict, and disappointments. Homecomings are much the same. So many quick adjustments need to be made by both the warrior and the family that it can be very hard for the reality to live up to the dreams. It is very important for everyone in the family to anticipate that there will be bumps in the road on the way to getting back on track as loved ones living together and to not make too much out of these challenges—they are to be expected and are normal.

- *Remember that a successful reunion takes time.* It may seem like a reunion is a single moment in time—meeting the warrior at the airport or the base— but reunions are really processes that take time. The warrior needs to adjust to being home—the time zones, the schedule, the responsibilities—and the family needs to adjust to having her there again. Especially after long deployments, it can take time—a few weeks or even a couple of months—to feel that things are back on a regular routine. Having a little scheduling flexibility in the early days of reunion is especially important. It is important not to be over-scheduled, in order to let everyone adjust to the warrior being home. Children sometimes show signs of anxiety and stress—this is often seen as them acting a bit younger than they have been acting before the warrior came home, or being irritable. Keeping a routine and giving everything some time to get back to normal will help.

- *Plan some free time for the warrior before she has to meet family or work obligations.* Adjusting to life in the United States after a combat deployment takes time. Warriors need to be on high alert in the battle zone, and there is no mental switch to just turn off the sense of needing to be watchful all the time when they return home. Feeling keyed up can interfere with sleep, appetite, sexual functioning, and feeling close to others. This situation is worse in individuals who have been diagnosed with PTSD or depression. The warrior's sleep pattern may be off and he may find it very difficult to relax or become connected with others; these problems usually improve over time so it is very useful to have the returning warrior be able to transition back to family and work roles slowly over a few weeks, rather than expecting that they can all be taken on at once. This will allow time for the warrior to be with the family and to have alone time—these are both important.

- *Embrace the changes.* It is likely that both the warrior and the other family members changed during the deployment—their values and life goals are likely different from what they were before. The immediate post-deployment period offers a wonderful time for all the family members to be curious about each other, what they want, and what they have learned during the separation. Concentrate on learning about each other again; ask a lot of questions and be open to what is new. Pay attention to any positive things that are happening.

- *Don't over-schedule time with extended family and friends.* It is natural to want to celebrate the warrior's homecoming with a party or get-together, but larger social gatherings can be overwhelming, especially for someone whose sleep is out of whack and who feels very hyped up. Let the warrior decide when or where the celebration will occur, and consider making this a very low-key event.

- *Schedule fun activities together.* During the reunion and after your warrior settles in at home make sure that you schedule recreational activities, date nights, travel experiences, and other fun times together as a couple and as a family, to help you rebuild your relationships in your family and to build new positive memories together.

- *Be careful about alcohol and substance use.* Many people use alcohol or drugs to relax and feel happier. Nevertheless, alcohol and drugs can make the stress of readjustment worse by increasing irritability and further disrupting sleep patterns. Many couples report that they are more likely to argue when they have been drinking. Keeping an eye on drinking levels and making sure they do not get out of hand increases the likelihood that the family can have a successful reunion. Plan ways to be together that do not revolve around alcohol or drug use.

- *Build on strengths.* Every family has strengths—things that go particularly well for them. Maybe they are good at having fun together, or talk easily together, or can pull together very well during a crisis. When things get tough, it is easy to forget the strengths and just focus on all the bad things that are happening— the fights, the worries, and the problems. Successful families are able to recognize and build on their strengths—to keep doing the positive things they do together—even when things are tough. It can be helpful for families and warriors to make a list of things they used to like to do together—take walks, go for picnics, go to movies, go to sports events—and make time for them on a regular basis.

- *Keep lines of communication open.* Many warriors are reluctant to talk about their war experiences; they may feel other family members will not understand, or they may be afraid they will contaminate their families if they bring the war back home. The family can help increase communication by: 1) listening carefully to what the warrior says, 2) being cautious about asking too many questions of the warrior but showing interest in whatever she offers about the deployment experience; 3) looking at videos or pictures that the warrior brings home or wants to view and discussing what they mean to her; 4) finding ways to spend time talking that are not too emotionally intense, like when taking a walk or sitting together outside in the evening, and 5) being nonjudgmental about the warrior's experience—showing interest and concern but not criticism.

  Warriors can be especially reluctant to talk to their children about their experiences, but the children are often curious about their parent's deployment. Warriors can talk with their children about what life was like in the country they were in—what the food was like, what games the children played, what the schools looked like—without talking about disturbing or traumatic events.

- *Manage irritability and conflict.* Many warriors are irritable when they return home, often because their sleep is disturbed and they are "wired." They may also be confused or unhappy about how the family has changed while they have been deployed. It can be hard to get back on a routine and even little things may seem to get on the warrior's nerves. This irritability can be hard to live with, but it is important that family members not take it personally and understand that it reflects the stress the warrior is under at least as much as it reflects his disappointment or unhappiness with other family members. It can be good to learn to take a "time-out" when the warrior seems stressed—taking a break before things get heated can help prevent small disagreements from blowing up into big fights.

  Many warriors keep weapons with them during the early post-deployment period so they can feel safer and protect themselves, but having a ready weapon can be dangerous for a person with a heightened level of irritability. It can be helpful for family members to discuss their own concerns if they are worried about the warrior having a weapon easily at hand, especially if there are children in the home or the warrior is struggling with substance use, PTSD, or depression.

- *Use all the available resources.* There are many books and online resources to educate families about how to have successful reunions; many of them are listed in this book. Learning about what to expect will help the adjustment go smoother. Also, participating in any base or service programs about post-deployment issues can be very helpful. It may become clear that, even after a few months, the warrior is still struggling with the post-deployment adjustment and things do not seem to be getting any better, perhaps because of trauma symptoms or other difficulties. The quicker someone gets help, the easier it will be for them to get back on track. Talking with the warrior in a calm and loving way, providing a few different treatment options (the U.S. Department of Veterans Affairs [VA], the Vet Center, Military OneSource at http://www.militaryonesource.com, for example), and offering to go with her to seek assistance can be very useful. Make it easy for the warrior to get help if she needs it.

Summary

Many families have successfully managed a reunion after a combat deployment, and become stronger for doing it. Deployments are hard but provide families with the opportunity to become more informed about what is important to them and give them a fresh start in living those values. Keeping open, keeping positive, and giving the adjustment time can all lead to the beginning of a new stage in your family's growth.

References

Bonanno, G. "Loss, Trauma, and Human Resilience: Have We Underestimated the Human Capacity to Thrive after Aversive Events?" *American Psychologist* 59 (2004): 20–28.

Office of the Deputy Undersecretary of Defense (Military Community and Family Policy). *2008 Demographics Profile of the Military Community.* Washington, DC: Office of the Deputy Undersecretary of Defense, 2008. http://www.militaryhomefront.dod .mil/12038/Project%20Documents/MilitaryHOMEFRONT/Reports/2008%20 Demographics.pdf (accessed 27 May 2010).

Palmer, C. "A Theory of Risk and Resilience Factors in Military Families." *Military Psychology* 20 (2008): 205–217.

Peebles-Kleiger, M. J., and J. H. Kleiger. "Re-integration Stress for Desert Storm Families: Wartime Deployments and Family Trauma." *Journal of Traumatic Stress* 7 (1994): 173–194.

Van Breda, A. D. "Deployment Resilience," in *Resilience Theory: A Literature Review.* Pretoria, South Africa: South African Military Health Service, 2001. http://www.vanbreda.org/ adrian/resilience/resilience8.pdf (accessed 19 August 2010).

Life after Military Service:

What You Need to Know and Do to Succeed as a Veteran Family

3

Michelle D. Sherman, Alan Doerman,
James A. Martin

The long-awaited ETS (Estimated Time of Separation) date has finally arrived, and your warrior is now officially out of the military. He has jumped through many hoops during the separation processes, including out-processing at the base, turning in all his military gear, balancing accounts at the bank, completing paperwork and long checklists, submitting military identification cards, and so forth. Your warrior has gotten a DD214 that lists his duty stations, deployments, awards, and other information, so the military separation is official! This is typically an emotional time for everyone in the family. There is often a sense of pride and joy that all family members feel from your family member's military achievements. It can be an exciting time, as families may feel free of the military's authority and control that has been such a big part of military service and military family life. However, sometimes there is a sense of sadness at the loss of military connections and friendships as well as apprehension about the future outside of the military. Your family member may experience a sense of loss at giving up the "warrior role." As a family member, you, too, may have had many goodbyes with your friends, neighbors, and colleagues at work or school.

Warriors often face this transition out of the military with much anticipation and excitement, perhaps even counting the days until discharge. It's not unusual for them to idealize how wonderful life will be like in the civilian world (only to be a bit surprised that life goes on and challenges exist in that world as well). Your warrior may have spent a lot of time and energy preparing for this transition, or may have delayed important life decisions due to her exclusive focus on duty and the mission. While transition issues will vary depending on your warrior's military career, education, training in the military, age, health, and other circumstances, major life questions and decisions often arise at this time of transition from military service to civilian life. These include:

- Will I go back to school? If so, can I use my GI Bill benefits?
- What kind of job do I want? Do I need specific training? How is the job market? Will I be under-qualified or overqualified? How will I interact with civilian peers and employers? How will a civilian employer be different from the military?
- Where should we live? (This may be the first time in many years that you, as a family, can decide where to live.) Do we want to move back home and live near our extended family (remembering there are likely advantages and challenges associated with doing so)?
- Can we afford to purchase a house? Could we use the U.S. Department of Veterans' Affairs (VA) home loan program?
- What kind of health insurance do we obtain and at what cost? Will we be eligible for TRICARE? Do we want to purchase a TRICARE supplement?
- Is there a VA hospital or clinic nearby? Does my family member want to establish care there?
- What day care and school system will be good for our children?
- Where can I find a good pediatrician for our children? A good soccer league for our star nine-year-old soccer player? A good music program for our talented twelve-year-old?

This list is just the beginning, and these decisions can feel overwhelming. For the veteran, even small issues such as "What clothes should I wear today?" are new decisions, since selecting the uniform of the day was a decision that was already made for him every day by unit leaders. Although you and your warrior may have craved independence, the lack of military structure in your new life and the associated responsibilities of the civilian lifestyle can be challenging.

This chapter addresses the experience of life after military service. It is written from the perspective of those entering veteran status but the discussion that follows will be very relevant to the "citizen soldiers," or those individuals and families from the National Guard and the other Reserve components who are coming from an active-duty tour of service back into civilian status. The goal of this chapter is to provide support for your veteran and family members as they navigate these many changes. After reviewing some key ideas about managing change, we will describe three fictional families, how they faced the transition from military service life back to civilian status, and the many resources that they found helpful along the way.

Change as a Necessary Part of Life

It has been said that "change is inevitable—except from a vending machine." Change is a necessary part of life, and we can grow and learn by facing changes head-on and dealing with them in healthy ways. Each person in your family, your relationships with each other, and your family as a whole can grow stronger as you face this change of leaving the military and reentering family and community life as a civilian. In fact, you have already coped with a lot of change, likely more than many families. Military life experiences (like relocations, unaccompanied military tours, deployments, reintegration after a separation or deployment, and return to civilian life) are all part of your family's individual and collective journeys. Regardless of the time frame, change is the one constant that has been shared by everyone in your family. Think for a few minutes about how you have successfully adapted to major life challenges in the past. For example, you may have had children, moved many times, resigned from a civilian job, or had your children leave home. What was helpful for you then? How did you get through those stressful times? The knowledge, skills, and the successful approaches you used to confront these challenges may be useful to you and your family now. With each of these major life events, your relationships and family functioning may have changed, and you reformulated a new way of life. Healthy families are always changing, responding to both internal changes (such as a new baby) and external influences (such as the tough economy), and sometimes facing several strong influences at once. How have you dealt with changes in the past, both individually and in your family?

With change, however, you may also grieve some losses for how things used to be or experience anxiety and worry about achieving your dreams or hopes for the future. It is important to acknowledge losses, but do not get stuck there and define your life by them. As Joan Wallach Scott said, "Those who expect moments of change to be comfortable and free of conflict have not learned their history." You may struggle to decide how your family will function now that you are out of the military. Negotiating many of the changes you are now facing can be stressful, and can test the entire family's communication and problem-solving skills. It may feel awkward for a while as family roles are re-established, so being patient and keeping a good sense of humor can be very helpful. If your warrior experienced a recent deployment or long Temporary Duty (TDY), you as a couple or family may be a bit rusty on these negotiation skills anyway, so it will be very helpful to commit to working on your relationship. We urge you to commit to using this transition time to renew and re-energize your shared commitment as a couple and as a family. (For more information about communicating and sharing intimacy as a couple, see chapter 14.)

Although it may feel like some days your entire world has been turned upside down, remember that much has actually stayed the same. You and your warrior are still the same people at the most basic level. You still have your personal possessions, relationship history, hopes and dreams for the future, and your family and friends. Family relationships can serve as an anchor during times of great change. As you are striving to be flexible in dealing with the many changes, balance this with the sense that much has stayed the same—especially those things that are basic, including your belief in yourself and your commitment to each other and to your family. If you have children, keeping a sense of continuity in their lives is especially important. For example, maintaining bedtime routines, family rituals, and predictable schedules are vital during times of big change.

"Life is change. Growth is optional. Choose wisely."—Anonymous

As you face these many life changes, we encourage you to view these challenges as opportunities. As the quotation above highlights, you can choose how you want to respond to these changes that arise. You can try to ignore them, deny them, and run away from their reality, or you can acknowledge them directly and embrace the changes as challenges and a chance to re-assess your situation and life course.

Change, for example, allows you the opportunity to re-assess and even alter many of your long-term goals and plans. Perhaps you have always dreamed of going back to school to get a teaching or business degree; you may be interested in a technical program to learn a trade skill; maybe you have wondered about living near your folks so they could spend time with their grandchildren; maybe you want to save money to purchase a boat for the great summer outdoor activities; perhaps you want to start investing in college savings plans for your children. In thinking about all of these things, have you and your veteran also taken the time to talk about your goals? Usually people change their long-term dreams over time, but sometimes they do not take the time to share them with important people in their lives. We encourage you to do so, and now is a good time.

As you are making these changes, consider these four suggestions:

- *Be hopeful and optimistic.* Retired General Colin Powell once said that "optimism is a force multiplier" and this definitely applies to managing change. Be open to different ideas, and avoid criticizing each other. Viewing this time of change in an open, positive manner will bode well for you and your future. Having a spirit of adventure rather than fear or anxiety can be helpful. Every day remind each other that you have successfully gotten through some big life changes in the past, and you will do so again.

- *Talk about and respect your individual dreams as well as your shared goals and your vision for the future.* As you do so, recognize and celebrate each other's strengths and how they can be useful in pursing future plans. Remember that attainment of some of these goals may be decades away, and taking small steps in that direction now can be empowering and hopeful.

- *Treat each other with tenderness, kindness, and respect as you embrace change together.* View yourselves as a team working together, not as opponents in a tennis match. When you remember that your family member is on your team, your negotiations go much more smoothly. Remember that strengthening your relationship is an important priority, as we human beings need each other in this journey called life. In the book *Tuesdays with Morrie*, the author's beloved friend and teacher, Morrie Schwartz, is quoted as saying, "In the beginning of life, when we were infants, we need [sic] others to survive, right? And at the end of life, when you get like me, you need others to survive, right? But here's the secret: in between, we need others as well." We think he is right. Allow yourself to draw on the strength of others as you embrace change. Ask yourself if your relationship is a place that helps both of you survive emotionally and physically. If the answer is yes, you have a great resource to draw on. If the answer is no then you have an important task that needs the commitment of both partners in your relationship.

- *Create and use a healthy support network.* In the military, both your warrior and the family often had a natural support system in place—especially if your unit had a strong family support group. You may have felt connected to members of other military families who were sharing in the same challenges, and going through deployments together does create powerful bonds. The transition to the civilian world can be experienced as a loss, but as that pre-existing social network disappears, you have to take the initiative to make friendships. We encourage you to find ways of getting connected in your community, such as through a house of worship, veterans' service organization, a gym or health club, or other community organization. (See the resources section in the back of this book for some suggestions.) If you're returning to your hometown, be prepared to know that, frequently, old friends have moved away, had their own families, and changed in ways that you might not expect. They may or may not be the social network you want to create for yourselves now. Remember that history demonstrates that we survive by banding together as tribes and families. Our relationships with others are very important. Today, we need each other not only to survive but to thrive. This is true for both individuals and for our families as well.

We close this chapter by describing three fictional case studies that highlight some common challenges of reintegrating from military into civilian life. In addition to reviewing the challenges faced by these families, we highlight some of the specific steps they took and services they sought and received that were helpful. Although every family's experience of the transition from military life to the civilian world is unique, we hope these stories help you better understand the common challenges we all face and give you hope that help is available and families can make it through stressful times.

Case Studies

Case Study One: Chuck

Chuck, a forty-five-year-old E6 (air ground equipment technician), retired from the Air Force six months ago after serving twenty years on active duty. He and his wife, Mary, have three teenage sons. This couple is navigating the transition to civilian life very well by being proactive in several important ways. First, Chuck submitted his paperwork to apply for VA disability while still on active duty. This early start was helpful because he realized that the processing of such claims can take some time. Secondly, the couple anticipated that they wanted to eventually settle on the East Coast. Therefore, when considering options for his last duty station, he elected an assignment in Virginia, and the family settled in Virginia Beach afterwards. Third, during the last few years of service, Chuck took online college classes to pursue his dream of being an alcohol/drug abuse counselor. This preparation was helpful in getting a position with a community agency shortly after discharge. Fourth, the family instituted regular family meetings with their teenagers before Chuck's retirement. These weekly meetings and family discussions after dinner on Sundays provided a regular venue for everyone in the family to share their feelings, concerns, and hopes for the upcoming changes. Finally, Chuck and Mary were actively engaged with their church. Church activities and the relationships that they established with other families in their congregation served as a stable factor for the entire family during the transition process.

Case Study Two: Connie

Connie, a twenty-four-year-old female, served in the Army National Guard (E6) in personnel administration. She was deployed to Qatar for one year, and returned home eighteen months ago. She and her husband have two children, ages three and five, and her husband cared for the children by himself during her deployment. Connie began experiencing some depressive symptoms while deployed, largely due to missing her children and feelings of loss and guilt for not being present at some critical moments in their young lives. This heavy sadness continued after homecoming. The couple chose to return to Oklahoma City to be part of a family business; however, they discovered that such employment involved very low pay and long hours. Due to the stress of separation, parenting challenges, financial difficulties, and Connie's depression, the couple has begun arguing more often and wondered if they should stay together. Upon the recommendation of a friend, Connie came to the Oklahoma City VA Medical Center, but really did not know what to expect or even what specific help to ask for from the VA. She was immediately referred to a case manager who works with Iraq and Afghanistan veterans. This case manager served as an advocate to connect her with many VA and community resources. In particular, she sought vocational rehabilitation services that helped her use the GI Bill to go back to school to study nursing. Also, Connie and her husband were given information on a range of mental health treatment options and began couples counseling to address some of their personal and family challenges. The counseling experience also provided the support both of them needed to address the numerous changes they were facing. Their case manager also told them about Veteran Parenting Toolkits (http://www.ouhsc.edu/VetParenting) that were useful for Connie in reconnecting with her children after being away.

Case Study Three: Frank

Frank, a forty-seven-year-old veteran, lives with his wife of twenty-five years, Susan, in rural Tennessee. He has one daughter and two grandchildren who live nearby. After completing almost sixteen years in the Army (including a deployment in the first Gulf War as an infantryman), Frank decided not to reenlist. Frank returned home and found employment where he worked two to three jobs, keeping extremely busy and having little time for his family. Although he never talked much about his deployment, Susan always said, "The guy who got off the plane is not the guy I married!" Although she coped with Frank's emotional distance by being busy with her daughter and grandchildren and with her own job and friendships, she has longed for greater connection with her husband. The impetus for Frank coming to the VA was an angry episode he had with Susan (which the young grandchildren observed and found quite frightening). Upon further assessment, Frank reports that he has been distant from his family, had nightmares, and been irritable ever since his deployment to Iraq. He revealed that his wife had given him an ultimatum that he either get help or she would leave him. He also admits that he missed watching his daughter grow up, but he truly wants to be a positive part of his granddaughters' lives. At the VA, Frank and Susan are now enrolled in a multifamily psycho-education program for families dealing with PTSD, addressing issues of symptom management, communication skills, anger management, and reconnecting as a couple. Although the couple was initially anxious and leery about coming to the VA, they are finding the support of other group members very validating. Susan repeatedly expressed the appreciation for having such support, noting, "I've not talked to anyone about this for twenty years!"

Conclusion

Each veteran and veteran family have their own unique story. As demonstrated by these three examples from thousands of stories, every service member and family coming home from military service face the challenge of transitioning back into civilian community life. For some it is a wonderful experience. For others, the challenge can be overwhelming. Many veterans struggle with physical and psychological injuries from their military services and the associated disruptions in their personal relationships—in their marriages, in their role as parents, in their extended families, as well as in their work and other community roles.

Regardless of your unique circumstances, it is important that you know that help is available. The federal government, through the U.S. Department of Veterans Affairs, as well as the efforts of many other federal agencies, is trying to ensure that all veterans and veteran families understand how to access help through VA representatives and facilities in their own communities, as well as through the many state and local government agencies and non-profit organizations that offer services. Our goal as a nation is to ensure that there is "no wrong door" for you. Wherever a veteran or veteran family turns, they will be connected to the helpful services.

This is not an easy task, and as our president and other national leaders have stated, "This is a challenge that we all share as citizens." Every community and every individual citizen needs to be a part of this welcome-home effort. Fortunately, many have already stepped up to help make this homecoming a success. Still, there is much that needs to be done. As a veteran family member, you know better than others some of these challenges and hopefully you have found an opportunity in your own community—at work, in school, in civic and faith-based settings—where you have been able to offer your knowledge and skills to help other families welcome their veterans home. Helping to make a difference in the lives of fellow veterans and veteran families can provide an important contribution to your own well-being.

Some of the resources and organizations available to support veterans and their families are listed in the resources section at the end of this book. Get to know them and share this information with others. When the fellow veteran or the veteran family member knocks on your door, open it and provide the welcome that you know they deserve.

Family and Friends as Care Providers for Disabled Service Members

4

Charles E. Drebing

We typically talk about illnesses or injuries as happening to us as individual people. "I got the flu" or "John broke his collarbone." The reality is that when we get sick or injured, it is rarely just one person who is affected. Family and friends are almost always impacted in small or large ways. Similarly, it is usually not just one person who acts to address the illness—we also do this as a group. Family and friends usually provide most of the care that is given for illnesses, helping support and heal people in their everyday life, either before they have to go to professionals or along with the care provided by professionals. In the United States estimates suggest that more than 44 million adults (14 percent of the population) are serving as caregivers at any one time to relatives or friends who are sick or injured or because of advanced age.

Doctors, researchers, and the broader field of medical professionals have increasingly recognized that the support of family and friends is a large and critical part of our healthcare system. There is growing research documenting the role of family and friends, usually referred to as "informal caregivers" (in contrast to "formal" or "professional" caregivers), the impact of their support, and how professional healthcare providers and these informal caregivers can best work together to heal patients. A steadily increasing amount of research shows that the medical field is recognizing the efforts of these family and friends and how critical they are in determining how a person recovers from an illness or injury. We review the published materials on informal caregiving to provide you with guidance that you can use with your own family member or friend.

The Concept of Informal Caregiving

The term "informal caregiver" is typically used to refer to people (usually family members) who provide care to others and who have a non-professional relationship with their patient. Though much has been written about spouses, there is plenty of evidence that informal caregiving often involves the entire family—with brothers and sisters, parents and children, and more distant relatives getting into the act. Non-family members are also increasingly recognized as playing a key role in caregiving. There is a wide range in what these caregivers provide, from physical care to emotional support, and from brief onetime support to large amounts of care every day for many years. The care requires a range of skills and is often a critical determinant of how well and quickly the patient recovers from an illness. Unfortunately, most informal caregivers have little or no formal training in how to provide effective care. A growing number of programs have been developed to ensure that informal caregivers have the skills and supports needed to do their job well, but there is still much to do.

Family and friends have been particularly important in the care of injured and disabled warriors. Abraham Lincoln's charge to "care for him who shall have borne the battle and for his widow and his orphan" was a call to action for the entire community, reflecting a shared obligation to provide care for the injured and disabled veterans, as well as their loved ones. Families, friends, and the entire community have an obligation to provide the support and care needed by those who have fought for us and those who depend on them. Military families have a long history of providing support and care for returning soldiers. The most recent wars in Afghanistan and Iraq have created a new generation of soldiers and a new generation of family and friends who have the opportunity and responsibility to provide the care that these returning veterans need.

What Do Caregivers Typically Do?

As we noted above, much of what family and friends provide in terms of support and care are typically things that they were never formally trained to do. No one usually tells family members when they are doing what is needed or if they are doing it correctly. The result is that family caregivers do not always know what to help with, and do not always know how to help most effectively. Informal caregivers do the following:

Assist in Managing Formal Care

Decisions about whether to seek healthcare, how and what to seek, how and what to communicate to professional caregivers, and how to manage the care people are receiving is probably the most common way that families and friends are involved. Informal caregivers are often part of the initial conversations about whether to contact professionals. They have a surprisingly large impact on whether the patient enters care and how quickly. There is clear evidence that in some situations family members actually discourage people with real needs from getting needed care, often resulting in significant delays in the start of needed treatments. It is important that family and friends recognize the important role that they play in determining whether patients get treatment and what treatment they receive. Once they are involved in care, family and friends continue to have a large influence on how well patients participate in their care. It is very important to stay fully informed about the needs of any patients in your family, the services that are available, and how best to be supportive of good care. It is also important to recognize the large influence that you can have in decisions about care and how you need to be thoughtful about how you can influence patients. We will talk more about how to be most effective in providing this support later in the chapter.

Provide Physical Assistance

For many people, one of the first and most vivid memories of receiving care from family or friends is that of being a child, at home in bed with a common illness, and having their mother or father taking their temperature or bringing them food and medicine. Physical assistance is a common part of informal caregiving, and can range from preparing food and helping the patient in walking or toileting, to providing more complex care such as changing bandages or checking blood sugar. The range of physical assistance needed varies widely and depends on the illness or injury, the skills of the caregiver, and the availability of professional help. Unless family members work in a clinical profession, they are not likely to have had a great deal of formal training in providing physical assistance. Even the decision regarding what types of help to provide is often made by family members who are not always certain what is best.

Provide Emotional Assistance

Being sick or getting injured often has an emotional impact on the person, and recovering from the impact of the illness on the patient's morale is often an important part, if not the most important part, of the healing process. Depending on the illness, patients often feel anxious or discouraged about being sick, whether they will recover, and how quickly. More serious illnesses or injuries can force a person to change their activities and relationships in a way that is also challenging emotionally. A sick child needs that bowl of chicken soup his mother or father brings, but possibly more important is the emotional support that it symbolizes and the caring and reassurance that takes place in the conversation around the soup. Having a loved one who is sick or injured can often have an emotional impact on the caregiver as well. The caregiver may also feel anxious or discouraged about the impact of the illness on her loved one. Being able to manage those emotions enough to effectively provide the emotional support the patient needs can be one of the most daunting challenges of caregiving.

Provide Behavioral Assistance

Some illnesses and injuries result in changes in the patient's behavior and in his ability to manage his behavior. For example, a person with post-traumatic stress disorder (PTSD) may feel irritable and depressed, and so may be more likely to be argumentative or to be more passive. A person with a head injury may be less able to recognize how his actions affect his children and so may be a less effective parent. Providing behavior assistance in situations like these may be among the most difficult forms of caregiving to provide, requiring some of the most advanced skills needed. There is research evidence that behavioral issues may be some of the most critical in terms of determining how much professional care is needed, and that these issues are the most difficult for family and friends as care providers.

Join in the Process of Receiving Care

In some situations, it is important for the caregiver to actually be part of the clinical treatment the patient is receiving. For example, there is emerging evidence that marital and family therapy can be a treatment that can benefit adults with mental health conditions like PTSD. Illnesses like PTSD can change the way the patient interacts with a significant other, so attending sessions of couples therapy may be a valuable option. Joining in the process of providing care can range from simply attending an occasional appointment with a doctor to being fully engaged in therapies and training designed to benefit the patient. Family and friends often have concerns about being involved in care themselves and may not know how it benefits them. For example, participating in treatment may give them a great opportunity to see firsthand the treatment that their relative is receiving and to have a closer working relationship with the treatment providers. It may also have some direct benefits for them, as they develop new skills and gain new knowledge about this illness.

What is the Impact of Caregiving on the Caregiver?

Early research studies examining informal caregiving focused almost exclusively on the negative impact of caregiving. This is understandable, as there was early recognition that caregiving is a significant challenge, particularly for some illnesses, and the loss of family caregivers was a significant barrier to quality care for the patient and may result in greater cost to the healthcare system. Many early studies focused on the concept of "caregiver burden," which has come to be defined as the "physical, emotional, social, and financial demands of caregiving." Studies have consistently shown that the degree of burden faced by caregivers for relatives with a range of illnesses and conditions is predictive of physical and psychological problems experienced by the caregivers themselves. Those caregivers facing the highest degree of caregiver burden were more likely to subsequently develop their own physical problems and were more likely to experience significant levels of depression and anxiety. This is a fairly serious issue that is often initially unrecognized by informal caregivers. Some studies have even shown that for older caregivers, higher levels of caregiver burden are associated with health problems that can result in a shortened lifespan. Clearly, in some situations caregiving can be stressful and can result in significant health risks that must be taken seriously. Those risks in turn undermine the ability of caregivers to fully support their relatives. Managing stress and quickly addressing health problems within caregivers clearly has to be a priority in those situations where caregiving demands are high. If you are an informal caregiver and are starting to feel burdened, check out the suggestions later in this chapter on how to ease this feeling.

While much of the initial research attention was paid to the risks associated with providing large amounts of care, there has been growing recognition that family and friends can benefit from providing care in a number of ways. Caregivers typically want to provide care and feel good about being able to support their family member or friend. They also report benefits such as having a stronger sense of making a contribution to the family, being able to stay in close contact with the patient, learning new skills, and having a greater sense of competence. They also can feel a personal sense of meaning that comes from providing care and support to another person. It is not surprising that so many people provide care and that many family members and friends are more than willing to provide support if asked. This simply underlines the benefits of sharing the caregiving responsibility among several people. Not only are the burdens divided, but the benefits are shared so that more people get a chance to make a contribution.

As citizens, taxpayers, and consumers of health insurance, it is important that we recognize the huge contribution that informal caregiving makes to our healthcare system. Looking only at those who need support resulting from the Operation Enduring Freedom/Operation Iraqi Freedom (OEF/OIF) conflicts, estimates of the cost of professional care and disability benefits range from $350 billion to $700 billion, with eventual costs likely to be much higher. Informal caregiving provides a huge portion of the care that would, in many cases, otherwise have to be provided by professional caregivers. We as taxpayers and consumers of health insurance carry the financial burden of care that is not provided by informal caregivers. When family and friends of severely ill patients can no longer provide support and care at home, many of those patients have to rely more heavily on professional care providers, either on an out-patient or in-patient basis. In this way, caregiving by family and friends protects the system from additional expensive care that people would rather avoid and that the healthcare system cannot really afford. There is also the positive and healthful impact on the patient who receives care from family and friends rather than from professionals who are strangers.

How to Be a More Effective Caregiver

Virtually all caregivers want to be helpful, but the degree to which they are actually effective varies by individual. Informal caregivers approach their task in a wide range of ways—with a wide range of results. My experience has been that effective caregivers share the following common approaches:

Take a Team Approach to Caregiving

Caregiving is by definition a team sport: Multiple people are involved, with at least one person receiving the care and one person giving the care. Effective caregivers recognize the need for efforts to be shared between patient and caregivers (with the patient doing as much as possible) in an effort to support independence and autonomy. They also recognize the need for responsibilities to be shared between the available caregivers. Since caregiving can involve a significant amount of work with a risk of burden and other consequences that are not good for the caregiver or the patient, sharing responsibilities between family members and friends often serves to divide the burden while multiplying the benefits.

Take a Practical Problem-Solving Approach

I have worked with thousands of patients over the years, almost all trying very hard to recover from very serious illnesses. One of the most active and motivated patients I have ever seen was an older business executive who had suffered a stroke and was working in a rehabilitation hospital to learn to walk again. He openly talked about his health problems and the likelihood that he may not live more than a year, yet he had a very positive attitude and was always looking for ways to get better. One day I asked him what kept him going and he told me: "I learned long ago that life is a series of problems that we are asked to solve. I take them one at a time and focus on how I can get to the best solution before I move onto the next problem." He had taken a perspective that had made him successful in his work life and applied it to his healthcare. He recovered more quickly from his stroke due in great part to this practical problem-solving approach.

This same perspective is very helpful for caregivers who can face an overwhelming set of challenges at times. Despite the array of problems, a simple problem-solving strategy is effective for many people:

Step 1: Identify a specific problem to address and be clear on what the problem is.

Step 2: Identify a list of possible solutions. Do not be too quick to settle on the first idea. Keep an open mind initially so that the full range of possibilities is considered.

Step 3: Identify the possible solution that is most likely to result in success and try it.

Step 4: Evaluate how it worked and if necessary revise the solution and try again.

Step 5: Repeat step 4 until the problem is solved and do not give up.

Taking a systematic approach to solving caregiver challenges often results in more success, more confidence, and reduced feelings of helplessness. Professional caregivers typically think about their work in this way and so it is easier to collaborate with them if family and friends take the same approach.

Be Proactive

Caregiving is usually caused by something that is not in our control such as the illness or injury that the warrior has suffered. Fortunately, how we respond is very much in our control, and caregivers who take the initiative in the caregiving process tend to do a better job and feel less stress. In contrast, those caregivers who take a more passive stance toward caregiving tend to find it more stressful, and are less effective.

Keep a Sense of Balance between the Patient's Care and Independence

Be careful to balance your patient's need for care with her need to maintain independence. Illness and injury threaten your patient's ability to manage her own life independently in small and in large ways. People need the care and support of others, but they also need to maintain as much independence as they can. Caregivers who focus only on providing the care needed and ignore their patient's psychological need for independence can create a situation in which their patient receives more care than she needs or receives care in a way that makes her feel more dependent than is necessary. This can lead to a range of difficulties, including the patient feeling incompetent and embarrassed and the caregivers feeling frustrated or resentful. On the other hand, caregivers who focus too much on the patient's need for independence can create situations in which the patient receives less care than she needs. This can happen when patients do not want to accept the support of others and so downplay their needs, or when the caregiver does not recognize the actual needs. Getting the right balance between providing care and supporting independence is critical in understanding the type and amount of care to provide.

Balance Your Relative's Need for Care with the Needs of Your Family

Caregivers need to provide support and care for the patient but they have their own needs as well, and caregivers must maintain active, rewarding lives. I have seen family caregivers who become so focused on meeting the needs of the patient that they neglect the needs of their children and other family members. More common may be the caregiver who is so focused on providing care that he begins to neglect his own needs and becomes ill. The needs of other family members and of the caregivers are all important parts of the overall picture that must be balanced. When caregivers become sick because they have not been taking care of their own needs then everyone—including the patient—ends up suffering.

Know When to Seek Professional Help

Informal caregivers and professional caregivers need to work together. While family and friends are often the first to provide support, effective informal caregivers know when it is time to get professional caregivers involved. This can be difficult, as most informal caregivers have little or no formal healthcare training, and so may not recognize situations that warrant a call for professional help. The increase in information made available for caregivers is making it easier for new informal caregivers to learn what they need to know in order to make decisions. For example, the Department of Veterans Affairs has a special Web page just for informal caregivers (http://www.caregiver.va.gov). On this page, caregivers are provided checklists to help identify situations in which professionals are needed. The most common situation in which caregivers need to seek new professional help is when new conditions arise or when existing conditions change or worsen such that additional professional help is needed. Situations in which the current professional providers need to be alerted may be even more common. Again, this typically happens when existing symptoms or problems change or new problems emerge. Safety issues can emerge in some situations, and informal caregivers are at times called upon to recognize when the patient is in immediate risk for urgent health problems (e.g., heart attack or stroke), or at risk for suicide or violence against others. Resources are available to help caregivers recognize and respond quickly to the range of urgent situations (see the appendix in this book).

Caregiving can be a challenging task, and caregivers at times need professional help for themselves. Effective caregivers know when to seek help. Unfortunately, caregivers often are slow to obtain professional help for themselves. In one study of family caregivers only 41 percent of those who had been identified as needing professional mental health care had received any specialty mental health care. Only 19 percent were receiving care from primary care providers, and 40 percent were receiving no professional care at all. There are a range of reasons this happens: 21 percent of these caregivers said they wouldn't know where to find help, 43 percent said it would be difficult to find the time to get help given other responsibilities, and 26 percent cited the expense as too much. Stigma is clearly another concern, as 22 percent said they would be seen as "weak" if they sought professional help for what was clearly a mental health need, while 21 percent said it would be "too embarrassing" to get care for themselves.

Strategies for Improving Your Caregiving

Learn Everything You Can

Information is power and lack of knowledge among caregivers is a key predictor of seeing stress in a caregiver. As in any other situation, we need information to respond effectively. Even in the most challenging situations having an understanding of what is happening helps us maintain a sense of control and of feeling that we know what we need to do.

Caregivers need to be educated on topics such as the patient's illness, common and uncommon treatment for it, the likely success rates of each treatment, the typical effects of the illness on the patient and family, local healthcare resources and how to access them, and local resources available for supporting caregivers and the family.

Fortunately, the healthcare field has recognized the importance of making information available to caregivers, resulting in an explosion in available printed and online information available to patients and their caregivers (see the appendix of this book). Caregivers will want to look for resources that are relevant to their situation, while being clear that just because something is in print does not mean that it is accurate. To help with common issues, we have included a small sampling of commonly used books and online resources in the appendix at the end of this book.

Develop the Skills You Need

Knowledge is not enough to ensure good caregiving. Having the skills relevant to the situation and having a sense of confidence in these skills are key determinants of success as a caregiver. Professional caregivers and experienced informal caregivers are usually more than happy to serve as a resource for skill development.

Common caregiving skills fall into the following clusters:

Providing Specific Care

This includes a wide range of skills, from helping a relative get into a wheelchair safely to managing medications and providing support for cognitive and behavior deficits. While many of these seem fairly simple, there are often ways to do them that are more effective than others—ways that other people have figured out over years of practice.

Coaching

Coaching the patient in successfully doing his part is often a pivotal skill for caregivers. One key area is coaching around care utilization. Patients are often slow to access professional help when they need it. This is particularly true of mental health services in military and veteran populations. A number of common barriers to care have been identified, including a group of practical barriers such as: "How do I find the right care?" "Can I afford it?" and "How can I find the time to participate?" These practical issues can be real or they can be excuses to avoid entering treatment that people feel uncomfortable starting. If these are true practical issues, caregivers can be a key to helping. The key to success often seems to be in engaging the patient in effective conversations about care—open and thoughtful discussions in which ideas and feelings are explored and decisions are made. Those types of conversations require good listening skills, the ability to understand and put the key issues into words, and the ability to encourage and confront others effectively when necessary.

Developing a System of Support and Self-Care

Caregiving is a team sport, and successful caregivers work effectively as a team. Part of being successful is finding ways to support each other and to connect with other caregivers who can provide support. This is particularly important given the challenges facing families and friends of returning military personnel. The process of a loved one returning from the military service can create challenges. Researchers have found that families often have some difficulty re-integrating the returning veteran. If the returning service member has mental health problems, there are frequently more difficulties in the family—sometimes resulting in more conflict, and more arguments, even more incidents of verbal or physical violence. The added challenge for family and friends who must start providing care can also create increased distance and conflict in some situations. Connecting with others, particularly other caregivers who are sharing similar experiences, can help break down some of these problems and reduce the strain and burden that people feel. Caregiver support groups are increasingly common in clinical and community settings. Web-based opportunities for connecting with other caregivers are becoming increasingly popular, as caregivers find the benefits of sharing with others in the same situation (see the appendix of this book).

Caring for a Family Member with PTSD or TBI (Traumatic Brain Injury)

Since post-traumatic stress disorder and traumatic brain injuries are so prevalent among returning service members, advice is presented below on how to provide care to relatives with these injuries.

Caregiving for a Relative with PTSD

PTSD is one of the most common mental health conditions among returning veterans, affecting up to 20 percent of those who have served in Iraq or Afghanistan in the last decade. The most common symptoms include anxiety associated with traumatic experiences and reminders of those experiences, intrusive memories of traumatic experiences, nightmares and sleep disturbance, agitation and over-arousal, avoidance of things that could remind the person of past traumas, and general emotional withdrawal. PTSD has only been formally recognized as a mental health condition in the past thirty to forty years, which is a relatively short period of time, and so there is a great deal of new research and our understanding is growing rapidly. Fortunately there are a number of treatments that have been shown to be effective, including forms of psychotherapy and medications. Unfortunately, about one-third of adults who have PTSD will continue to have symptoms for many years, creating a challenge for the service member and her caregivers.

Because of the nature of the symptoms, PTSD tends to have a significant impact on marriages and families. Adults with PTSD often have difficulties in dealing with intimacy and anger, in talking about their feelings, and with sexual intimacy, all of which can strain relationships within families. (See chapter 14 about reconnecting sexually and rebuilding intimacy after deployment.) There is evidence that the high levels of stress and the associated adjustment problems commonly experienced by combat veterans with PTSD can be also be seen in their partners. This is not surprising once we understand that family members of veterans with PTSD are more likely to be facing repeated crises, conflict and tension within the family related to the relative with PTSD, challenges in helping relatives manage their symptoms and their increasing social isolation, and financial problems. All of these stressful situations start to have an effect on the family. Here are some techniques that will help you help your veteran with PTSD:

Helping the Patient Enter Treatment

Effective treatments for PTSD are increasingly available to the public, but many people with PTSD are slow to enter treatment. This results in unfortunate delays that can create opportunities for symptoms to do more damage to the veterans' lives and to their families. Sometimes this is simply an issue of not knowing where the services are or how to set up an appointment. These are tasks that family members can easily help figure out. Unfortunately, the barriers to treatment entry can be more complex. This is not surprising, given the fact that most treatments require participants to talk about their symptoms and their trauma, and adults with PTSD typically work very hard to avoid any situation in which their symptoms and memories of their trauma will be brought up. Family and friends can play a particularly important role in helping victims of PTSD take the difficult step of beginning treatment. This has to be done in a thoughtful way. One potential strategy is to respectfully help your veteran think through the costs and benefits for entering treatment compared to the costs and benefits of continuing to avoid treatment

Helping the Patient Manage the Most Difficult Symptoms

By definition, PTSD involves having symptoms that are interfering with daily life. Anxiety, anger, irritability, depression, and emotional distancing are all common symptoms that are often difficult to manage. Family members can help the service member find ways to reduce the impact of these symptoms. This often happens within the context of family or couples therapy, where a professional can help coach the family member. Success in this effort often includes the following elements:

1. Recognizing the behavior as a symptom of PTSD
2. Identifying the specific impact of the symptoms on the person and the family's life
3. Generating possible strategies for reducing the negative impacts
4. Selecting a strategy or strategies to try
5. Trying the strategy and evaluating how effective it was
6. Reviewing progress and changing strategies until the best outcomes are achieved.

There is a growing public recognition of the existence of PTSD, resulting in greater opportunities for veterans with PTSD and their caregivers to come together to support each other. Caregiver support groups and support groups for victims of PTSD can be found in many settings and should be part of the support structure for many effective families (see this book's appendix for some examples).

Caregiving for a Relative with TBI

Traumatic brain injury (TBI) affects an estimated 10 million people worldwide and causes significant physical, emotional, and cognitive disabilities. TBI has been described as the signature injury of the military operations in Afghanistan and Iraq. It has been estimated that more than 20 percent of all military personnel who have been involved in these conflicts acquired a TBI, and that as many as 60 percent of the soldiers who are injured in these conflicts will have a TBI as part of their injuries.

There is wide variation in how a TBI affects people. The way that the person is injured and how severe that injury is, coupled with a range of factors specific to the individual and her background all influence the various problems that TBI patients have. Similarly, the response to treatment varies and is influenced by factors such as age, gender, prior injuries, and genetics. One of the best predictors of how a TBI will affect someone over time is the severity of the initial injury. Severity is generally graded in degree, with clinicians typically using the terms "mild," "moderate," or "severe." Determining severity is often based on the early effects of the injury such as how long the person is unconscious and the length of the amnesia period. The great majority of TBIs are mild (also referred to as "concussions"), identified by a brief initial period of confusion or unconsciousness. While most people fully recover within weeks from mild TBI, some may experience both short-term and long-term effects including changes in their cognitive abilities like the ability to remember or to concentrate. The course of recovery from "moderate" or "severe" TBI is longer, with greatest recovery of function occurring within one to two years of injury for many people with TBI, though a small fraction may actually get worse over time.

Longer periods of TBI symptoms can impact marriages and families in many ways that are similar to PTSD. Adults with TBI often have difficulty managing feelings of anger and irritability, and in being emotionally close to others. In more severe TBI cases the personality change can be so distinct that family members and friends may feel that the person with TBI is a different person. The impact on memory and concentration may be dramatic in many cases, resulting in additional strain for family members as they often try to help compensate for these lost abilities. Cognitive and behavioral symptoms are typically a common cause of the strain that the family experiences. In particular, when the TBI leaves the person unable to recognize his own symptoms, family members tend to have a much more difficult time coping. Family distress can build over time, though networks of families and friends who support each other seem to have protections against many of these negative effects.

Here are some key caregiving strategies that you can keep in mind while working with a family member with TBI:

Work with Treatment Providers

While adults with moderate or severe TBIs almost always enter treatment early, those with mild TBI can go unrecognized for some time. The symptoms of mild TBI can be subtle and many adults conclude that they do not need treatment. Unfortunately, many adults with TBI also have poor awareness of the effects of the TBI on their behavior and abilities, adding to the likelihood they will not seek treatment. Family and friends can be of great assistance in helping veterans find appropriate professional caregivers and programs. Treatment and rehabilitation resources for adults with TBI are varied and at times difficult to find. Caregivers can work with their relative and the clinical providers to help identify the right resources and advocate for entry into those services. Resources for caregivers are included in the appendix of this book.

Help the Patient Manage the Most Difficult Symptoms

Changes in personality, behavior, and cognitive abilities like memory and attention can be challenging to address. In some cases, adults with severe TBI have diminished awareness of their deficits, leaving much of the burden for finding ways to manage the symptoms to others. Cognitive symptoms (such as impaired memory or concentration) vary widely but in a small portion of patients can be quite debilitating. While many TBI victims recover cognitive abilities either spontaneously or as a result of their treatments, some do not. In these situations, the patient and their informal caregivers typically look for ways to work around those deficits. In some cases the person uses other abilities to make up for the cognitive deficit. For example, a person whose memory is so impaired that he cannot remember what bills to pay each month may start to rely on his ability to use a detailed calendar to guide his actions so that he does not have to rely on his memory. A second strategy is for someone else to take over a task that has become too difficult for the person with TBI. For example, a family member or friend could take over paying his bills. This is not ideal in that it results in more dependence by the TBI victim and more work for others, but in some cases it is necessary.

Conclusion

Friends and family often play a key role in the recovery of veterans from the wounds of war. They may be called upon to provide care, to help manage professional care, and even to engage in care with the service member. This is often a critical role that has important implications for the service member's health, as well as that of the family. Successful informal caregivers are those who recognize the need to help, are careful to prepare themselves for the task of providing support, and who work closely with the patient, with the professionals, and with other informal caregivers to ensure that everyone recovers successfully together. In that way, we can all help fulfill our part of President Lincoln's charge to us to care for those who "have borne the battle."

5 | Emotions and Their Impact on Families

Kristy Straits-Troster, Monica Mann-Wrobel,
Erin M. Simmons

Military service members and their families become experts in adapting to change. Whether it involves moving due to a change of station, training for additional duties, or being deployed to a war zone, members of our all-volunteer fighting force and their partners and other family members must meet these challenges head-on throughout every stage of the deployment cycle. In addition to the specific mission- and family-related tasks associated with deployment, emotional tasks are also associated with each stage of deployment. Even the most prepared and committed military families experience stress and tension along the deployment cycle, since one definition of a stressor is anything that requires us to change or adapt. The possibility of interpersonal conflict is even greater with multiple deployments, as families may find their personal and social support resources more limited with each deployment or their service member's personality changing after a previous deployment. Understanding the context of these stressors across the deployment cycle, and how they relate to resilience and potential problems with reintegration after deployment, can help families identify successful strategies for coping with emotional issues. This chapter will describe emotions that can emerge during the deployment and reintegration processes and will describe how your family can cope with these emotions.

Emotions and Pre-Deployment

There is great variability in the amount of notice, training, and danger associated with each deployment. The first step in the process of deployment is getting ready. After the initial notification it can sometimes take a while for the reality of the upcoming deployment to sink in among family members. Emotional reactions among family members may range from denial to anticipatory grief and feared loss. Generally this is a busy time because of the need to take care of multiple details

and the increased workload both at work and at home as part of the preparation for deployment. Balancing these "mission-focused" activities against the pressure of making time for your family can be further complicated by an emotional
withdrawal between spouses in anticipation of the separation, or by your children
reacting to the upcoming deployment. Even well-prepared and experienced families may experience sadness and anger in anticipation of the separation. This can
lead to the shutting down of emotions or a perceived numbness, perhaps to protect from the pain of separation or to prevent interpersonal conflict.

Emotions during Deployment and Sustainment

From the date of departure through the first month of deployment, your service
member and your family will adjust to altered routines and communication strategies. These early adjustments may be accompanied by a sense of confusion or
feeling overwhelmed. Sometimes the emotional reaction after the deployed family member departs is one of relief as the preparations and perhaps increased tensions end (at least for a while). Sometimes there is excitement associated with this
latest transition, especially for the service member, which can trigger resentment
in the family. This stage is followed by a sustainment period that lasts until the
final month of deployment, and is characterized by families recognizing that they
are able to cope and develop new routines as they increase in confidence over
time. Some may need additional help and support as they juggle home and work
responsibilities and strive to communicate with the deployed family member.

Although the use of e-mail, Skype, Facebook, and satellite phones serves to
increase communication options for families, it also provides nearly immediate
access to news about problems on the home front, with few options for action on
the part of the deployed service member. Some spouses left behind may experience
loneliness and anxiety about the welfare of the service member and expect what
might be felt by the other spouse as an unreasonable amount of contact or reassurance. Additionally, both you and your service member may have concerns about
trust and intimacy. These issues can be complicated by suddenly realizing you are
now a single parent or that you are facing major life events like the death or serious
illness of a family member without your deployed spouse's presence and support.

Emotions and Redeployment

The redeployment stage starts thirty days prior to the homecoming of your
deployed family member. In addition to being a busy time of preparation, emotional reactions may also include some anxiety as more realistic plans are made

and expectations for the reunion become known. Everyone—your service member, you, and your family members—will have changed over the months of deployment. Renegotiation of family roles and routines will be part of the adjustment process and this process will also bring out strong emotions. One of the authors of this chapter, Lt. Cdr. Erin Simmons, developed a set of tips for successful reunions that can be viewed on the Web as "Erin's Six Rules of Thumb for Successful Homecomings," http://www.youtube.com/watch?v=Gh_lHPKnbDE.

Emotions and Post-Deployment

During the first three to six months after the homecoming, couples and families are usually able to reset their expectations and renegotiate family roles through the use of good, open communication. Barriers to a smooth transition include factors that might interfere with good communication, such as profound fatigue, or feeling irritated, guarded, or isolative. Sometimes the effects of combat stress can negatively impact reunion or reintegration, particularly when emotional numbing and avoidance behaviors are present. These challenges are only exacerbated by other life stressors, such as unemployment or other financial issues, and potential separation from supportive unit members or family readiness–based support if relocation occurs. For National Guard and Reserve members, community support such as that found near military bases may be lacking altogether, resulting in further layers of isolation and limited support resources across all phases of the deployment cycle. Service members and family members may be concerned about stigma should they seek mental health or other resources, especially if your service member is planning to continue in his military career.

Role of Emotions Down Range and Back Again

Although a great deal of training is provided to service members for success in combat scenarios, comparatively little training is involved in preparing warriors to transition these skills to the civilian world. For example, hypervigilance for danger can save lives during deployment through early identification of insurgents or scanning for improvised explosive devices (IEDs), but these same automatic skills can interfere with sleep at home and safe driving as a civilian. Over time this can even lead to chronic physical problems that are associated with insomnia and hyperarousal, including cardiovascular events. Similarly, having everything squared away and well-organized prior to a mission is highly valued and important to a mission's success, but at home an insistence on perfection, coupled with anger or irritability over relatively minor deviations or infractions, can result in heightened family conflict.

Particularly for those warriors with high levels of combat exposure, education about how specific skills that served them well in combat need to be adapted for the transition home can help prevent subsequent symptoms of depression and post-traumatic stress disorder (PTSD). The Army's resiliency training for soldiers and family members (previously known as "Battlemind Training") can provide help to relearn these skills. The program is located on the Web at https://www.resilience .army.mil. People going through this resiliency training have seen that having a better understanding of transition issues and emotions can help families transition successfully and experience more pleasure and less conflict in daily life. (For more information on building resiliency in your family, see chapter 7 in this book.)

Another resilience training intervention called "Families Overcoming Under Stress" (FOCUS) has been developed as a family-centered public health intervention designed to prevent reintegration problems among distressed service members and their families post combat deployment. It was first adapted for the United States Marine Corps at Camp Pendleton and later standardized for further dissemination throughout the Navy. The core components of FOCUS are psychoeducation (learning about how deployment affects all family members across the deployment cycle), emotion regulation skill-building, training in goal-setting and problem solving, and practice using traumatic stress reminder management techniques. All of these techniques are done within a framework designed to increase and improve family communication. One example of a strategy to increase both family communication and awareness of stress and other emotions is the use of a "feeling thermometer." All family members are encouraged to identify their feelings and intensity by rating them on a 0–100 scale, or more simply whether they are "stressed" in the yellow (low), orange (moderate), or red (high) range. Because service members in the Navy and Marine Corps and their families have found the FOCUS interventions to be helpful, FOCUS services were expanded to also be available to Army and Air Force families at selected installations.

Is Anger an Adverse Emotion?

Anger can be adaptive and may play a positive role during deployment by helping the warrior stay focused and on task despite fatigue and difficult conditions. Anger can be activating and can help motivate constructive action. At home, anger in response to threats to one's self or family members can serve to protect those threatened, rally resources, or energize implementation of a fighting or coping plan. Anger is an emotion that can range from mild irritation to intense fury and rage. It is a natural response to feeling threatened, betrayed, or frustrated when our needs or goals are not met. Anger is not the same as aggression, which is a behavior that is intended to cause harm or damage property. Hostility is another construct that is not the same as anger, but rather is an attitude that involves disliking others and evaluating others negatively, which can lead to judgments that may motivate aggressive behaviors. An individual can feel angry without acting aggressively, but when anger is felt too intensely, too frequently, or acted upon with aggression and increased hostility, negative consequences occur.

The physical strain of frequent anger takes its toll on the body through increased blood pressure and heart rate and may be related to problems like hypertension, heart disease, and immune system insufficiency. When anger is directed at others such as family members or coworkers, the result may be alienation from individuals as fear, resentment, and lack of trust develop in response to angry outbursts. When anger expression moves beyond verbal abuse or intimidating behavior to violence or physical aggression, risk of physical injury or being arrested and jailed is increased. The risks can be fatal if firearms are accessible and if impulse control is limited, such as when one is under the influence of alcohol or other substances. Unfortunately, high anger expression can be effective as a way to control or intimidate others in the short run. As a strategy to get children to comply with demands, for example, an angry tone or outburst may result in compliance with the parent's demands, but can result in the children's emotional detachment and future avoidance of the parent altogether over the long run, if such anger occurs frequently over time.

For the returning combat veteran, there is often an awareness of having "a short fuse" or going "from 0 to 60" in a flash. This responsiveness may have served the warrior well in combat situations, but having these automatic responses can be frightening when they occur in civilian interactions. Among possible symptoms of PTSD, hyperarousal symptoms were found to be most closely related to anger and hostility among troops returning from Iraq and Afghanistan. When angry outbursts occur with family members or co-workers, the consequences for the warrior may include guilt and shame over the perceived loss of control, as well as fear of losing close relationships or important relationships at work. If left unexamined, chronic anger problems may lead the veteran to avoid social contacts and interactions altogether, and to try to avoid feelings by resorting to numbness and emotional detachment. Unfortunately, use of these avoidance approaches is closely related to the development of depressive symptoms and of PTSD among combat veterans. Further, studies have found that military service alone is not related to aggression, but PTSD symptoms are related to both physical aggression in general and psychological aggression in intimate relationships specifically. In addition to negatively impacting couples' adjustment post-deployment, PTSD symptoms are also associated with greater perceived parenting challenges. Thus, skill building in managing emotions is the key foundation in most preventive interventions tailored for returning service members and their families.

Strategies for managing anger involve interrupting the cycle of anger escalation and aggressive behaviors using behavioral strategies like taking a "time-out" and leaving the triggering situation, or cognitive strategies that involve increasing one's awareness of a range of angry feelings and identifying triggers to anger. It can be helpful to carefully consider what situations or kinds of events seem to trigger angry feelings. When specific events are identified then it may be possible to reflect and identify early cues in the situation, including thoughts or even physical sensations that preceded the episode and might serve as cues for increasing awareness in the future. The advantage to seeing the episode coming even a few seconds earlier is that it gives you the opportunity to be proactive rather than just reactive. For example, if a couple recognizes that a conflict situation is escalating, either one can ask for a time-out. If this plan is discussed when the couple is calm, the time-out process and expectations can be anticipated, including the expectation for when the time-out will end and the couple will be able to reconnect. The use of time-outs is one of the best ways to prevent interpersonal violence and keep your relationship on track when arguments become heated or could escalate out of control. Here are some tips for a successful time-out plan:

Tips for Successful Use of Time-Outs

- Ask for a time-out when an argument is escalating.
- Initiate a time-out before either person says or does something he or she will regret.
- Be specific and clear: "I want to take a time-out."
- Say clearly when you will be back (e.g., "I'll be back in half an hour").
- Leave the situation immediately and return when you said you would.
- Blow off steam safely—brisk walking is good, drinking alcohol is risky.
- When you return, remember to speak in "I" statements instead of blaming. Consider "I feel . . . ," "I need . . . ," and "I want . . ." statements instead of those that begin with "You . . ." (e.g., "I feel that you did not respect my judgment," rather than "You don't respect my judgment").
- Remember that time-outs can increase trust and respect by honoring the agreement, so once you have made a plan, stick to it.
- Never try to physically stop someone from leaving for a time-out.

Numbness/Avoidance

In the heat of a firefight, there is no room for a service member to have emotional reactions—there can be no hesitation in accomplishing one's mission and following orders. This is true when the task at hand involves high levels of danger, fearful civilians, killing insurgents, or even when providing medical care to the injured. That does not mean that feelings and reactions to such events do not occur, but the warrior develops an ability to "compartmentalize" or turn off such feelings in favor of being able to perform her duty without hesitation. This may be a skill that is developed and practiced throughout several months of combat deployment. When the warrior returns home and automatically uses these same overdeveloped skills, such as showing no emotion when there is a death in the family or a when a distressed spouse is crying during an argument, the picture changes. No longer is the lack of emotion and potential numbness a sign of competence. Instead, the warrior may be perceived as cold, unfeeling, and uncaring. This is usually not the case. As with any other skill, it may take time and effort to experience emotions safely again. Counseling can often be helpful on the personal journey to regain awareness of emotions beyond anger (the easiest or the safest for a warrior to feel) and to recognize subtleties or variations in emotional intensity.

One of the problems with emotional numbness or avoidance of emotional experience is that it is really hard to change because it works so well for the person who feels numb. Feeling no pain can even be adaptive in a crisis. Among symptoms of PTSD, the hardest symptom to change is the avoidance of triggers that cause discomfort, because avoidance again works so well in the short run. However, over time a lack of emotional connection can be devastating to family relations, as parents, spouses, and children may progressively become more emotionally disconnected too.

Another issue with avoidance strategies for dealing with stress is that sometimes avoidance is healthy. If you know that the sight and sounds of fireworks are going to ruin your night, staying home on July 4th may be a good idea. The way to know whether avoidance has become a problem is to look to see if the avoidance is causing any problems or deficits in valued areas—like limiting family activities, the ability to work or travel, or the loss of hobbies, activities, or social support contacts.

Other Emotions

Guilt and shame are feelings often kept to oneself that can lead to avoidance coping and habits such as drinking alcohol excessively. Trying not to think about certain experiences may contribute to increased social isolation, substance use, or more anger—which can then circle back to more guilt and shame. Family members may also get caught up in this cycle. They may worry about not having supported their deployed spouse enough, worry about how they handled money during the deployment or provided parenting on their own. Even if spouses and family members are pleased with how they dealt with home/work/family issues while the warrior was deployed, they may still experience guilt over not thinking about him enough when they were caught up in day-to-day life.

Feeling down or depressed is also not unusual post-deployment. In addition to having to negotiate a series of important adjustments to routine and how the family system works with the return of the service member to the home, most returning warriors have sleep difficulties, which can also impact mood, concentration, and general irritability. Profound fatigue coupled with difficulty sleeping through the night and perhaps occasional nightmares can all take a toll on one's mood and ability to successfully problem-solve without conflict. One study found that over 40 percent of service members returning from Iraq or Afghanistan reported sleep problems, and those with sleep problems reported significantly more PTSD severity three months after deployment. When substance use is added to this scenario, both the risk of dependence and the potential of suicide are increased. Adhering to a regular sleep regimen, using good sleep hygiene habits, and settling into a healthy diet and exercise routine can potentially help with reintegration and may support resilience and reintegration.

Ways to Manage Emotions

As Jon Kabat-Zinn famously said, "You can't stop the waves, but you can learn to surf!" Service members, veterans, and their families need to know what to expect in transition, how to manage the ups and downs, and find ways to surf the stress rather than be pulled down. If emotions are well managed, good conflict resolution and problem-solving efforts can occur, and life can seem more meaningful.

Tips for Managing Emotions and Promoting Family Resilience

- Take care of yourself—pay attention to your own needs, feelings, and values.
- Build emotional awareness and emotion regulation skills.
- Engage in activities you enjoy and find meaningful or relaxing.
- Exercise regularly—it will help you improve your patience, focus, and mood.
- Eat and drink healthy food and drink—provide your body with positive fuel.
- Use good sleep hygiene. Limit your intake of caffeine, alcohol, and nicotine drugs during the day and especially before bed.

- Make connections with others outside the family and develop good relationships with close family, friends, and others.
- Schedule activities for fun and positive interaction rather than just expecting them to happen.
- Communicate—tell people what you feel, make eye contact with them, listen well, and do not interrupt them when they are speaking.
- Be flexible and open to negotiation and compromise.
- Take time-outs as needed.
- If you fight, fight fair. Avoid name-calling, bringing up the past, running away from issues, or having to get the last word in.
- Consider mindfulness exercises to improve concentration and being in the moment, such as meditation, yoga, or tai chi.
- If you need medical or psychological help, get it. Family members will likely be the first to know when help is needed.

Mindfulness

Mindfulness has been defined by Kabat-Zinn as the process of "paying attention in a particular way: on purpose, in the present moment, and nonjudgmentally." Although the formal practice of mindfulness is rooted in Eastern religious traditions, mindfulness can be practiced without adoption of specific religious or spiritual practices, and its secular application is growing, particularly among veterans and service members. Mindfulness techniques typically involve seated meditations that focus on increasing observation and awareness of bodily states, thoughts, and feelings that are experienced in the present moment. Meditation helps to reduce thoughts or judgments about emotions, such as, "Feeling anxious means I'm weak." Generally, mindfulness refers to focusing attention openly to whatever is present, without fixating on any particular aspect of experience, engaging in secondary thought processes, or indulging, or acting on, thoughts or emotions. The practice encourages individuals to simply observe their experience for what it is. While most mindfulness exercises involve sitting quietly in meditation, individuals are commonly encouraged to practice mindfulness during daily activities, such as walking, eating, or at any time during a normal day.

Mindfulness techniques are emerging as promising methods for helping individuals cope with negative, and often unwanted, emotions or problematic thoughts. Mindfulness skills have been found to be associated with a reduction in psychiatric symptoms, such as anxiety, depressive symptoms, substance abuse, and chronic pain. Mindfulness can lead to improved emotion regulation, awareness of the present moment, and nonjudgmental acceptance of distressing emotions, and can assist with decreasing physiological arousal and stress. Also, mindfulness practice is suggested to foster approach-oriented coping and psychological flexibility, or the ability to address challenges consciously rather than reacting to them, as well as skillfully moving between accepting internal experiences or distracting from them, based on what the situation affords and what is valued by the individual.

The use of mindfulness-based therapies is expanding and increasingly applied to a range of psychological conditions, particularly conditions characterized by high levels of negative emotional experience. Mindfulness skills are being increasingly offered and utilized within the Veterans Affairs Health Administration for the treatment of PTSD, as well other related mental health conditions among veterans. A new program called Warrior Mind was recently implemented that incorporates mindfulness techniques to help service members cope with the unique mental health challenges faced at all stages of service. (Information on this program is available at http://warriortraining.us/index.php.) In addition, an application for the iPhone was recently developed, called PTSD Coach, which includes mindfulness exercises for those struggling with symptoms of PTSD (http://www.ptsd.va.gov/public/pages/PTSDcoach.asp). The evidence base for use of mindfulness-based approaches as well as evidence regarding the relationship between mindfulness and emotion regulation is relatively small but shows promise and is accumulating.

Brief Mindfulness Meditation

- Find a quiet and comfortable place to sit. Congratulate yourself for taking time to practice mindfulness.
- Notice as much as you can about your breathing—the rate, the depth, the temperature of the air, where you feel your breath most prominently in your body.
- Do not alter your breath or try to figure out your breath. Do not visualize, count, or distract yourself.
- As you breathe in and out be mindful of the rising on the inhalation and falling on the exhalation. From time to time, your attention will wander away from the breath and back onto different thoughts and emotions. When you notice this has happened, simply thank your mind for doing its job and then gently and kindly return your awareness back to the natural rhythm of your breath and the sensations in your body.
- As you come to the end of your allotted meditation time, congratulate yourself for taking this time at all, no matter how easy or difficult the exercise may have been.

Back on Track Program

Many of the strategies described in this chapter are included in the two-week intensive outpatient program "Back on Track," originally created by Lt. Cdr. Jim Langenfeld, Lt. John Christian, and HM2 Joe McDaniel at Naval Hospital Camp Lejeune, North Carolina, and further developed by Lt. Cdr. Erin Simmons. The program is given to eight to twelve active-duty combat veterans at a time, and instruction is provided by representatives from eight to ten disciplines or agencies.

The Back on Track program content includes psycho-education, recreational activities, relaxation training, exposure therapy, group discussion, skills training, and pastoral care. In addition to helping participants learn to regulate emotion and improve relationships, problem-solve effectively, and improve sleep hygiene and basic life skills, this program also integrates physical fitness, meditation, and spirituality into mental health. Movie clips and games are used to illustrate concepts, and weekly follow-up groups offer continuing treatment and support. Preliminary results indicate that distress and PTSD symptoms significantly decrease following participation in the program, and written feedback from participants suggest that Back on Track adds unique and beneficial interventions to a service member's treatment program. Back on Track planners are currently considering ways to increase the inclusion of family members. Service members can currently attend this program with a referral from their mental health provider if they are in the area or can obtain transportation to Camp Lejeune Marine Corps Base (North Carolina), Cherry Point Marine Corps Air Station (North Carolina), or Portsmouth Naval Medical Center (Virginia). Other military treatment facilities on the East Coast are in the process of implementing similar types of programs.

Conclusion

Emotions are associated with all life events, including those experienced along the cycle of deployment. Service members and their families will react to circumstances in different ways, depending upon their experience and personal resources, including their skill level in managing emotions and in problem solving. Some of the same skills that make an individual a good warrior during combat deployment will cause problems at home and must be adjusted or transitioned as part of reintegration. Hyperarousal, the numbing of emotions, and the avoidance of social interactions can all be problematic in family and work or community relationships, despite their prior usefulness in the field as ways to cope with combat stressors. There are a host of ways to improve emotion management, communication skills, and problem-solving abilities. In addition to the information and tips provided here, several tailored programs are described that may be available in your area. The Department of Defense (DoD) and the VA offer group and individual treatment for combat stress-related issues, as do many other community resources, which are listed in the appendix of this book.

References

Adler, A. B., P. D. Bliese, D. McGurk, C. W. Hoge, and C. A. Castro. "Battlemind Debriefing and Battlemind Training as Early Interventions with Soldiers Returning from Iraq: Randomization by Platoon." *Journal of Consulting and Clinical Psychology* 77, no. 5 (2009): 928–940.

Baer, R. A., ed. *Mindfulness-Based Treatment Approaches: Clinician's Guide to Evidence Base and Applications.* San Diego, CA: Elsevier, 2006.

Brown, K. W., and R. M. Ryan. "The Benefits of Being Present: Mindfulness and Its Role in Psychological Well-being." *Journal of Personality and Social Psychology* 84 (2003): 822–848.

Chambers, R., E. Gullone, and N. B. Allen. "Mindful Emotion Regulation: An Integrative Review." *Clinical Psychology Review* 29 (2009): 560–572.

Elbogen, E. B., R. H. Wagner, P. S. Calhoun, P. M. Kinneer, MIRECC Workgroup, and J. C. Beckham. "Correlates of Anger and Hostility in Iraq and Afghanistan War Veterans." *American Journal of Psychiatry* 167 (2010): 1051–1058.

Gerwitz, A. H., M. A. Polusny, D. S. DeGarmo, A. Khaylis, and C. R. Erbes. "Posttraumatic Stress Symptoms among National Guard Soldiers Deployed to Iraq: Associations with Parenting Behaviors and Couple Adjustment." *Journal of Consulting and Clinical Psychology* 78, no. 5 (2010): 599–610.

Hayes, S. C. "Mindfulness: Method and Process." *Clinical Psychology: Science and Practice* 10, no. 2 (2003): 161–165.

Hofmann, S. G., A. T. Sawyer, A. A. Witt, and D. Oh. "The Effect of Mindfulness-based Therapy on Anxiety and Depression: A Meta-analytic Review." *Journal of Consulting and Clinical Psychology* 78 (2010): 169–183.

Kabat-Zinn, J. *Wherever You Go, There You Are: Mindfulness Meditation in Everyday Life.* New York: Hyperion, 1994.

Lester, P., C. Mogil, W. Saltzman, K. Woodward, W. Nash, G. Leskin, B. Bursch, S. Green, R. Pynoos, and W. Beardslee. "Families Overcoming Under Stress: Implementing Family-Centered Prevention for Military Families Facing Wartime Deployments and Combat Operational Stress." *Military Medicine* 176 (2011): 19–25.

McLay, R. N., W. P. Klam, and S. L. Volkert. "Insomnia Is the Most Commonly Reported Symptom and Predicts Other Symptoms of Post-Traumatic Stress Disorder in U.S. Service Members Returning from Military Deployments." *Military Medicine* 175 (2010): 759–762.

Pincus, S. H., R. House, J. Christenson, and L. E. Adler. "The Emotional Cycle of Deployment: A Military Family Perspective." *U.S. Army Medical Department Journal* 4/5/6 (2001): 15–23.

Reilly, M., and M. S. Shopshire. *Anger Management for Substance Abuse and Mental Health Clients: A Cognitive Behavioral Therapy Manual.* DHHS Pub. No. (SMA) 07-4213. Rockville, MD: Center for Substance Abuse Treatment, Substance Abuse and Mental Health Services Administration, 2007.

Sheppard, S. C., J. W. Malatras, and A. C. Israel. "The Impact of Deployment on U.S. Military Families." *American Psychologist* 65, no. 6 (2010): 599–609.

Vujanovic, A. A., M. O. Bonn-Miller, A. Bernstein, L. G. McKee, and M. J. Zvolensky. "Incremental Validity of Mindfulness Skills in Relation to Emotional Dysregulation among a Young Adult Community Sample." *Cognitive Behaviour Therapy* 39, no. 3 (2010): 203–213.

Vujanovic, A. A., B. Niles, A. Pietrefesa, S. K. Schmertz, and C. M. Potter. "Mindfulness in the Treatment of Post-Traumatic Stress Disorder among Military Veterans." *Professional Psychology: Research and Practice* 42, no. 1 (2011): 24–31.

Wachs, K., and J. V. Cordova. "Mindful Relating: Exploring Mindfulness and Emotion Repertoires in Intimate Relationships." *Journal of Marital and Family Therapy* 33, no. 4 (2007): 464–481.

Walser, R. D., and D. Westrup. *Acceptance and Commitment Therapy for the Treatment of Post-Traumatic Stress Disorder and Trauma-Related Problems: A Practitioner's Guide to Using Mindfulness and Acceptance Strategies.* Oakland, CA: New Harbinger Publications, 2007.

The Effects of Repeated Deployments on Warriors and Families

6

C. Alan Hopewell, Denise Horton

For the spouse of a military member, the words OPTEMPO ("operating tempo") and deployment are consistent with challenges and opportunities of many kinds. This chapter will focus on how repeated deployments can impact your family and offer ideas and resources available to help your family make the constant adjustments needed to remain healthy. If you are a family member or a service member, we hope that this chapter will encourage you to obtain help to sustain you through what could be difficult times.

How Did We Get Here?

Since the end of the first Gulf War, our military has shrunk by 40 percent. The number of Army divisions has dropped from eighteen to ten. The Army has reduced its ranks by more than 630,000 soldiers and civilians and closed over seven hundred installations at home and overseas. Since 1990 the Air Force has shrunk from thirty-six fighter wings (Active and Reserve) to twenty. The Air Force has downsized by nearly 40 percent while simultaneously experiencing a fourfold increase in operational commitments. At the height of the Reagan administration buildup, the Navy had 586 ships. As of 1999, it had only 324. The Clinton administration's blueprint called for that number to drop even further to 305. If the rate of ship construction and retirement by the current administration is continued, that number could fall to only 200 ships by 2020.

In our nation's history we have seen a cycle of military successes (i.e., the Revolution, the Civil War, World War I, World War II, etc.) followed by significant and sometimes severe reductions in the nation's military preparedness, followed by a new military challenge requiring a rapid and precipitous increase in military preparedness to bring the armed forces back up to strength. Not only did the military need to add people each time but it also went through paradigm shifts as the new challenges were always different from the previous ones. As the old saying puts it, "We are always fighting the last war."

Such was the cycle during the 1990s as the military was not only reduced but still configured to Cold War expectations. The terror attacks against the World Trade Center, the Pentagon, and other targets in Washington, D.C., on 11 September 2001 forced the military into another complete paradigm shift as we faced a dispersed and asymmetrical enemy like no other. In previous wars, a significantly higher percentage of the population generally deployed, achieved victory, and then returned home to demobilize. The paradigm shift was now a much smaller percentage of the U.S. population deploying multiple times. The burden of sustained combat is therefore borne by a very small percentage of the general population (about 1 percent) and this population deploys over and over again. This asymmetrical burden of combat is borne by not only the Active and National Guard/Reserve components, but also by their families. The small percentage of families impacted in this conflict compared to previous ones gave rise to the comment that after the terror attacks of 9/11 "the military went to war, but U.S. civilians went shopping."

It has been estimated that since 9/11 American service members have deployed nearly 3.3 million times to a combat zone. In 2009, the *Army Times* reported that over 800,000 service members have deployed multiple times. This suggests that approximately 40 percent of the 2-million-person force has experienced multiple deployments. Although the percentage of those who have left the military through the "burn out" of multiple deployments is not known, it must also be assumed that this has been considerable, and that the costs of replacing those experienced veterans with new recruits has also been extensive. Consider the children in these families: If you are ten years old or younger, you have known nothing else except your parent at war. If you are a family member, it can feel like a roller coaster or a merry-go-round of family responsibilities that are accepted and rejected. Just as the family organizes and reorganizes with each deployment, the whole way the military system operates has changed as more and more service members go out for more and more deployments.

Change Is All We Know

This rapid mobilization and re-organization has markedly changed the way the military operates as an entire system. The organizational culture of the military switched from a large force geared toward conducting operations like those of the Persian Gulf War in 1991 to more of a combined, smaller force consisting of Active, National Guard, and Reserve components. Each now defends the nation's interests via multiple combat and non-combat deployments. There is a much higher reliance upon Special Forces and other military techniques such as drone surveillance and assault. While many Active Component service members signed up for this work as a contingency of their career, National Guardsmen and Reservists did not necessarily see this as a way of life. Multiple deployments therefore tend to have more of a cumulative and increasingly negative impact upon their primary careers. In addition, the dramatic changes in U.S. strategic defense policy have placed increased demands on members of the Reserve components, with them to some degree being "cross-leveled" into the entire deployment and defense cycle as never before. As noted, though the changes in military structure have reduced the total number of personnel available to do the work of protecting America in the age of terrorism, there has at the same time been a substantial increase in the amount of work to be done.

With fewer people and more missions in the military, most service members have had to serve several times in various theaters of operation. While undergoing his pre-deployment training, the first author of this chapter overheard two female non-commissioned officers (NCOs) talking about their impending divorces. They did not wish to divorce, but both were married to servicemen and out of seven years' active duty, one NCO had only spent three years with her husband. She was heard to state, "We don't really want to get divorced, but there is no way we can have a life together as a couple."

The other author of this chapter works on a Reserve installation that mobilizes troops routinely. One fifty-six-year-old senior NCO Reserve soldier had broken his back when he fell from a three-story building the unit was clearing. When asked about going home to his family after his deployment, he stated that he would rather stay on orders to help the younger troops who needed him rather than go back to his family who had been managing well without him.

Deployment Is Not Just Combat

While most think of combat when they hear the word "deployment," a large number of separations can also include peacekeeping, humanitarian aid, counter-drug operations, noncombatant evacuation operations, support to insurgencies and counterinsurgencies, and support to domestic civil authorities. These are all operations that are, in fact, increasing in number. These are all examples of what are called "military operations other than war." While these are relevant and important military missions, the average citizen often may not see the point of these operations. It may feel like these types of operations are less relevant than combat missions. The Army and Air Force Reserve components complete missions that are mundane and boring or outside the type of training they received. The family may resent the mission and seem less than supportive, while the children may only see their parent leaving again. While there is pride in the service the parent provides, it is also sad to see the parent depart yet again. These military operations clearly require strength and support to make it through the transitions these operations create for families. At-home time, also known as *dwell time*, between missions is critical to the health of the family system.

Dwell Time—What Does It Mean?

Dwell time is commonly referred to as the time spent at home following a deployment. The amount of dwell time can vary depending on the type of mission. The Mental Health Advisory Teams that have surveyed service members in Iraq and Afghanistan recommend that the baseline for the mental health of a unit's service members to return to normal may take as long as twenty-four to thirty-six months. The Army Health Promotion, Risk Reduction, and Suicide Prevention Report in 2010 suggested that the amount of dwell time is related to the amount of risk for the service member and the family. For combat and operational deployments of twelve months or longer, a service member should not be deployed for at least twelve months without a waiver. We have talked to families who are happy to have their warrior home for ninety days before returning to the Reserve Center. In the economic times we live in, the need for a consistent income is challenging families to try to sustain the military need. How much time is spent at home depends on the type of job the service member does for the military and what the need is for that work. What the military is learning is that there is also a need to reset the family. Reducing the amount of dwell time has been seen to increase stress, depression, and anxiety symptoms among both service and family members. Sufficient time for recovery and restoration is needed to be able to face the next transition.

Frequent Deployments and the Warrior

Frequent mobilizations have also pointed to several areas of unpreparedness such as members being physically unfit, inadequately trained, and improperly equipped, as well as unit leadership problems, worries about family and civilian jobs during deployment, adjustments to returning and reintegration, post-deployment post-traumatic stress disorder (PTSD) and related symptoms, and suicide.

To the service member reading this: At reintegration trainings we have heard from you that the stress of being cross-leveled is tremendous; that the leadership you have encountered is lacking; that the fear of facing your child is worse sometimes than facing the enemy; that pain issues you are facing seem endless; and you are concerned about the number of blasts and concussions you have experienced but you do not want to ask. For the family members of service members:

we know that you have taken up the hassles of daily living; you do not understand the mission but continue to function, and may feel angry at the military, yet know that your spouse's service to the country is important to him. The military system seems impossible to negotiate and it feels like there is no common sense in the processes, but you stand ready to do what needs to be done too.

Traumatic Brain Injury (TBI) and Post-Traumatic Stress Disorder (PTSD)

The demands of frequent deployments along with the use of remotely detonated explosives by an asymmetrical warfare enemy (i.e., individuals and small groups attacking our forces) increased the number of mild traumatic brain injury (mTBI) and psychiatric casualties among deployed troops. Such injuries affect both your service member and your family.

Early media reports on mTBI were significantly inaccurate and did little but increase anxiety among the troops and their families. Such early reports were most often based upon "self-reports," questionnaires that included questions worded so that almost every service member involved in combat or even indirect fire incidents could answer "yes" to the questions. Estimates of mild traumatic brain injury reached levels that even exceeded the number of security incidents in Iraq during the five-year period reviewed—meaning that there were more estimated brain injuries than there were documented attacks during the period from 2003 to 2008. One published report indicated that over 2,700 veterans at Fort Hood alone had been "missed" with brain injuries, and assertions were made that essentially an entire brigade of soldiers might be non-deployable due to such injuries.

These numbers were quite surprising to the first author of this chapter, who at that moment was the Fort Hood brain injury consultant and who had documented that far fewer soldiers than these estimates actually had "brain injuries" worth reporting or that would impact medical readiness in any way. Continuing to sensationalize this story, the media often portrayed such injuries as if they had never previously been seen in the history of medicine, that providers had no idea how to identify or treat such "invisible" injuries, and that these disorders might lay hidden for years, only to erupt at some future date to destroy the lives of the service members and the family. Soldiers, families, and commanders became increasingly concerned.

Carefully validated studies have now shown that the true estimate of brain injury among all OIF/OEF veterans is much lower. Rather than the questionable screening methods previously reported, current estimates are based upon the actual number of injuries tracked by the Defense Veterans Brain Injury surveillance from 2003 (the invasion of Iraq) through the first quarter of 2011 (a total of 177,479 injuries) and the total number of military personnel deployed (2,302,237). The vast majority (77 percent) of such injuries are mild or minor TBI (mTBI), or concussions. Follow-up studies also document that not only have evidence-based treatments long been available for these concussions, but that from 90 to 95 percent of all uncomplicated concussive injuries show good outcomes and resolve without symptoms. The early exaggerated estimates of the number of injuries as well as of the severity of the injuries only served to increase the concerns of both the soldiers and their family members. However, a remaining and valid concern is the effect of both repetitive concussion as well as the occurrence of additional problems faced by the returning soldier, or "co-morbid" conditions, which at times may occur more than four times as frequently as actual concussion.

While most concussed soldiers experience only single uncomplicated injuries, some experience repetitive damage. The outcome of multiple minor head injuries over a prolonged period has not been well studied and is not well understood. The preponderance of data assessing the impact of repetitive head injuries on short- and long-term neurologic (cognitive) performance has been focused on boxing and American football. These are sports that, over the span of a career, have the capacity to produce many more repetitive concussions and also those of a greater severity than are experienced by most soldiers, so direct comparisons cannot be made. Numerous studies of professional boxers have shown that repeated brain injury can lead to chronic brain problems, the scientific term for which is *encephalopathy*. Evidence from other sports that involve head impact (such as studies of soccer players who have had multiple minor concussions) has demonstrated that these individuals performed worse on neuropsychological tests compared with a control group.

Other investigations of retired professional football players have shown a three-fold increase of depression in players with a history of three or more concussions. Military regulations now generally mandate withdrawal from combat operations and medical evaluation after at least three injuries.

In addition, other research has established that combat mTBI is essentially a dual or co-morbid diagnosis disorder. Almost always, wartime military injuries are accompanied by co-morbid problems such as sleep disturbance, operational stress, or PTSD. The result of these studies are that families should not have excessive fear that their soldier has some type of untreatable brain injury unless this has been diagnosed by a qualified doctor, but should rather ensure that their soldier obtains adequate treatment for all disorders that may have occurred during their deployment(s).

Impact of Frequent Deployments on the Family

In 2007, the American Psychological Association (APA) Task Force noted that 700,000 children had experienced a parental deployment at that point in time. Other researchers one year later put the number of children at over 2 million. Although there is very little good research on the impact to families, there are some things we have known for a while.

As a normal course of family life, military children face moving every two to three years. Family cohesion, the relationship with the other parent, and length of time in residence appeared to be more important to the children's psychosocial functioning than the sheer number of moves. The research has shown that the better the quality of the relationship to the caregiving parent and the better the ability of that parent to manage the family, the better the outcomes for the children. However, it is that very cohesion and quality of parental relationships that are now threatened by the deployment OPTEMPO itself, the sheer number of deployments, and the rising stress and injuries to which the deployed soldiers are subjected.

Children's experiences often depend on their own developmental abilities. But many children internalize their feelings so that they will not show on the outside. Children are the next generation of soldiers. How likely will it be for them to want to join after seeing what their parents are going through? We encourage you to speak with your children, keep your lines of communication open, and encourage your children to open conversations with you if they have concerns. If they are old enough, we encourage you to share this book with them and see if they see themselves in any of the descriptions on these pages.

Deployment as a Process

What distinguishes deployments from other types of stressors for military families is *uncertainty*. The military member of the family is separate and apart, often for an unknown period of time at a location they cannot divulge to their families. A number of problems are encountered by families at each stage of deployment.

In the *pre-deployment phase*, many difficult decisions have to be made. Wills, power of attorney, and financial support are areas that the family needs to understand. The family may struggle to prepare psychologically and emotionally for the impending separation and try to make sense of the absence.

During the *deployment phase*, the re-organization of the family responsibilities can be hampered by several factors: (a) not knowing how long the deployment will last, (b) scheduling of time for mid-tour return of the service member to the family, (c) ever-changing information given (or not given) by the chain of command and news reports, and (d) the loneliness of missing each other.

In the *post-deployment* or *reunion phase* of the cycle, renegotiation of family roles is an adaptation that is often difficult to manage.

Many veterans often consider their unit members as family. But when they return to their primary family the effects of the mission and the closeness of their comrades-in-arms may not be understood or accepted. The service member may even express sadness or regret that they cannot go back to the fighting or military situation. The loss of duties and responsibilities for returning veterans may present a hardship that needs to be worked through. It has been seen that when the family and the spouse are supportive of the mission, the reunion and the overall adaptation are improved. Families with poor communication, financial problems, and behavioral or mental health issues in one or more members of the family prior to deployment tend to get worse with the departure of the military member. A spouse who is young, knows little about the military, and is unable to manage daily tasks alone may struggle with deployments. Other spouses may demand everything from the military and will have expectations that are out of sync with reality. These tend to be families or spouses who have an entitlement attitude (e.g., they joined the military solely for educational or other benefits, and they seem to be surprised when they are called upon to perform their actual military duties).

Reintegration of the service member into the family means re-working roles and boundaries. How the everyday living arrangements have changed since the service member's departure may require discussion and normalization. The expectations of romance and increased intimacy may not be realized. Social support networks depended on by the family, especially the spouse, may be given up as a sign that they are now not necessary.

Reconnecting with the children is a task often feared and uncertain for military parents. Some soldiers returning from Iraq have noted that often terrorists have used children to gather intelligence about the military strength or weapons in a unit, placed children physically to block roads so that units may be ambushed, or, as happened during the tour of the senior author, were sold by hospitals to serve as human IEDs. Some of these children may be the same age as the service member's own children. These experiences may well contribute to PTSD symptoms and create problems for the service member with relating to other children or even their own.

Children will also continue to grow and develop as their parent is gone. The children may worry about the potential for the military parent to be harmed or injured, psychologically or physically. If the fear is realized, special circumstances may present the family with more difficult changes than they imagined.

The Impact on the Spouse

Research has shown that spouses of deployed military, compared to spouses of those who had not deployed, showed increased prevalence rates for disorders such as depression, anxiety disorders, sleep disorders, acute stress reaction, and adjustment disorders. These problems could become more prevalent with each subsequent deployment. The prevalence of major depression in spouses in primary care has been shown to be almost 20 percent. Risk factors for mental health problems in spouses may also include the absence of military partners during critical periods such as pregnancy. Deployment during pregnancy correlates with an almost threefold increased risk of postpartum depression in partners. Family life is also replete with other critical periods in which fathers and mothers are needed, such as graduations, illness of children, and incidents of behavioral acting out of children under stress and with perhaps inadequate supervision and support.

Research on the effect of multiple deployments on overall marital health is conflicting and the interaction between deployment, combat exposure, homecoming, and marital health is complex. Whereas the effects of deployment or combat exposure alone on marital health may be unclear, military personnel who return with PTSD and other problems are at significantly greater risk of having problems in their relationships with their spouses.

What Is Available for Families?

There has been long-standing concern for the career status of the Active Component soldier who seeks help. It is an ingrained cultural notion that help-seeking behavior is a career-ending move. National Guard members or Reservists are often geographically distant from actual installation assets, and by virtue of living off post may have increased difficulty in benefiting from assistance programs. Families may also be fearful of making their family problems known to the chain of command. New marketing programs like the Real Warriors Web site (http://www.realwarriors. net) are attempting to counter these long-standing myths. The creators of this program used the .net extension rather than a .mil extension in hopes that it would lessen the fear of being identified. Programs like Military OneSource (http://www. militaryonesource.com) were also put in place to provide alternative sources of professional counseling/therapy/daily living assistance. For those living in or close to a military installation, military-resourced programs have been in place for more than thirty-five years.

Military Programs

Those who have seen the movie *We Were Soldiers* will never forget Madeleine Stowe's moving portrayal. Mrs. Moore, portrayed by Stowe, was among the wives of the 7th Regiment of the First Cavalry Division who were entirely on their own as word of the casualties experienced in the Ia Drang Valley filtered back to them— and were often delivered by a taxi driver. So that this would not happen again to military families, the Army in particular has offered programs and services to families since the early 1980s to assist them in adapting to the military lifestyle and to provide much-needed support that was often missing during the Vietnam era. Most military families do adapt well to the varying mission requirements. In fact, the service member's retention in the military has been correlated to the positive attitude the spouse and the family have toward the mission of the military member. Recognition that families are a critical piece of the military mission leads to the creation of supportive programs and services, including the Family Support Centers and Army Community Service Centers. Most of these services are made available on military installations around the world. The National Guard and Reserve components that are located away from installations have developed Family Assistance programs, but the linkage to the families and funding for these programs are problematic. While these programs are intended to offer preventative and immediate assistance for a variety of problems, the cultural notion in the military of asking for help is still a negative norm. These families may not feel the sense of belonging to the larger social community of the military.

Family Life Education

Family life educators can offer support and self-help groups to cope with the transitions associated with moving. Understanding the cultural changes families must navigate can be eased with the help of a family life educator. Education about the military structure, culture, pathways, and traditions are needed to increase a family's understanding of where they fit in the mission. Family life educators can assist in keeping the deployed parent in touch with the children as well as offer discipline and guidance advice to the non-military parent left at home. Employment issues for the non-military spouse have been improved through the use of Family Support and Army Community Service Center staff. Prevention of social problems such as spouse and child abuse is handled through Family Advocacy staff at these centers. Families with special-needs children or adults can access advocacy and assistance through the Exceptional Family Member programs. Many families undergo changes in financial circumstances with moving and deployment. At Family Support Centers, staff members are available to guide or advise the families on how to handle their financial concerns. With deployment, the income of the service member may dramatically change.

Over six hundred family assistance centers were created during the First Gulf War to assist National Guard families. Technologies like e-mail and video conferencing have been made available at most Family Support Centers to help keep the lines of communication open between the family and the service member. One simple thing needed to help National Guard and Reserve families is to inform them of existing services and how to access them. With so little in the way of choice for these families due to mission or operational requirements for the service member, having support and choice is quite important.

The newest offering to service members and their families is the Comprehensive Soldier Fitness Program. Because of the disgraceful way in which earlier Vietnam veterans were treated, strong efforts were made to reverse this toxic trend and to focus on the resilience that most service members and trauma survivors actually experience. This emphasis uses the tenets of positive psychology to help service members, families, and civilian employees become and remain resilient in the face of stress. Positive psychology is a way to focus on the strengths and assets of a person. Instead of focusing on the deficits and shortcomings of a person, it focuses on the qualities of strength and coping, building on the optimism and resilience of that person.

The Comprehensive Soldier Fitness Program instituted by the Army utilizes the Global Assessment Tool (GAT) as a starting point toward health and wellness. Families can participate in using the GAT, attend training, or have one of the trainers offer sessions geared toward family issues. It is a way to leverage technology (the GAT is an online anonymous assessment), while also including a human component for team building.

Increasing Use of Technology

With the increasing use of technology for training service members, it is no surprise that computer-based programs are springing up to increase the efficiency of training time and to encourage service members to access treatments. Self-help aids and products that offer independence to service members seem to have practical applications. A Department of Defense (DoD) team from Joint Base Lewis-McChord in Washington developed the T2 Virtual PTSD Experience (http://t2health.org/vwproj/). This Web site includes videos and self-screening tools to allow service members to decide whether there is a need for treatment.

Developed by DoD and the Veterans Administration, the PTSD Coach is a smartphone application that offers self-assessments and tips to manage behaviors that are daily stressors. One of the reasons this application is helpful is that it offers a way to connect veterans to mental health professionals if they choose to make contact. Companies like Hazelden (http://www.hazelden.org) also offer smartphone applications to track one's mood and give daily meditation readings to reduce stress.

Summary

The current wars and their repeated deployments have stretched the military members and their families in many ways we have yet to truly understand. In some ways, the responses to deployment demonstrate a resilient force that has faced great demands. Frequent deployments have created the need for more research on the long-range impact on families, especially children. Issues like dwell time, injuries, and retention need more attention and understanding. Technology is offering new ways to allow service members choices for help-seeking. The on-post military programs continue to offer assistance, but there need to be fewer stigmas attached to looking for help. Leadership and command emphasis on wellness programs and preventative measures need to be the norm instead of the exception. The bottom line is that each service member should feel free and safe to give, to offer, and to receive help in ways that make sense for him. Our hope is that it will make a real difference in their lives and their families.

References

ABC News. Transcript of "ABC News/Facebook/WMUR Republicans Debate." St. Anselm College, Manchester, New Hampshire, 5 January 2008, http://abcnews.go.com/Politics/Vote2008/story?id=4091645.

ALARACT (All Army Activities) 253/2007. *Individual Dwell Time (IDT) Deployment Policy*. U.S. Army, Chief Distribution and Readiness Division, http://www.carson.army.mil/Moblas/CustomerOriginals_Revisions/Changes-Needed/Changes_01_2010/ALARACT%20253%202007.pdf (accessed 10 August 2011).

Allen, E. S., G. K. Rhoades, S. M. Stanley, and H. J. Markman. "Hitting Home: Relationship between Recent Deployments, Post-Traumatic Stress Symptoms, and Marital Functioning for Army Couples." *Journal of Family Psychology* 24 (2010): 280–288.

American Psychological Association, Presidential Task Force on Military Deployment Services for Youth, Families, and Service Members. *The Psychological Needs of U.S. Military Service Members and Their Families: A Preliminary Report*, Executive Summary (2007), http://www.apa.org/ (accessed 21 June 2011).

Army Suicide Prevention Task Force. *Army Health Promotion, Risk Reduction, and Suicide Prevention Report* (2010), http://csf.army.mil/downloads/HP-RR-SPReport2010.pdf (accessed 21 June 2011).

Beaussart, M., and L. Beaussart-Boulengé. "'Experimental' Study of Cerebral Concussion in 123 Amateur Boxers, by Clinical Examination and EEG before and Immediately after

Fights." *Electroencephalography Clinical Neurophysiology* 29, no. 5 (November 1970): 530.

Bell, D. B., and W. Schumm. "Providing Family Support during Military Deployments." Chapter 9 in *The Military Family: A Practice Guide for Human Service Providers*, ed. J. A. Martin, L. N. Rosen, and L. R. Sparacino, 139–152. Westport, CT: Praeger, 2000.

Bowen, G. L., J. A. Mancini, J. A. Martin, W. B. Ware, and J. P. Nelson. "Promoting the Adaptation of Military Families: An Empirical Test of a Community Practice Model." *Family Relations* 52, no. 1 (2003): 33–45.

Burkett, B. G., and G. Whitley. *Stolen Valor*. Dallas, TX: Verity Press, 1998.

Cornum, R., M. D. Matthews, and M. E. P. Seligman. "Comprehensive Soldier Fitness: Building Resilience in a Challenging Institutional Context." *American Psychologist* 66, no. 1 (2011): 4–9, doi: 10.1037/a0021420.

Cozza, S., R. Chun, and J. Polo. "Military Families and Children during Operation Iraqi Freedom." *Psychiatric Quarterly* 76, no. 4 (2005): 371–377.

Christopher, R., and C. A. Hopewell. *Psychiatric Correlates of Combat Trauma in Military Personnel: PTSD and TBI TESI Statistical Analysis, Operation Iraqi Freedom and Operation Enduring Freedom*. Reno, NV: Psychological, Clinical, and Forensic Assessment, 2007.

———. *Quantitative Analysis of Military Trauma Symptomatology*. Reno, NV: Psychological, Clinical, and Forensic Assessment, 2007.

De Burgh, H. T., C. White, N. Fear, and A. Iversen. "The Impact of Deployment to Iraq or Afghanistan on Partners and Wives of Military Personnel." *International Review of Psychiatry*, 23 (2011): 192–200, doi: 10.3109/09540261.2011.560144.

Defense Veterans Brain Injury Center, "DoD Worldwide Numbers for TBI—Totals at a Glance," http://dvbic.org/Totals-at-a-glance.aspx.

Drummet, A. R., M. Coleman, and S. Cable. "Military Families under Stress: Implications for Family Life Education." *Family Relations* 52, no. 3 (2003): 279–288.

Eaton, K. M., C. W. Hoge, S. C. Messer, A. A. Whitt, O. A. Cabrera, D. McGurk, and C. A. Castro. "Prevalence of Mental Health Problems, Treatment Need, and Barriers to Care among Primary-Care-Seeking Spouses of Military Service Members Involved in Iraq and Afghanistan Deployments." *Military Medicine* 173 (2008): 1051–1056.

Glantz, K., A. Rizzo, and K. Graap. "Virtual Reality for Psychotherapy: Current Reality and Future Possibilities." *Psychotherapy: Theory, Research, Practice, Training* 40, nos. 1/2 (2003): 55–67, doi: 10.1037/0033-3204.40.1/2.55.

Griffith, J. "Decades of Transition for the U.S. Reserves: Changing Demands on Reserve Identity and Mental Well-being." *International Review of Psychiatry* 23 (2011): 181–191, doi: 10.3109/09540261.2010.541904.

Guskiewicz, K. M., S. W. Marshall, J. Bailes, M. McCrea, H. Harding, A. Matthews, M. J. Register, and R. C. Cantu. "Recurrent Concussion and Risk of Depression in Retired Football Players." *Med Sci Sports Exerc* 39, no. 6 (2007): 903–909.

Guskiewicz, K. M., M. McCrea, S. W. Marshall, R. C. Cantu, C. Randolph, W. Barr, and J. A. Onate. "Cumulative Effects Associated with Recurrent Concussion in Collegiate Football Players: The NCAA Concussion Study." *Journal of the American Medical Association (JAMA)* 290 (2003): 2549–2555.

Johnson, J. "Organic Psychosyndromes Due to Boxing." *British Journal of Psychiatry* 115, no. 518 (1969): 45–53.

Kaste, M., T. Kuurne, and J. Vilkki. "Is Chronic Brain Damage in Boxing a Hazard of the Past?" *Lancet* 2, no. 8309 (27 November 1982): 1186–1188.

Kelly, J. P., J. S. Nichols, C. M. Filley, K. O. Lillehie, D. Rubinstein, and B. K. Kleinschmidt-DeMasters. "Concussion in Sports: Guidelines for the Prevention of Catastrophic Outcome." *JAMA* 266, no. 20 (1991): 2867–2869.

Knox, J., and D. Price. "Total Force and the New American Military Family: Implications for Social Work Practice." *Families in Society: The Journal of Contemporary Human Services* 80, no. 2 (1999): 128–137.

Lanning, M. L. *Vietnam at the Movies.* New York: Fawcett Columbine, 1994.

Laster, J. "Five Things that Every Sailor Should Know about Virtual PTSD Help." *Navy Times*, 21 February 2011.

McCrea, M. A. *Mild Traumatic Brain Injury and Post-concussion Syndrome.* Oxford: Oxford University Press, 2008.

Moore, H. G., and J. L. Galloway. *We Were Soldiers Once, and Young.* New York; Random House, 1992.

Petraeus, D. *Testimony of General David Petraeus to Congress on the Situation in Iraq.* Defense Government Publications. Council on Foreign Relations. 8 April 2008.

"Phone App Aims to Help Troops with PTSD." *Navy Times*, 9 May 2011.

Robrecht, D. T., J. Millegan, L. L. Leventis, J. B. Crescitelli, and R. N. McLay. "Spousal Military Deployment as a Risk Factor for Postpartum Depression." *Journal of Reproductive Medicine* 53 (2008): 860–864.

Ryan, A. J. "Intracranial Injuries Resulting from Boxing." *Clinical Sports Medicine* 17, no. 1 (January 1998): 155–168.

Sheppard, S., J. Malatras, and A. Israel. "The Impact of Deployment on U.S. Military Families." *American Psychologist* 65, no. 6 (2010): 599–609.

Spinrad, P. S. "Patriotism as Pathology: Anti-Veteran Activism and the VA." *Journal of the Vietnam Veterans Institute* 2, no. 1 (1993): 42–70.

Tan, M. "A Million Soldiers Deployed since 9/11." *Army Times* 12 (20 December 2009), http://www.armytimes.com/news/2009/12/army_deployments_121809w/.

Tanielian, T., and L. H. Jaycox, eds. *Invisible Wounds of War: Psychological and Cognitive Injuries, Their Consequences, and Services to Assist Recovery.* Santa Monica, CA: RAND Corporation, 2008.

United States Army. "Military Operations Other than War (MOOTW)." (1992), http://www.dtic.mil/doctrine/jrm/mootw.pdf.

Wild, D. "Coming Home from War: A Literature Review." *Emergency Nurse* 11, no. 2 (2003): 22–28.

Zoroya. G. "Pentagon Tally Omits 20,000 Vets' Brain Injuries." *USA Today*, 23 November 2007.

Building Resilience in the Military Family during and following Deployment 7

*Stephen V. Bowles, Liz Davenport Pollock, Colanda Cato,
Monique Moore, Shelley M. MacDermid Wadsworth,
Vasiliki Anagnostopoulos, Kathleen K. Sun, Mary Campise,
William P. Mueller, Daniel Freeland, Malvis Tarney, Katalin
Brogdon, John Brogdon, Alexis A. Alvarado, Mark J. Bates*

Since 2001 approximately 2 million U.S. service members have been deployed to Afghanistan and Iraq. Multiple tours, prolonged separations, and the stress associated with every deployment have presented innumerable challenges for members of the military and their families. The challenges of coping with military life do not end when the family member comes home. Indeed, for many that is when the difficulties of maintaining a family are greatest. Family resilience—the family's capacity to adapt and grow in the face of adverse stressors and changing demands—plays a critical role in how military families cope or thrive with the challenges of deployment and reintegration. In addition to all the stressors of deployment and reintegration, military families also have to cope with the routine challenges that civilian counterparts experience, such as financial concerns, relationship problems, and health and work-life stressors. The extent to which families overcome such challenges will be connected to the overall resilience of the family. While most military families are remarkably resilient, even the strongest families experience ups and downs.

This chapter describes the stressors that can impact your service member and your family members in the areas of deployment and reintegration, relationships, children, finances, and injuries. It provides tips and suggestions on how to cope with these stressors and then concludes with three types of resilient skills you can utilize to cope with all of these stressors. To save space, we mention all of the reports, documents, and individuals we used in the reference section at the end of this chapter. We also conducted a focus group with deployed service members; the work and resources that we drew upon for this chapter are mentioned in the acknowledgments section at the front of this book.

Resilience is a process of adapting to adverse events and is influenced by heritable characteristics, learned behaviors, and environmental factors. Some people seem to be born with a natural sense of resilience and seem to be able to adapt to anything. Others may not have this heritable resilience but may be fortunate to be in an environment that helps them become more resilient (such as being surrounded by a strong community of other service members or having close family relationships). If you do not have the heritability for resilience or the environmental factors there are still learned behaviors that you can develop and strengthen, and tools that you can utilize to help to develop resilience.

Deployment Stressors, Coping, and Reintegration Strategies for Families

A family has the potential to be either a source of support, love, and comfort or a source of stress for each member. Oftentimes it is both. Like their civilian counterparts, military families rely on the support of family and friends to mitigate stress. Whether or not your home offers these supportive qualities usually depends on the relationships within a family and the stressors it faces. While all families face some level of discord at times, the distance of a military deployment places additional stress and demands on the entire family of each service member. Everyday living for a civilian family brings routine stressors including financial, relationship/marital, parental (e.g., children's behavior and schedules), mechanical (e.g., car breakdowns and home repairs), health, and work-life balance–related issues. Furthermore, conflicts, disagreements, and misunderstandings occur in any family. These challenges can spill over into the work and school environments and generate additional stress with work/school-family balance. Military families must deal with these everyday stressors in addition to military-specific ones generated by the strain of deployment.

The family members of service members, who remain on the home front, face a unique set of challenges. They struggle with worrying that their service member is in constant danger and with the fear the service member will be killed or injured. A spouse at home may also struggle to manage the household and juggle multiple responsibilities that were formerly divided between two people, while trying to maintain a strong connection with the deployed spouse. For military families with children, added challenges for the at-home spouse include finding proper and sufficient child-care services in the neighborhood and balancing work while dealing with all the children's needs in the absence of their deployed spouse. Additionally, parents of service members may find it challenging to communicate and maintain a strong relationship with their child while deployed. Other stressors surrounding the deployment of a service member may strain all members of the family. For instance, a short home-to-deployment dwell time—the amount of time spent at home compared to the amount of downtime during deployment—may not provide a service member adequate rest or time to reconnect with his family. In addition, the uncertainty about deployment and redeployment dates (i.e., when a service member leaves for or returns from deployment) can generate anxiety in family members.

As the service member's family at home reacts to stressors, the stressed family will in turn create stress for the deployed service member. As an example, in 2010 the Joint Mental Health Advisory Team 7 found that 25 percent of soldiers reported that stress at home caused them to be distracted at work while they were deployed. In addition, 19 percent of deployed service members also reported anxiety and tension that made it difficult for them to do their jobs because of concerns for their family back home.

General Tips to Cope with the Stressors of Deployment and Reintegration

Coping with the separation of deployment can be very challenging for the military family. The following tips are offered as specific strategies your family members can engage in to help maintain your resilience as you cope with deployment separations and reintegration.

Communicate Regularly

Communication is crucial during and after deployment. Communicating regularly, staying connected, and adjusting to changed roles are all critical strategies that can help family members manage stressors associated with deployment. This in turn will help you build resilience to cope with the challenges of deployment.

Do Not Isolate

Social support groups are key to helping family members stay connected, manage their emotions, and maintain resilience during times of stress. Activities with other service members' families, extended family, and friends are not only useful while your service member is away but will also provide important support during the reintegration period and afterwards. You can find these groups through your local military base (if you live near one), houses of worship, in your local community, and by contacting the veterans' service organizations listed in the appendix of this book.

Manage Stress

Keeping stress under control through the practice of stress management techniques can also be helpful in maintaining family resilience. Service members in the focus group organized by the authors of this chapter offered the following general stress management suggestions to help service members and family members cope with separation and reintegration:

- Ensure adequate sleep and rest.
- Practice breathing exercises and meditation.
- Exercise and participate in other recreational activities as time allows.
- Maintain a regular routine as much as possible.
- Enjoy the times you spend interacting with members in your unit, including family and friends.
- Read for enjoyment.
- Maintain regular communication with family members while away and continue to stay involved upon your return.
- Make plans to do social things to help lessen the amount of time spent strictly at work—making set plans can help establish clear boundaries between work and home. This in turn helps build a good social network.
- Do not put your life on hold—remain engaged and active by starting activities or continuing existing ones.

How Relationships Are Impacted by Deployment and Reintegration

During deployment, your family may have had a difficult time adjusting to the absence of your service member. As the stay-at-home spouse, you might have assumed new roles and responsibilities including employment, oversight of family finances, and childrearing. Some spouses who chose to leave a military base and stay with parents or in-laws may feel less connected to their military community and its attendant support. Spouses' reactions and behaviors during deployment may range from thriving on the independence to struggling with depression, anxiety, increased alcohol or substance use and abuse, and other conditions related to stress.

Communication issues often develop during deployment due to distance and the inability of service members and their family members to speak daily. Spouses are unaware of what loved ones are encountering and may become frustrated and concerned when they cannot talk to them while they are away. Likewise, deployed service members may not always be aware of what is happening at home. Resilience can be built if a couple can address issues through communication and can adjust their communication skills when the service member returns home.

Building a strong marital friendship, keeping in touch, and sharing feelings and thoughts are essential for couples to maintain strong relationships and mitigate stress during deployment and reintegration. Relationship problems, especially when left unresolved for long periods of time, can potentially impact a service member's or a spouse's or partner's well-being. If you find yourself having issues in your relationship, do not hesitate to seek help from a support group, counselor, or chaplain. We have highlighted in this chapter the ways that military deployment can place enormous strains on even the best relationship. If you have issues with your relationship you will not be alone—help is available for your family.

When your service member returns you should be prepared to adjust and work together as a couple to redevelop intimacy (if necessary) since people change and grow during the time spent away from each other. Couples' retreats can be useful to help you build communication skills so that you can discuss intimacy and strengthen your relationship. For more information on sex and intimacy after the deployment, see chapter 14.

In addition to intimacy issues, you as a spouse will need to manage home-life activity changes upon the return of your service member. Both you and your service member should be patient and willing to slowly adapt to the changes in your family's finances, daily routines, members' roles, and other home-life activities that may occur during the transition period. It may take time as it may be difficult for your service member to discuss all these issues right away, so dealing with things together in a steady manner may be the best way to help your service member reintegrate back into the family. Outcomes are best if you and your service member are receptive, open-minded, and patient; it can take several months to a year before service members can get on a regular home-life schedule.

Other common stressors on marriages and relationships include:

- Worries about infidelity.
- The spouse's lack of familiarity with the military lifestyle and lack of understanding of the communication difficulties while the service member was deployed.
- Difficulty communicating due to phone and Internet connection problems in a foreign country (as well as mission requirements).
- Changes in sexual and intimacy interest due to the separation and physical and mental effects of the war.
- Lack of preparation or foundation for the responsibilities of marriage, especially when service members and their spouses marry at a young age.
- Difficulty dealing with roles changing during the post-deployment process.

Tips for Couples Coping with Reintegration Stressors

For spouses and partners, the following coping strategies may help you build resilience during the reintegration period:

- Anticipate the challenges and sacrifices associated with post-deployment. Knowing what to expect can help prepare you for difficult decisions regarding work-life balance and career transitions.

- Communicate openly and consistently.
- Surround yourselves with people with whom you enjoy spending time both as a family and as a couple.
- Engage in hobbies.
- Take time for yourself.
- Avoid overusing alcohol and over-the-counter medications, using illegal drugs, engaging in aggressive driving, or engaging in sexually promiscuous behaviors.
- Remain connected with your own social network.
- Take advantage of professional services, such as your chaplain, installation's family support center, and Military OneSource (http://www.militaryone source.com).
- Try to be open-minded, flexible, and adjust to the unexpected. Try practicing relaxation techniques or mindfulness through audiobooks or classes. This can help foster flexibility and greater tolerance for uncertainty.
- Prioritize your time with family and friends. Do not stay at work if you are not truly needed.
- Upon return, try to treat family members as you normally would or adjust your interactions with them depending on how they have changed (e.g., perhaps the children have grown).
- Be patient. Slowly transition into roles; avoid rapid changes in roles or responsibilities, since transitioning too abruptly can cause friction and disrupt relationships.

How Children and Teens Are Impacted by Deployment and Reintegration

Deployments and reintegration will impact your children but there are techniques that can help them be more resilient as well. For more information and tips about how deployment affects children and how you can help them with these changes, see chapters 10, 11, and 12. A recent RAND study of military spouses in 2008 indicated that children with parents in Reserve components reported more readjustment difficulties, while children of active-duty parents reported more anxiety with their home caregiver. During deployment, children miss their deployed parent and feel the stress of the parent left behind. Each child will react differently—some may feel the need to act older and take on responsibilities such as the role as a co-parent for younger siblings, while others may exhibit more behavior problems during the parent's deployment and display increased attachment behavior during the reunion.

The RAND study also found that the longer the deployment, the greater the amount of stress the family is likely to experience, and that children may feel resentment toward their deployed parent if they only see the parent's absence. Upon the service member's return home, sometimes the problems that the children encountered during deployment may worsen without focused attention from parents. The feelings and behaviors children have toward their parent's deployment may also vary depending on the child's age; if the child is very young when the parent is deployed, the child may not recognize the parent upon return. The parent and child may need to spend time getting reacquainted with each other and re-forging a relationship.

Following deployment, disciplinary roles may change as they become shared between both parents. Service members and their children need to readjust after the parent's absence. Just as children who took on more responsibility during their parent's deployment or relied heavily on the parent at home may find it difficult to re-shift some of those responsibilities and expectations back on the returning parent, the returning service member may need to recognize his children's greater independence and maturity.

Children of service members who may be suffering from a physical or psychological injury may find it hard to understand and relate to their parent's behavior. Children may feel responsible for the parent's changes or worry that the injured parent no longer loves them; the non-injured spouse will need to reassure the children and help them see they are not at fault. During these times, self-awareness and awareness of others' behaviors, as well as frank communication, may help individual family members understand and enhance family bonding.

Teenagers of deployed parents often worry about the safety of their deployed parent or consequences from deployment and may experience changes in sleep, diet, and emotions. The stress of having a parent deployed may cause greater irritability, disrespectful behavior at home and school, or changes in academic performance. Under stress, teenagers may adapt initially by keeping their feelings to themselves; however, over time this can become isolating and perpetuate problems.

Many children born and raised in military families learn to adapt to their parent's deployment and reintegration and become more resilient as a result. However, no family is immune to stress. The resilience strategies in this chapter can provide valuable support and protection against stress over the long run.

How Family Finances Are Impacted by Deployment and Reintegration

Military spouses experience a range of unique financial stressors associated with military life, including spousal underemployment and unemployment. Spouses may also often face stark challenges to finding employment and building a career.

Most spouses want to work, but their career development and opportunities may be limited as a result of their spouse's multiple relocations. When a family relocates, the service member already has a new position waiting for her, while the spouse often must find a new one in an unfamiliar environment.

Work-life balance can be an ongoing stressor for military families. It is important to communicate and discuss career expectations and aspirations with your partner. A shared vision and commitment to your future and joint decision-making may help prevent career goals from generating relationship conflicts.

Budgeting issues can also arise during a service member's deployment and can carry over when the warrior returns home. Spouses may also have trouble budgeting at home. Sometimes family members may have limited skills and abilities in managing their own finances or simply cannot be trusted to manage money. Unexpected repairs, childcare costs, or other services can also upset a family's budget.

Tips for Addressing Family Financial Concerns

The following tips by Ryan Yarnell and Lee Aker can help your family reduce your financial stressors and in turn improve your family's resilience against these stressors.

- *Have "the Money Talk."* Discuss your financial dreams and ambitions with your family. What are you trying to achieve with money? Who will be the day-to-day money manager? How will you make decisions when there are competing goals?

- *Save for emergencies.* Murphy's Law states: "Anything that can go wrong will go wrong." Setting money aside for the inevitable financial emergency creates a strong foundation for financial security and helps "Murphy-proof" your life. We recommend earmarking a minimum of $1,000 for the unexpected, though ideally you should increase that amount to account for three to six months of total monthly expenses.

- *Pay off debt.* Paying off debt is one of the best things you can do to improve your financial situation. Not only are you saving on interest, but you also free up cash flow as you pay your debts off. Develop a plan to work through your debts, starting with the lowest balances and working your way up the list.

- *Create and use a budget.* The budget is the most useful tool to ensure a strong financial future. The budget will drive most of your financial decisions, small and large, and it should be prepared monthly to account for variations in spending throughout the year. A budget is only as good as the information put into it, so be sure to track your spending to make your budget more accurate. Additionally, the budget is only useful if you follow it, so set realistic goals and work to stay on target. Families should be prepared to make lifestyle changes if necessary (e.g., eat out less, take fewer vacations, switch to generic brands, etc.).

- *Save for retirement.* Traditional pensions are almost nonexistent, and the future of Social Security is unknown. The only way to ensure a comfortable retirement is to save money on your own. Tax-sheltered investment vehicles, such as the government's Thrift Savings Plan (TSP) and Individual Retirement Accounts (IRAs), are great tax-advantaged ways to set aside money for your future retirement. A good rule of thumb is to save 10–15 percent of your gross income into retirement accounts. Save early, and save often. The best time to start saving for retirement is today, no matter how old you are, and set up your contributions to occur automatically on a regular basis, such as monthly or every two weeks. A little cash saved today will be a lot of money saved tomorrow.

- *Check your credit.* Your credit information is used for other purposes besides deciding whether or not you can borrow money. Everyone is looking at your credit: your landlord, your insurance companies, the military, and even future employers. There are many reasons, such as the increased incidence of identity theft, for learning about what is included in your credit file. By federal law, you can obtain a copy of your credit report once every twelve months from each of the credit reporting agencies (Experian, Equifax, and TransUnion) by going to http://www.annualcreditreport.com, which is the only site where you can get your reports absolutely free. Instead of pulling all three reports at the same time, pull them at different times throughout the year; this way you will not have to wait twelve months to see your credit report for free.

- *Get insured.* Make sure that you have all the right insurance for your needs: life insurance for all the contributing adults, health care insurance reviewed by your provider, auto insurance, and homeowners or renters insurance.

- *Create a will.* Setting up a will is necessary. Consult with free legal services (available on most military installations for active-duty military and family members) for other necessary documents, such as those for appointing powers of attorney or guardians for children or special-needs relatives. Creating a will can bring much-needed help and peace to loved ones in the case of unfortunate events.

War-Related Physical and Mental Health Conditions

Injuries sustained during deployment (including physical ones such as combat wounds, traumatic brain injury [TBI], and psychological ones including post-traumatic stress disorder [PTSD] and depression) will have an impact on family members, who may be prone to their own trauma, burnout, and compassion fatigue by virtue of the care they provide for their family member. Spouses who care for a wounded warrior will need to attend to their own well-being to keep up their own resilience and should not feel guilty in doing so.

PTSD often presents difficult challenges for families. An injured service member may forget important family events or be unable to do previous home chores or recreational activities to the fullest extent. The family may be unable to participate in activities they once loved to do together. Family members may feel unsafe if behavior is unpredictable. At times the family may feel there is no one that they can reach out to during stressful events, and will need to seek counseling to help cope with the changes in family dynamics. The family may feel sad, angry, or worried about the service member and his future. Stress and depressive feelings occurring for one or more of the family members may decrease the family's potential for cohesion and functioning.

Building resilience after a physical or mental injury is critical. Military families need to understand the unique circumstances and health conditions of the service member in order to maintain strong family units and resilience. Several obstacles make it difficult to maintain optimal health in military life and culture. Moving frequently and changing health care providers can sometimes make it challenging to establish continuity of care. Some younger military couples and parents are under greater stress because they may be newlyweds or first-time parents living apart from each other. The stress can be exacerbated by the lack of support or distance from extended family. More established families might face various challenges throughout the family life cycle. Loved ones may have difficulty understanding complex regimens or health instructions from providers, which may result in unintended problems for family health care.

Dealing with Individual Stress Responses and Risky Behaviors

A service member's involvement in high-stress situations such as combat may trigger a stress response or stress injury. This stress response is the body's natural reaction to stress in the environment and places the individual's body and mind at alert for danger. This response can often keep individuals alert and quicken reaction time in dangerous situations, thus increasing the likelihood of staying alive. But after being under stress for a prolonged period of time many individuals find it difficult to calm down and "reset" after stressful experiences. Family members should be aware that their service member could display some of these difficulties postdeployment. These difficulties may involve sleep problems (e.g., problems falling asleep, getting restful sleep, staying asleep, waking up too early, or having nightmares); restlessness; increased startle reactions; feelings of anxiety, depression, and anger; pain from injuries; and hypersensitivity to environment and ambient noises—objects and locations may be seen as threatening. Service members may also withdraw, avoiding social situations and preferring to be alone rather than interact with family and friends.

Returning from deployment, service members sometimes develop unhealthy risk-taking behaviors as attempts to reduce their stress level. This may occur through first-time alcohol use or an increased use of alcohol in an attempt to soothe the emotional pain that stems from combat. The start of or increase in cigarette smoking may serve a similar purpose. Service members may also engage in risky sexual behavior or aggressive driving. These behaviors may be in combination with alcohol use, over-the-counter drug abuse, or illegal drug use. These behaviors can directly or indirectly affect a family's health. More specifically, mixing anger and alcohol in the context of troubled relationships can result in mental or physical abuse. When families are placed at risk in this way, immediate medical attention and assistance are necessary to address mental and physical health concerns.

Family members should be aware of the more easily treatable common symptoms of stress injuries or traumatic stress so that they can spot possible warning signs and get the help they need with the PTSD symptoms. Those suffering from stress injuries, traumatic stress, or PTSD may experience flashbacks, nightmares, or upsetting memories from a traumatic event. They are also subject to intense physical responses to reminders of the traumatic event(s) (e.g., increased heart rate, rapid breathing, sweating, etc.). Those with PTSD may avoid remembering details of their trauma or avoid thoughts, places, and feelings that remind them of the event. Research has found that service members returning from the recent conflicts with trauma symptoms, sleep issues, or sexual problems displayed lower levels of satisfaction with their marriages and relationships. It is not uncommon for those with stress symptoms to experience a loss or reduction in sexual desire.

Depression is different from the normal disappointments or dissatisfactions that one typically experiences in life. Depression is a long-term response that may cause changes in a person's normal routine and personality. Someone suffering from depression remains consistently unhappy or "down in the dumps" for an extended period of time. Symptoms may include difficulty concentrating, making decisions, sleeping, and eating; irritability; loss of interest in activities and hobbies; loss of sexual interest; feelings of guilt, worthlessness, and helplessness; persistent aches or pains; and thoughts of or attempts at suicide.

The time needed to heal from TBI caused by head injuries will depend upon the severity and location of the injury, as well as the age and general health of the service member. It should be noted that symptoms of TBI often mimic the symptoms of stress injuries and that the presence of both can change the treatment. For example, some medications commonly used to help with stress injuries are not advisable for use with someone who has a TBI as well. Some common conditions include problems associated with thinking (concentration, memory, and decision making), senses (vision, sound, touch, taste, and smell), communication (speech and under-standing), mental health (anxiety, depression, personality or mood changes, aggres-sion, irritability, and socially inappropriate behavior), and physical health (sleep difficulties, headaches, trouble with balance, and numbness in limbs). There can also be a reduced desire or inability for intimate relations and sexual behavior.

Tips for Families with Wounded Service Members

Here are some tips to help your family build resilience and cope with some of the stressors associated with having a service member in your family who was injured or disabled during deployment:

- Surround the service member with people with whom he enjoys spending time.
- Join social organizations that support the conditions suffered by the service member.
- Be flexible—things may not return to exactly the way they were before in terms of both family activities and work; your service member may have outbursts of anger, and engage in socially inappropriate behavior in public.
- Facilitate your service member's engagement in social activities, but increase them gradually.
- Children may feel responsible for the parent's changes or worry that the injured parent no longer loves them. The non-injured spouse will need to reassure children and help them see they are not at fault.
- Stay connected with your social network and self-care routine.
- Ensure children are involved in age-appropriate activities in school, camps, and other recreational activities.
- For service members with depression or TBI, write things down to help them remember or encourage them to do so when appropriate.
- Become involved with as many of your normal activities as possible.
- Find new hobbies.
- Be patient—it takes time for wounds to heal and to adjust to changes that have occurred in military operations.
- Consistent routines can give a child a sense of safety. Continuing to meet the needs of children during this difficult time is important for ensuring family strength in the long run.
- Recognize that children will feel the stress caused by the absence and sub-sequent injury of the service member. They may simply display it differ-ently. In babies, the stress may manifest itself as a disruption in feeding and

sleeping patterns. Slightly older children may be more prone to temper tantrums or complain of physical ailments, which are representative of their internal emotional ailments. Teenagers may lash out, confused by their feelings and torn by their growing desire for independence and their need for a connection to their family due to their parents' combat injuries.

- Adults who are good role models for their children discuss their children's feelings with them, help them express their feelings, and model good behavior for their children.
- Parents can use this opportunity to serve as good role models for children and youth regarding health care–related behavior and responsibilities such as nutrition, exercise, and stress management.

Resilience Building Skills

Three skill sets can help your family build resilience to be better prepared to take on all of the stressors described above: (1) mind-body skills, (2) cognitive skills (i.e., cognitive reframing), and (3) communication skills. While other variations exist, these three approaches are easily learned and applied for resilience-building. Each of these skills is detailed below, along with concrete examples of how to apply each skill.

Resilience Skill #1. Relax: Incorporating Mind-Body Skills

Being able to manage stress and intense emotions is a key factor in promoting resilience. As described above, stress can place individuals at risk of being less able to manage negative emotions such as anxiety, anger, and depression and can strain your family relationships. Increasingly, integrative health practices such as diaphragmatic breathing, yoga, mindfulness, meditation, and guided imagery are being used in military communities as effective tools aimed at building resilience (e.g., the Army's Comprehensive Soldier Fitness and the Air Force's Comprehensive Airman Fitness programs). In particular, a variety of breathing exercises that trigger the body's relaxation response can often be quickly learned and can provide immediate relief for feelings of anxiety, stress, and anger, and can be practiced by individuals to de-escalate stress during times of high tension and conflict. Regular practice of one or more of these techniques may increase feelings of relaxation and reduce feelings of anxiety. There are even some couples meditation and yoga classes as well as parent-child meditation and yoga classes. See the appendix of this book for information about these types of resources.

Resilience Skill #2. Think: Incorporating Cognitive-Behavioral Skills

Building resilience within the family can also be accomplished by using cognitive-behavioral skills. These skills show you how to recognize faulty or unproductive ways of thinking (called cognitive distortions) and develop alternate thoughts and behaviors to promote healthy, realistic thoughts, and positive emotions (called cognitive reframing).

Cognitive Distortions

Cognitive distortions are a type of thinking that can lead to misinterpretations of events, situations, and behaviors. Here are some of the most common distortions:

- *Jumping to conclusions* involves assuming the worst outcome without having any supporting evidence or information. Two examples of jumping to conclusions are *mind-reading* and *fortune-telling*, which involve making assumptions about another person's behavior or an event without doing a reality check of the situation or with the person to see if your thoughts are accurate.
- *Magnification* involves over-stating or under-stating the importance of an event or action and focusing on the aspects that put you or another person in the most negative light possible.
- *"Should" statements* focus on beliefs about what you or others ought to, have to, or should do or be to have a particular positive result.
- *Labeling* is a form of rigid, "black or white" thinking, in which you label yourself or others as bad or awful because of a single individual event or isolated situation.
- *Personalization of blame* involves assigning blame to yourself or someone else for something over which you or the other person had little or no control.

Any one of the above distortions could seriously hamper your ability to think realistically or positively about a situation or person and result in negative family interactions.

Cognitive Reframing

Cognitive reframing is a cognitive behavioral strategy that refers to a person's ability to critically identify, examine, and correct distorted thinking. It involves examining the thoughts a person is having, questioning whether the thoughts are realistic, helpful, or supported by outside evidence, and then mentally rephrasing the thoughts for a more positive outcome.

The following example highlights a number of challenges and demands military family members may face, many of which were described in detail in previous sections of this chapter. Using cognitive reframing, unhealthy conclusions drawn from specific actions in the scenario are reframed into healthier, more positive conclusions. Such steps are likely to improve resilience, enhance family interactions, and result in improved family reintegration processes post-deployment.

Case Example

Not long after returning from his third deployment, MSgt. John Smith, an Air Force Security Forces first sergeant, knew that something wasn't right. He was having trouble sleeping due to intrusive memories of a young airman his unit lost in a convoy ambush in Iraq, and began to wonder why he was spared. He was easily startled by noises around the house, and began shutting his door to be alone. His wife noticed the changes first, including a withdrawal from normal activities that he used to enjoy, such as going out with his friends, reading, and working out. Although he remembered his wedding anniversary, he forgot other daily chores, including picking up groceries, clothes from the cleaners, or dog food. Easily angered and short-tempered, he and his spouse argued frequently about things that had never bothered them in the past. His spouse believed that he was withdrawing to avoid being around her and the kids and that he was angry at her.

The clinical symptoms depicted within the above scenario could be interpreted in a number of ways. Using the cognitive reframing strategy, specific cognitive symptoms associated with depressive disorders, PTSD, and TBI are described in the table below. The table below also describes unhealthy perceptions and identifies alternative healthy perceptions that can be substituted through reframing unhealthy perceptions. Specific cognitive distortions are noted within the unhealthy perception column to illustrate negative interpretations of potentially neutral or innocuous events.

Resilience Skill #3. Communication: A Key Family Resilience-Building Skill

Communication can be a lifeline for service members and their families after deployment since it can ease tough times, help resolve problems, and maintain feelings of closeness and love, and thus serve as one of several family factors that can promote resilience in the military family.

Stress can blur and destroy communication in families and hinder family members' abilities to effectively engage in problem solving. This in turn can potentially deteriorate the quality of the family's relationship. Communication between couples can often take some time to re-adjust or reset once back home.

Each individual within the family will have their own experiences of deployment and the reintegration process. Therefore, it can be helpful during reintegration for families to collectively share and listen to each family member's experiences. For example, the Families Overcoming Under Stress (FOCUS) program has family members discussing "deployment narratives," and places these narratives on a timeline so that each member can gain a good understanding of the other members'

Table 7.1 Reframing Common Clinical Symptoms Associated with Depression, Stress Injuries, and TBI

Cognitive Behavioral Strategy	Case Example Symptom	Unhealthy Perception	Healthy Perception
Reframing Depressive Symptoms	Trouble sleeping	He's avoiding coming to bed at night because he doesn't find me attractive. **(Personalization of blame)**	He's really tired after a long day, and he's trying to catch up on work unit activities after being away on a long deployment.
	Decreased interest in activities	He's withdrawing from activities, because he doesn't want to spend time with the kids or me. He's going to leave me and file for divorce. **(Magnification)**	He may need some additional help from a professional, or perhaps I could plan some activities that he might enjoy, such as a family movie night.
Reframing PTSD Symptoms	Withdrawal from friends	He doesn't want to be a part of our lives anymore or socialize with friends we've had for years. It's going to be like this forever. **(All-or-nothing thinking)**	This might be part of a larger issue related to his PTSD or stress injuries and is not a direct result of anything I've said or done. After he's had some time to adjust being back, he may be more interested in socializing with others again.
	Hyper-arousal; exaggerated startled response	He's angered so quickly because the kids and I are annoying him. It's totally my fault that he gets so angry all the time. I am an awful spouse because I keep saying the wrong thing to upset him. **(Labeling)**	If I obtain more information about PTSD, perhaps I can learn how his hyper-vigilant behavior in a war zone was very adaptive there. It may take some time before he's able to adapt to not being in a war zone.
	Numbing	He ignores me and acts as if I'm not even there. **(Jumping to conclusions)**	He's going through a tough time dealing with his PTSD or stress injury. This is likely another part of the disorder that I'm not aware of. He's not intentionally ignoring me, but really trying to cope with the problems he's experiencing.

continued

Cognitive Behavioral Strategy	Case Example Symptom	Unhealthy Perception	Healthy Perception
Reframing TBI Symptoms	Forgetfulness	He forgets everything and just doesn't care. He should be able to remember simple things. How hard is it to remember to pick up dog food? **(Should statements)**	Perhaps this is part of the health issue he is experiencing. Just because he's become more forgetful lately doesn't mean that he doesn't care.

feelings and experiences. The program is available online at http://www.focusproject .org. Additionally, military family resilience programs all include some focus on the importance of communication as a central aspect of family strength-building both during deployment and post-deployment. Borrowing from these programs, as well as from findings from research with military families, the following tips can help protect or rebuild communication to strengthen relationships.

Tips for Family Communications

Use the following guidelines to help you effectively communicate with a loved one when there is something important that you want to discuss:

The *person speaking* should follow these guidelines:

- Use "I" statements when describing your thoughts and feelings. "I" statements help your listener not feel attacked and helps him hear what you are saying.
- Be specific—only discuss one main issue at a time.
- Pick a good time and place for expressing thoughts and feelings.

The *person listening* should then follow these guidelines:

- Summarize and restate what you heard.
- Do not ask questions, react to what the speaker said, offer solutions, or interpret the meaning of her comments.
- Assess your tone of voice, facial expressions, and your posture to indicate that you are open and not defensive.
- Put yourself in the speaker's shoes.

Once one small issue has been expressed and heard, partners switch roles. These guidelines can help break communication down to the basics so each member can feel heard. Being able to have a dialogue and discuss serious issues is important in relationships. Research indicates that around 70 percent of the problems that couples face remain the same throughout the relationship (implying that only about 30 percent of problems are solvable). Therefore, learning how to solve the problems that are solvable and engaging in an ongoing discussion around perpetual problems is key to optimally functioning relationships.

General Communication Tips

- Start the conversation gently. Choose the right tone, and choose the right time wisely. Most of the time the first minute of conversation will predict how the rest of the conversation goes.
- Avoid the following four attitudes when communicating with your loved ones: 1) making global negative statements about each other (*criticism*), 2) being sarcastic (in a mean way) or mocking your loved one (*contempt*), 3) responding without listening to defend your behavior (*defensiveness*), and 4) withdrawing from or ignoring your loved one (*stonewalling*). Having high levels of these characteristics is linked to unhappy relationships over the long term.
- In conflict conversations, try to use a "repair attempt" that defuses the conflict or stress of the argument. This is when one or both members try to defuse the disagreement, calm down, and connect with each other through agreeing to disagree, bringing humor into the conversation, gentle statements, or other ways. Sometimes what will work as a repair attempt in one conflict will not work as well in another situation.
- Remember to compliment each other. You want to show you care for, are thinking of, love, and respect your loved ones on a daily basis. Studies suggest that couples who have at least five positive interactions for every negative interaction (a 5:1 ratio) are more likely to have long-term, happy, successful marriages than unhappy couples who tend to have one positive interaction for every negative interaction (a 1:1 ratio), or even less (sometimes as low as a ratio of 0.8:1).
- Foster a good friendship with your partner—discuss your goals and dreams for the future, listen to the small daily things that interest each of you, and try to do things you like together occasionally. A marital friendship is an important part of long-term marital satisfaction.

Summary

A variety of coping tips have been identified for family members as they reunite after deployment. The utilization of mind-body, cognitive-behavioral, and communication skills can allow family members to more accurately interpret and understand potentially negative events, communicate and respond to loved ones' needs more effectively, and exhibit lower levels of stress and higher levels of family functioning. Effective communication, developing positive cognitive skills, and learning mind-body exercises can be important for family resilience building.

The Way Ahead

Applying family resilience tips can strengthen your family. Be aware of each family member's needs, as well as your own—and be patient and compassionate with each other. Increase your family's confidence through communicating love, praise, encouragement, and in-person support at every opportunity you have in order to build a good foundation for everyone in both good and difficult times. Just as in a sports team, each member of the family team has an important role and function—and everyone needs to work together to get to the other side of the field. Like all successful teams, bring your family together for regular routines (e.g., eating together), celebrations (e.g., graduations, birthdays), and traditions (e.g., holiday events) that will strengthen your family, build cohesion, and create fond memories. Make sure your team has available experts such as coaches, Family Readiness Group advisors, therapists, counselors, and spiritual leaders to provide valuable advice, assistance, and support. Surround yourself with positive people and participate in activities that make you happy, serving as examples for your family. All athletes need rest days and periods to recover from high-intensity training; therefore, make sure you plan and take time to remove yourself from your hurried life and reflect for a couple of minutes to regroup or to think about how you can strengthen yourself and your family. Make sure you are doing fun activities, enjoying yourself, resting and recharging. The more rested and stress-free you are, the greater the likelihood you and your family will be more flexible to meet the challenges of life.

References

Allen, E., G. Rhoades, S. Stanley, and H. Markman "Hitting Home: Relationships between Recent Deployment, Post-Traumatic Stress Symptoms, and Marital Functioning for Army Couples." *Journal of Family Psychology* 24, no. 3 (2010): 280–288.

Barker, L. H., and K. D. Berry. "Developmental Issues Impacting Military Families with Young Children during Single and Multiple Deployments." *Military Medicine* 174 (2009): 1033–1040.

Bates, M., S. Bowles, J. Hammermeister, C. Stokes, E. Pinder, M. Moore, M. Fritts, M. Vythilingam, T. Yosick, J. Rhodes, C. Myatt, R. Westphal, D. Fautua, P. Hammer, and G. Burbelo. "Psychological Fitness: A Military Demand-Resource Model." *Military Medicine* 175, no. 8 (2010): 21.

Bowles, S. V., C. Cato, E. D. Pollock, M. Moore, K. Sun, J. Dekle, B. Mueller, and M. J. Bates. "Military Family Fitness Model." Poster presentation at the American Psychological Association Convention, August 2011, Washington, DC.

Bowles, S. V., M. Moore, C. Cato, E. D. Pollock, and M. J. Bates. "Family Fitness Model." 2011 DoD/USDA Conference Proceedings Presentation at the Family Resilience Conference, April 2011, Chicago, IL.

Burns, D. D. *The Feeling Good Handbook.* Rev. ed. New York: Plume, 1999.

Center for the Study of Traumatic Stress. "Courage to Care: Health Literacy Addressing Communication Barriers to Foster Patient Self-Care and Family Care." Bethesda, MD: Uniformed Services University of the Health Sciences, 2012.

Chandra, A., R. Burns, T. Tanielian, L. Jaycox, and M. Scott. *Understanding the Impact of Deployment on Children and Families: Findings from a Pilot Study of Operation Purple Camp Participants.* Santa Monica, CA: RAND Corporation, 2008.

Epstein, N., and D. H. Baucom. *Enhanced Cognitive-Behavioral Therapy for Couples: A Contextual Approach.* Washington, DC: American Psychological Association, 2002.

Esposito-Smythers, C., J. Wolff, K. M. Lemmon, M. Bodzy, R. Swenson, et al. "Military Youth and the Deployment Cycle: Emotional Health Consequences and Recommendations for Intervention." *Journal of Family Psychology* 25, no. 4 (2011): 497–507.

Goff, B., J. Crow, A. Reisbig, and S. Hamilton. "The Impact of Individual Trauma Symptoms of Deployed Soldiers on Relationship Satisfaction." *Journal of Family Psychology* 21, no. 3 (2007): 344–353.

Gottman, J. M., J. S. Gottman, and C. L. Atkins. "The Comprehensive Soldier Fitness Program: Family Skills Component." *American Psychologist* 66, no. 1 (2011): 52–57.

Gottman, J. *The Marriage Clinic: A Scientifically Based Marital Therapy.* New York: Norton, 1999.

———. "Psychology and the Study of Marital Processes." *Annual Review of Psychology* 49 (1998): 169–197.

———. *Why Marriages Succeed Or Fail . . . And How You Can Make Yours Last.* New York: Simon & Schuster, 1994.

Huebner, A. J., and J. A. Mancini. *Adjustments among Adolescents in Military Families When a Parent Is Deployed: A Final Report Submitted to the Military Family Research Institute and the Department of Defense Quality of Life Office.* Falls Church, VA: Department of Human Development, Virginia Polytechnic Institute and State University, June 2005.

———. "Supporting Youth during Parental Deployment: Strategies for Professionals and Families." In supplement, *Prevention Researcher* 15 (June 2008): 10–13.

Human Resources Strategic Assessment Program (HRSAP). "2008 Survey of Military Spouses: Impact of Deployment on Spouses and Children." *Human Relations Surveys,* No. 2009-019.

Joint Mental Health Advisory Team 7 (J-MHAT-7): Operation Enduring Freedom 2010, Afghanistan. http://www.armmedicine.army.mil/reports/mhat/mhat_vii/J_MHAT_7.pdf (accessed 23 June 2011).

Lester, P., C. Mogil, et al. "Families Overcoming Under Stress: Implementing Family-Centered Prevention for Military Families Facing Wartime Deployments and Combat Operational Stress." *Military Medicine* 176, no. 1 (2011): 19–25.

MacDermid Wadsworth, S. M. "Family Risk and Resilience in the Context of War and Terrorism." *Journal of Marriage and Family* 72 (2010): 537–556.

———. "Supporting Family Resilience: What Does The Evidence Say?" 2011 DoD/USDA Conference Proceedings Presentation at the Family Resilience Conference, April 2011, Chicago, IL.

Meis, L. A., R. A. Barry, et al. "Relationship Adjustment, PTSD Symptoms, and Treatment Utilization among Coupled National Guard Soldiers Deployed to Iraq." *Journal of Family Psychology* 24, no. 5 (2010): 560–567.

Meredith, L. S., C. D. Sherbourne, S. J. Gaillot, L. Hansell, H. V. Ritschard, et al. *Promoting Psychological Resilience in the U.S. Military*. Santa Monica, CA: RAND Corporation, 2011.

Merolla, A. J. "Relational Maintenance during Military Deployment: Perspectives of Wives of Deployed U.S. Soldiers." *Journal of Applied Communication Research* 38, no. 1 (2010): 4–2.

Moore, M., D. Brown, N. Money, and M. Bates. "Mind-Body Skills for Regulating the Autonomic Nervous System." Arlington, VA: Defense Centers of Excellence for Psychological Health and Traumatic Brain Injury, June 2011. http://www.dcoe.health.mil/Content/Navigation/Documents/Mind-Body%20Skills%20for%20Regulating%20the%20Autonomic%20Nervous%20System.pdf.

Sanchez, E. "DOD Launches Military Spouse Employment Partnership." American Forces Press Service. http://www.defense.gov/news/newsarticle.aspx?id=64509 (accessed 10 July 2011).

Savych, B. *Effects of Deployments on Spouses of Military Personnel*. Santa Monica, CA: RAND Corporation, 2008.

Taft, C. T., J. A. Schumm, J. Panuzio, and S. P. Proctor. "A Prospective Examination of Family Adjustment among Male and Female Operation Desert Storm Veterans." *Journal of Consulting and Clinical Psychology* 76 (2008): 648–656.

8 | Suicide and Suicide Prevention

Michael Russell

Suicide is a significant problem for the military. It is the third leading cause of death for males of service age, and the stresses of war have increased the suicide rate substantially. For about twenty years (from the 1980s to 2001) the rate of suicide among active-duty military held fairly constant at 11.5 incidents per 100,000 people each year. As the war has progressed over time that number has more than doubled for service members exposed to combat, recently rising above 24 incidents per 100,000 people for both Marines and soldiers. (See Figure 8.1.) During the month of June 2010, the Army alone experienced more than one active-duty suicide per day.

What explains this rise? I worked as an active-duty Army psychologist for twenty-four years and my duties included conducting psychological autopsies of anyone on active duty who had committed suicide. Later in my career I became the suicide prevention "subject matter expert" for the Army Medical Department. We studied suicide deaths to figure out what had gone wrong and why the deaths happened, and in doing so collected the data on every active-duty suicide. Over all this time several things have become clear that make suicide in the military a unique problem and I offer suggestions on how you can help the service member in your family if you suspect she may be suicidal.

What Suicide Is Not

Having worked with suicide for a quarter century, I have come to realize that some of the common wisdom about suicide in the military does not hold up to close scrutiny. A great deal of emphasis of suicide prevention is often placed on new recruits or junior members of the military, but they actually have among the lowest per capita rates of suicide. The most at-risk rank is actually at the E-8 level (e.g., senior chief petty officer, master sergeant, or first sergeant). Depression is a

Figure 8.1 U.S. Army Active Duty Suicide Rates, as of November 2011:
Convincing evidence of the effect of multiple deployments on suicide rates, which have more than doubled from peace-time levels, rising from 9.6/100,000 in 2004 to a projected 24.6/100,000 in 2011

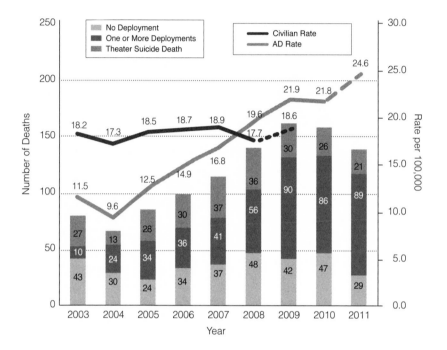

real issue in suicide, but most of the people who kill themselves in the military are not actually depressed. Alcohol and drug abuse is common among people who commit suicide, but most people who kill themselves are neither alcoholics nor drug addicts. The typical role substance abuse plays in suicide is to disinhibit people and make them more likely to be able to act out their darker desires. People call it "liquid courage"—implicit in that phrase is the concept that the impulse to suicide came first and then the drug or drink was added to assist in the process, rather than the other way around. My point is not to dismiss these co-morbidities (i.e., depression and alcohol and drug abuse), but rather to put them in context. Mental health professionals lock onto familiar territory and onto things that they have already built structures to address. We know how to treat depression, and we know how to treat substance abuse. That it rather misses the point is one of those inconvenient truths. To understand suicide, and to prevent suicide, you have to get to a deeper truth.

What Suicide Is: An Impossible Choice

So what really is going on with military suicide? It does appear that suicide clusters around different themes at different stages of life. For the elderly, who are still the highest risk populations in the nation, suicide is about a loss of meaning and purpose in life, declining health, and isolation. So if you look at suicide in America as a whole, this is the answer you will get. But for active-duty service members or more recent veterans (who are usually younger men and women in the prime of their lives), suicide is usually about facing an apparently impossible choice. In study after study, the number-one precipitating event for active-duty suicide is defined as "loss of love object." The number-two reason is the parallel perception of a "loss of career." Just these two reasons alone account for 85 percent of all suicides among those actively serving as members of the armed forces. The things we seem to mainly worry about, namely the mental diseases and addictions, are tucked away in the remaining 15 percent.

Suicide seems often to be about a situation: The suicidal person is faced with an often self-imposed "impossible choice." The psychological quandary goes something like this: The love object (spouse, partner, or lover) leaves. The service member affected by the loss says to himself: "I can't live without her." He then ruminates on it and repeats that phrase (or variations on it) over and over. Eventually he will come to really believe he cannot live, or does not want to live, without her. This process is very painful. The idea of suicide starts to seem like a reasonable solution to make that pain go away. Strangely, once the decision is made to actually die, the person will feel a sense of relief, because the unsolvable problem of how to live without his lost love is now solved. He may actually become quite cheerful leading up to his death.

This is all distorted thinking, and becomes increasingly irrational. Pointing this out to the person is our first point of intervention to prevent his suicide. People on the outside of this whole internal dialogue are often completely unaware that this process is taking place in their friend or loved one's head. To them it seems so obvious that he can indeed live without that former lover. In fact they might even be relieved, or think he is better off without her, and it is overall a good thing that they broke up. But the people on the outside are not the ones whose world is shattered. To the person affected, it really may seem like the end of the world.

The same sort of tragic logic comes into play with the loss of career. Many people derive much of their self-esteem from their employment or profession and they strongly identify with that career and define themselves as being their job (i.e., "I am a sergeant major"). If a job is suddenly taken away, then what is left for that person? As with the loss of an intimate partner, the same irrational thought process begins to occur to a person who lost her job (i.e., "I can't live without my job,"

"I am nothing without my position," or "My life is not worth living without my career"). In one six-month time span I performed a psychological autopsy of two suicides: The first was a West Point officer, the son of a general, who was passed over twice for promotion and given ninety days to get out of the military. The second was a first sergeant relieved of his position, who hanged himself on the Fort Lewis golf course near his favorite hole.

These are real people so affected, and I have seen it played out over and over. E-8 is the highest risk rank for suicide in the military because that is the rank at which hard-charging, dedicated career service members face mandatory retirement. I once attended an event for a person who put on their biography "I am married to the Army." If you are married to the Army, then breaking up with her is potentially as hard as losing a spouse.

The military's culture feeds into this. Sayings like "Death before dishonor" are mottos in the military. We are only a few generations from hara-kiri (ritualized suicide) in the Japanese military. The perception of failure, and of dishonor, goes strongly against the grain of the military mind, which also has prepared itself for the idea of death.

Understanding these psychological processes is really the key to recognizing people at risk for suicide and also the key to helping them. This is why it falls on the family and friends to do the heavy lifting in recognizing and preventing suicide. We are ultimately looking for a loss as the reason for a suicide, as both of the above reasons really boil down to a service member reacting to a loss.

How You Can Help

Pain and emotional distress make people withdraw into themselves, and they become increasingly self-focused and unaware of the world around them. Pain makes them focus on themselves as it puts on psychological blinders. They really lose all perspective. If your friend or loved one is a person headed toward self-murder, she is just going to withdraw further and further, obsess more and more, and finally come up with exactly the wrong "solution" to the loss. Some really irrational stuff can start to seem reasonable inside one's head at this stage. What is needed is a "reality check" that allows her to bounce her ideas off someone else who is really listening. It will thus fall to you to help your friend or loved one get the blinders off, because you may be the only one in a position to see the storm that is brewing inside her.

If there is a break-up, or loss of love object, do not let your friend or loved one completely withdraw and disappear. Maintain some daily contact with her. The Army recommends three steps in its "ACE" (Ask, Care, Escort) approach that you can take in dealing with a service member who might be suicidal (see the text of the ACE program card distributed to all soldiers reprinted below). The first step is to *ask* her how she is feeling and what she is thinking. Listen for irrational statements and gently dispute them. Help her start by seeing beyond the present loss. Many people do return from combat, deployment, and military service strengthened with a better appreciation for life. A situation of loss can actually be turned from a potentially tragic situation to one in which the person grows and becomes a better and stronger individual. Unfortunately "growth experiences" are high-risk, and not everything that does not kill us makes us stronger.

The next step in the ACE program is to control the situation by removing things away from the service member that could be used in a suicide (such as weapons, pills, or rope) and *care* for her by actively listening to her concerns. If the service member appears or sounds determined to end her life, the final stage of the ACE program is to *escort* her to someone with the training to provide her with help.

Figure 8.2 ACE Program Card

Ask your buddy
- Have the courage to ask the question, but stay calm
- Ask the question directly: Are you thinking of killing yourself?

Care for your buddy
- Calmly control the situation; do not use force; be safe
- Actively listen to show understanding and produce relief
- Remove any means that could be used for self-injury

Escort your buddy
- Never leave your buddy alone
- Escort to chain of command, Chaplain, behavioral health professional, or primary care provider
- Call the National Suicide Prevention Lifeline

National Suicide Prevention Lifeline:
1-800-273-8255(TALK)
USAPHC http://phc.amedd.army.mil/

The card below, which lists the common risk factors for suicide, is used by the Army to assess the potential for suicide in a soldier. You can use it as a checklist to determine if your service member could be suicidal and what you can do to help him. The situations in rows seven through twelve represent very high risk situations that merit immediate attention.

Figure 8.3 Suicide Prevention Risk Factor Assessment Card

#	Risk Factors:	ACTION REQUIRED
1.	Is the Warrior a male, age 25 or under? Has the Warrior just reported to his or her permanent duty assignment in the last 3 months?	☐ Know your Soldier! ☐ **Ask, Care, Escort!** ☐ Be willing to intervene!
2.	Has the Warrior had one or more previous deployments to Iraq or Afghanistan? Is the Warrior cross-leveled for deployment purposes? New to the unit?	
3.	Has the Warrior displayed a noticeable change in behavior recently, such as a decline in work performance or withdrawing from friends and/or co-workers?	☐ Know your Soldier! ☐ **Ask, Care, Escort!** ☐ Be willing to intervene! ☐ Mandatory informal counseling with Unit Leadership ☐ Refer to Unit Chaplain or Behavioral Health Provider
4.	Has the Warrior had significant problems with anger control in the past year, including road rage, domestic violence, or verbal and physical outbursts?	
5.	Has the Warrior had any drug or alcohol-related incidents in the past 12 months?	
6.	Does the Warrior have a personal history of Behavioral Health needs?	
7.	Is the Warrior pending nonjudicial punishment, under investigation by CID or any other agency, or facing UCMJ?	☐ Mandatory counseling with Company CDR &/or 1SG ☐ Refer to Unit Chaplain or Behavioral Health Provider ☐ Consider Precautionary Watch
8.	Has the Warrior recently experienced any stressful relationship problems? (This may include conflict within a marriage or dating relationship.)	
9.	Has the Warrior experienced the loss of a significant relationship in the past month, such as a divorce, legal separation, break-up or death of a loved one?	
10.	Is the Warrior currently expressing any thoughts of hopelessness, worthlessness or depression? Showing signs of disturbed appetite, sleep, interest or motivation?	
11.	Is the Warrior currently having thoughts or talking about Suicide as an answer?	■ Initiate Escort Watch Protection Procedures ■ Mandatory Command-Directed Referral action to Behavioral Health ■ Mandatory CCIR to higher echelon
12.	Has the Warrior thought or talked about Homicide as an answer?	

The "Dear John" Letter

The" Dear John" letter (written to tell the service member that the relationship is over) was first described in World War II and is actually probably as old as military service and the human ability to write. Prolonged separation leads to temptation, and many of the players involved are not mature. The life of a military family may also lead to a "Dear John" letter.

The nature of today's military requires families to move frequently, so spouses and partners of military members are therefore often relocated far from their homes and extended family, which would be able to support them and their union. Further, the recent pattern of base closings and realignments have increasingly isolated military complexes in rural areas, as the base realignment rules almost seem designed to strain marriages by giving preference to places that have a low cost of living and where the loss of a facility would have "a severe impact on the local community" (meaning there is nothing else going on there beyond the military, which would translate into fewer employment and educational opportunities for spouses). A typical "military town" is often not an attractive place for a military spouse unless they grew up in one. As few spouses in modern America sign up to be exclusively housewives anymore, this lack of opportunities in many military communities creates geographic separations, high spousal unemployment, and thus strains marriages from the very start.

These are all things beyond an individual service member's control. That does not mean that the unhappy spouse does not blame the service member for dragging her to one of the choice garden spots of today's military complexes. And it does not mean the spouse is not bombarded with requests to stray. It is a miracle that the divorce rate is not higher. The spouse is tired of waiting, and wants to move on. Unfortunately the service member, if deployed, is usually trapped in a situation that does not allow him to move on. This can lead to the "Dear John" letter being sent to the service member.

Our service member has most likely received the "Dear John" via an e-mail. Most psychologists would advise against breaking up with someone via e-mail or letter while she is in a distant land. However, the people who write these letters are not necessarily the most responsible or mature members of society. If you are the person who receives this letter you will hopefully be able to recognize that the "I can't live without you" thinking is an irrational statement. Of course you *can* live without that person, and probably should, because he was neither particularly loyal nor faithful. It is unfortunate that he lacked character. It is unfortunate that he is immature. But those things are beyond your control. What you can do is try to choose better next time.

When such a person comes into my office thinking in such black-and-white terms and devastated by loss, I try to help him think of possibilities beyond the thing he is so focused on. I try to challenge his thinking that he cannot live without the other person. If I can get the fellow who got the Dear John letter to put up a dating profile and begin corresponding with other women, he is probably past the crisis point of believing life is over. He might still be in love with that person, and might still prefer that person over all others, but at least he now realizes that there are other people out there. (While running the suicide prevention office, I once even proposed to the military the concept of a Web site called something like "dearjohn.com," which would be free to any service member with an overseas deployed address and open to any woman in America who would like to become a pen pal and keep a dumped and potentially despairing deployed soldier company. I think it would have done wonders to lower the suicide rate. Unfortunately I could not interest the military in operating a dating site.)

Career Loss as a Cause of Suicide

The same thing holds true for loss of career: If you can find something that the person could be passionate about, and could enjoy as much as she enjoyed the military, then goals and ambitions beyond the military could be ignited or at least sparked enough to keep her going until she gets past the crisis. One of the best things that the United States Navy does to prevent suicide is recognize the need for someone to soften a blow. After a Captain's Mast (the Navy's equivalent of an Article 15 or an adjudication and punishment of an offense by a ship's captain or commanding officer), the standard operating procedure is to take that sailor or Marine out the door and straight to the chaplain. I wish all of the services did that.

Preventing suicide is very hard. It is relatively easy to spot depressed people and help them treat their depression. Substance abusers come to the attention of police by driving under the influence or other misbehaviors, and can be treated for the substance abuse. Truly suicidal people usually use very lethal means, and you may only get one chance to intervene.

If you are the person outside of the crisis, it is important to be there for the person who suffered a loss. What you are listening for is that irrational belief about "not being able to live" without a person or job. If that comes up, you need to help the person dispute that irrational belief and to engage other help so that the outcome does not rest solely on your shoulders. If the distressed person suddenly looks a whole lot better, inquire why. Hopefully there is an answer that justifies the change other than "I've decided to die." The giving away of things is also something to discuss if it happens after a loss: If a person cares about something and is not going to be around to care for it, he often wants to leave it with someone he cares about.

Traumatic Brain Injury (TBI) and Suicide

Concussion produces post-concussive syndrome, and although most people will heal within a few months, a few people go on to have chronic symptoms. Chronic traumatic encephalopathy (CTE) is the result of repeated concussions and its symptoms closely resemble those of post-traumatic stress disorder (PTSD)—especially depression, apathy, substance abuse, and risk of suicide. Neurological treatment of TBI symptoms will closely mirror what a psychiatrist would do for depression, but it is important to realize that after an injury these symptoms can truly be part of a neurological organic brain syndrome, and not just a psychiatric disease. If this is the case in your family, contact your local Veterans Administration (VA) Polytrauma Center (http://www.polytrauma.va.gov) or a Department of Defense (DoD) TBI clinic or program (http://www.dvbic.org) for assistance.

The Effects of Multiple Deployments

Multiple deployments wear people down. The graph below is from the present war, but I have no doubt any deployment wears on one because of the loss of normal support mechanisms such as the service member's family and friends; note that morale, and with it resilience, declines with each new deployment. For more information on how repeated deployments can impact your family, see chapter 6 in this book.

Figure 8.4 The Toll That Multiple Deployments Take on Service Members

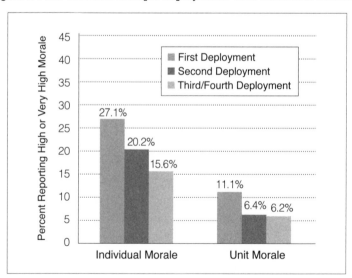

Building Resiliency

A key part of preventing suicide is building resiliency. Combat adds to losses, and sometimes can deplete an individual's resilience, which is an ability to absorb damage. People deployed to combat zones do not sleep well, their diets are often poor, and there is altogether too much adrenaline racing through their bodies. The phenomenon of "survivor guilt" (a person feels badly because they were spared while others were killed) is not uncommon. The DoD today is focusing many efforts on how to go about building resilience, essentially emphasizing how a warrior can recharge her batteries to help her better deal with her stress. The DoD has also established "resiliency campuses" on many bases and posts and is in the processing of creating a virtual one that can be accessed by any computer. You can help build resiliency in your service member by helping him get enough sleep and proper nutrition and ensuring that he feels your support. For more information on building resiliency, see chapter 7 and the resources in the appendix.

Depression and Suicide

It is a fact that depressed people lack joy and do kill themselves more often. I have tried to tease out the difference between an "adjustment reaction" (i.e., adjusting to a loss), which is more of a reaction to a crisis, versus a clinical depression. Adjustment disorders come on fast and they clear up fast so there is scarcely time for an antidepressant to kick in. Depression is more biological, more cyclic, and much more treatable with pharmacology.

Determining Depression

Depression is the common cold of mental illness, and it is very treatable. Your regular primary care provider is your first stop in seeking help for depression. Most providers are quite knowledgeable about depression, and there are several good medications now that have few if any side effects. Research has shown that antidepressant therapy is more effective if you also talk to someone about your problems. Your doctor can help you make that connection to other health professionals who specialize in mental conditions.

Are you or a family member depressed? The PHQ 9 (Patient Health Questionnaire) is a simple depression rating scale used in the DoD and Veterans Administration. Answer the questions to determine the potential for depression. If more than a few items are endorsed, depression may be present. Please speak to your primary care provider about getting help—depression is quite treatable with the right help. The text is reprinted below.

1. Over the last two weeks, how often have you been bothered by any of the following problems? Read each item carefully, and circle your response.

   a. Little interest or pleasure in doing things
      Not at all/Several days/More than half the days/Nearly every day

   b. Feeling down, depressed, or hopeless
      Not at all /Several days/More than half the days/Nearly every day

   c. Trouble falling asleep, staying asleep, or sleeping too much
      Not at all/Several days/More than half the days/Nearly every day

   d. Feeling tired or having little energy
      Not at all/Several days/More than half the days/Nearly every day

   e. Poor appetite or overeating
      Not at all/Several days/More than half the days/Nearly every day

   f. Feeling bad about yourself, feeling that you are a failure, or feeling that you have let yourself or your family down
      Not at all/Several days/More than half the days/Nearly every day

   g. Trouble concentrating on things such as reading the newspaper or watching television
      Not at all/Several days/More than half the days/Nearly every day

   h. Moving or speaking so slowly that other people could have noticed, or being so fidgety or restless that you have been moving around a lot more than usual
      Not at all/Several days/More than half the days/Nearly every day

   i. Thinking that you would be better off dead or that you want to hurt yourself in some way
      Not at all/Several days/More than half the days/Nearly every day

2. If you checked off any problem on this questionnaire so far, how difficult have these problems made it for you to do your work, take care of things at home, or get along with other people?
   Not Difficult at All/Somewhat Difficult/Very Difficult/Extremely Difficult

Major depressive syndrome is suggested if:

- Of the nine items, five or more are circled as at least "More than half the days"
- Either item 1a or 1b is positive, that is, at least "More than half the days"

Minor depressive syndrome is suggested if:

- Of the nine items, b, c, or d are circled as at least "More than half the days"
- Either item 1a or 1b is positive, that is, at least "More than half the days"

Getting Help

The recent media attention on suicide has prompted the DoD and VA to dramatically improve services. Every veteran's hospital now has a suicide prevention coordinator, and the Veterans Administration alone has hired two thousand new psychologists in the past few years to help with increased demand.

I have worked in mental health for many years, and I know the system is far from perfect. It can be very difficult to get a routine appointment with a specialist. It is sometimes hard to know even who to call. But in cases of life and death, for potential suicide there is no reason not to get help. The final fallback is always the emergency room since by law a patient presenting with suicidal ideation must be evaluated, and if a doctor determines that the person is a danger to himself or to others he will be retained for treatment. If the patient is actively suicidal he must be hospitalized and stabilized regardless of his ability to pay. Therefore, in a worst case scenario head for the emergency room if you find yourself at the "E" ("escort your buddy") end of the suicide prevention ACE card presented above.

In the case of a veteran, you can get help 24/7. There is a Veterans Crisis line at 1-800-273-8255 that is available around the clock. If the hotline cannot help you directly they will know someone who can. You can call that same number if you are a civilian as well, as it is also the national suicide prevention hotline. The Veterans Crisis Web site is online at http://veteranscrisisline.net.

Hopefully these things can be dealt with before the situation becomes a crisis, and once again I suggest using your primary care provider as a resource. If it is an urgent case she will often have same-day appointments in reserve and may be able to help. If not, use the hotline mentioned above or, if necessary, go to an emergency room.

It does get better but everyone just needs to stick around to see that this is true.

9 | Self-Medication and Drug Abuse

David S. Greenawalt, Sandra B. Morissette,
Suzy Bird Gulliver

Returning from a war zone and readjusting to civilian life can be very stressful for military personnel and their families. Although most returning service members are able to make this transition smoothly, some turn to alcohol and other substances to self-medicate symptoms of post-traumatic stress disorder (PTSD), anxiety, and depression. We know from research that service members coming home from the conflicts in Afghanistan and Iraq are more likely to have alcohol problems than others their age. This is particularly true of the youngest veterans (under the age of twenty-five). Developing PTSD also greatly increases the risk of developing alcohol- and drug-related problems. In addition, veterans are more likely to smoke than non-veterans, putting them and their families at higher risk for the health problems associated with smoking.

It is likely that veterans with PTSD turn to substance use as a way of coping with distressing thoughts and feelings. Substance use may initially provide relief, but in the long term it can maintain or worsen symptoms because the user fails to adopt more effective ways of coping. Over time, he may need to keep taking the substance to achieve the desired effect, reinforcing the addiction. This may be a particular vulnerability for veterans experiencing chronic pain from physical injuries, who may end up misusing painkillers and other prescription drugs. Prescription drug use can be harder for family members to detect because they may not be aware that the service member is taking more than what was prescribed.

A Special Note on Suicide

Although suicide is not a focus of this chapter, we highlight the importance of suicidal risk because alcohol and drug use can lower inhibitions, and users may be more likely to make impulsive and drastic decisions. Suicide is more thoroughly addressed in chapter 8, but there are special concerns about suicide for those who have addictive behaviors. Veterans struggling with addictive behaviors not only have ready access to substances, but often keep weapons in their homes—a particularly dangerous combination. In addition, because returning soldiers frequently take pain medication for physical injuries, alcohol and drug use can increase the chance of accidental or intended overdoses. Do not be afraid to ask if someone is feeling suicidal—it may be a critical safety issue to negotiate having another family member keep or dispense medications or hold the key to where weapons are locked.

Risk Factors

Several factors can put someone at risk for substance problems. Environment can play an important role. For example, one large study revealed that higher levels of work stress or family stress were related to substance abuse for military men. For military women, on the other hand, the amount of stress experienced from being a woman serving in a primarily male military was related to using illegal drugs and smoking. A history of PTSD, traumatic brain injury (TBI), or high levels of chronic pain may put one at higher risk for misuse of prescribed medications. Overall, high levels of life stress or experiencing a traumatic event can increase the risk for substance abuse. In addition, once substance abuse sets in, it can heighten stress because of resulting problems with finances, work, health, and social relationships. Stress and substance abuse problems can thus feed on each other and create a vicious cycle.

Low involvement by parents in their children's lives, high levels of family conflict, and a lack of family cohesion all increase the risk of substance abuse. On the other hand, positive, loving relationships between parents and their kids can decrease this risk. Since loving families with involved parents sometimes struggle with having a family member with an addiction and those in low-involvement families may not have addiction, we see that there is no perfect rule to determine who will develop a substance abuse problem. Some circumstances make individuals more or less vulnerable to developing problems.

Genetics and family background also can play a strong role. For example, having a family history of alcoholism is one of the strongest predictors for developing alcoholism. Children of alcoholics are about four times more likely to become alcoholic than children whose parents were not alcoholic. In addition, studies of identical twins indicate that some people have a genetic vulnerability to nicotine dependence. Although certain genes probably increase the risk for addiction, there's a temptation for someone with an addiction to conclude, "Well, I'm born with it and there's nothing I can do." This could not be further from the truth, as evidenced by the many people who enter recovery or quit smoking every day. Most genes only represent vulnerability and not a determination. Many factors influence whether or not the gene is expressed or "turned on." For this reason, there are many people with strong family histories of alcohol and drug abuse who never go on to develop addictions.

When Should Family Members Be Concerned?

Family members often become concerned long before they try to do something about alcohol and drug use with loved ones. This can happen for many reasons, including not wanting to admit that a loved one has a problem or not knowing what is "normal." Aside from this, people with addictions often hide their alcohol or drug use, making it difficult to know if there really is a serious problem. We put drinking and drug use into perspective in the sections below to guide families about when they should consider intervening.

What Is Normal Drinking?

According to the National Institute of Alcohol Abuse and Alcoholism (NIAAA), "sensible" drinking means consuming, on average, no more than one drink per day for women and two drinks per day for men. One drink is equivalent to twelve ounces of beer, five ounces of wine, or 1.5 ounces of 40-proof alcohol. These quantities are important to keep in mind because higher levels of drinking lead to increased health risks. Often someone will say, "But I only had *one* drink" and not be aware that his mixed drink with six ounces of alcohol was actually equivalent to four drinks.

The NIAAA defines "binge drinking" as five or more drinks in a two-hour period for men, and four or more drinks in two hours for women. The cutoffs are lower for women because women metabolize or "clear" alcohol more slowly and become more intoxicated from smaller amounts. Repeated binge drinking is associated with harmful behaviors such as impaired driving, higher rates of injuries, unintended pregnancies, fetal alcohol spectrum disorders, higher risk of contracting sexually transmitted diseases, poor control of diabetes, cardiovascular disease, and liver disease. Young adults are more likely to engage in binge drinking than older adults; half of adults aged eighteen to twenty who drink alcohol report binge drinking. While it is important to bear in mind that binge drinking is not the same as alcoholism—a chronic dependence on and compulsive use of alcohol despite serious impairment and consequences—binge drinking is a serious health and social problem.

Two common instruments that are used for screening for alcohol problems are the Alcohol Use Disorders Identification Test—Consumption (AUDIT-C) and the CAGE test (the acronym is for "cut down, annoyed, guilty, and eye-opener"). These tests are mostly used in health care settings where they then can be interpreted by health care professionals, but the types of questions can be useful for family members to consider when assessing whether their loved one might have a problem. First, you can observe whether your loved one is drinking within normal ranges. Second, you can assess how the drinking is interfering with the person's life. CAGE questions help the person remember areas that they should assess to determine problems: C) "Have you ever felt you should *cut down* on your drinking?"; A) "Have people *annoyed* you by criticizing your drinking?"; G) "Have you ever felt bad or *guilty* about your drinking?"; and E) *eye opener*: "Have you ever had a drink first thing in the morning to steady your nerves or get rid of a hangover?" If the answer to any of these questions is "yes," the person may have a problem with alcohol.

Warning Signs of Drug Abuse

Some potential warning signs of drug abuse are listed below. While it is important not to ignore warning signs, beware of jumping to conclusions based on seeing one or two of the signs, as they may be related to other psychological problems, such as depression or PTSD.

General warning signs:

- Decline in appearance or physical grooming
- Reduced interest in family activities
- Deterioration of ethics
- Sudden mood swings or increased irritability
- Changes in memory or attention span
- Increased withdrawal, secretiveness, and time alone
- Lying about activities and whereabouts
- Frequent excuses for irresponsible behavior
- Poor performance at work
- Disappearance of valuable items
- Frequently needing money or having unexplained, excessive amounts of money
- Not coming home on time
- Changing the type of friends with whom one spends time
- Sudden increases or decreases in appetite
- Verbally or physically abusive behavior
- Paraphernalia such as digital scales, syringes, pipes, baggies, and vials

In addition to noticing general signs, it may be helpful to know signs of abuse and paraphernalia associated with specific drugs listed in the table below.

Table 9.1 Drug Abuse Warning Signs

Drug	Warning Signs	Paraphernalia
Cocaine (including "Crack"), amphetamines, and other stimulants ("Uppers")	nervousness; sweating or chills; weight loss; nausea or vomiting; hyper-alertness; shaking; dilated pupils; reduced sleep; increased heart rate and blood pressure; skin rashes or marks from picking at skin	clear glass pipes or Pyrex tubes; aluminum foil for freebasing cocaine; small mirrors; razor blades; small spoons; lighters; wax paper "bindle" containers—folded over like an tiny envelope
Opiates (heroin, morphine, opium, methadone, codeine, Oxycontin, hydrocodone, Fentanyl)	slurred speech, excessive fatigue, apathy, lack of coordination, trouble standing or sitting straight, constricted pupils	injection needles, prescription bottles for painkillers
Marijuana and Cannabis ("pot," "weed," hashish, THC)	Bloodshot eyes; apathy; increased appetite; dry mouth; difficulty walking; memory problems; sleepiness; feelings of paranoia	Glass apparatus that has a vertical pipe and bowl filled with liquid (bong); pipes (sometimes made out of fruit); cigarette rolling papers; lighters; metal clips to hold marijuana cigarette ("joint"); small plastic baggies; disguised boxes or containers to store marijuana; air fresheners
Hallucinogens (LSD—"Acid," "Mushrooms," psilocybin, peyote, MDMA or "Ecstasy," "STP")	very dilated pupils; warm, clammy skin; excessive perspiration; dry mouth; low appetite; odd body odor; confusion; paranoia; anxiety; false sense of power; mood swings and erratic behavior; euphoria	LSD *Paraphernalia:* small squares or circles of paper (blotter paper), colored gelatin; *MDMA ("Ecstasy") Paraphernalia:* glow-sticks or safety light sticks for visual stimulation; pacifiers for teeth grinding; lollipops and hard candy to relieve dry mouth

Drug	Signs/Symptoms	Paraphernalia
Anxiolytics, hypnotics, depressants ("Downers")	Decreased inhibition, slowed motor coordination, tiredness, relaxed muscles, staggering, poor judgment, slurred speech, and glassy eyes	prescription bottles; plastic baggies; glass vials
Inhalants ("Whippets," "Poppers," solvents, nitrous oxide or "'Laughing Gas'")	Dizziness; lack of coordination; slurred speech; unsteady walking; blurred vision; repetitive, uncontrolled eye movements; euphoria	nitrous oxide canisters; canister "cracker" tool used to open containers; large balloons; small bottles or vials containing liquid; whipped cream containers; rags; or odd collection of household products (with propellants)
Phencyclidine and dissociative anesthetics (PCP, ketamine, "Angel Dust")	Sometimes violent or bizarre behavior; paranoia; anxiety; aggressive or withdrawn behavior; dilated pupils; jerky eye movements; skin flushing; sweating; dizziness; total numbness; and impaired perceptions	foil or paper packets, stamps (from which PCP is licked); needles, syringes, and tourniquets (for injection); may be used with marijuana
Tobacco use	smoke smell on clothes and breath; stained teeth and clothing; coughing; reduced physical endurance	cigarette boxes, cigars, pipes, smokeless tobacco or "dip"

Impact of Substance Abuse on the Family

Substance abuse is often a family problem that not only changes the user's behavior, but also the behavior of those closest to that person. Family members frequently find themselves in the position of being angry at the user, yelling, turning a cold shoulder, or making biting comments or jokes out of frustration with a loved one's drinking. Concerned family members may plead with a loved one to change. They may try to limit her drinking or drug use and feel that she should be able to control the problem. Family members might find themselves monitoring her substance use and whereabouts. Another common behavior is enabling, trying to cover up so the user will not lose her job, suffer embarrassment, or experience financial problems. Over time, a family member's drug and alcohol use can become the main focus of life, replacing previous interests, activities, and goals. This can be especially difficult for children, as the family's focus can shift from taking care of the child's needs to worrying about and coping with the user's behavior. In time, everyone in the family may feel like they are carrying a secret that makes them different from "normal" families. An underlying feeling of anger, helplessness, or sadness can set in, particularly if the user is in denial about her problems.

Some other possible changes in a family member's behavior that you might notice include:

- Not inviting people to your home because you are embarrassed about the user's behavior or worried what the user might do
- Wondering if the drinking or drug use is your fault
- Staying up at night worrying
- Making threats or ultimatums to get the user to change
- Searching for hidden drugs or alcohol
- Getting angry at and blaming the user's friends
- Hiding money and valuables so the user will not take them
- Loaning the user money to pay off his debts
- Taking over the user's unmet responsibilities
- Feeling hopeful when the user makes promises and then crushed when the promises are broken.

The effects of alcohol and drug misuse can extend beyond the user and her partner to their children. Chronic alcohol and drug abuse by parents or guardians can have lasting emotional and cognitive effects on children. According to the NIAAA, children of alcoholic parents score lower on IQ tests and are at a greater risk for academic problems than other children. Children of alcohol and drug abusers report higher levels of depression and anxiety, and are more likely to develop behavior problems such as lying, stealing, fighting, and truancy. In addition, drinking and drug abuse runs in families, and children in these homes are at greater risk than the general population for becoming alcoholic or addicted to drugs themselves. It is important to help a child to get appropriate services as early as possible if you are a parent or caring adult in the child's life and you notice that he is having behavioral changes or difficulties.

Getting Better: Al-Anon, Nar-Anon, and Detachment

If you are concerned about another person's drinking, one resource is Al-Anon, an organization that is similar to Alcoholics Anonymous (AA) but is specifically for families and friends of problem drinkers. Al-Anon describes itself as "a fellowship of relatives and friends of alcoholics who share their experience, strength, and hope, in order to solve their common problems." You do not have to be certain that a friend of family member is an alcoholic to attend an Al-Anon meeting. Meetings are free (members typically contribute a dollar), confidential, and open to anyone affected by someone's drinking. Most Al-Anon groups welcome those affected by someone's drug use, even if alcohol is not the main problem, although in larger cities you may also find a Nar-Anon group for families and friends of drug abusers. Nar-Anon meetings are similar to Al-Anon meetings and use the same twelve-step program. The easiest way to find an Al-Anon or Nar-Anon meeting is to search for "Al-Anon meetings" or "Nar-Anon meetings" in your area on the Internet, or to look for Al-Anon or Nar-Anon in the phone book.

One concept that Al-Anon and Nar-Anon stress is *detachment*. Detachment is gaining emotional distance from substance abuse and the behaviors that accompany it. Part of detachment, according to Al-Anon, is seeing drug addiction or alcoholism as a "disease" rather than a deliberate and controllable behavior. Al-Anon maintains that people can recover from the effects of alcoholism or drug addiction, but the underlying illness is always there and will resurface if an alcoholic or a drug addict starts drinking or using drugs again.

Understandably, many people have difficulty accepting that some drinkers or drug users have little control over their behavior. It generally takes time to see that problem drinkers or drug users, even when they are aware they have a problem, have tremendous difficulty controlling their drinking or drug use once they start. In fact, one of the hallmarks of addiction is drinking or using more of a substance than was intended. Viewing addiction as an illness may help you to have compassion for the drinker or drug user and to take her behavior less personally.

However, seeing addiction as an illness does not mean that the drinker or drug user should not be accountable for his actions. Just as a diabetic learns over time that he must avoid certain foods if he wishes to remain healthy, many problem drinkers/drug users must stop using to regain their health. Often they need to experience the painful consequences of their drinking in order to commit to change. Many drug users and problem drinkers cannot stop using on their own through sheer willpower. Treatment programs, including but not necessarily limited to AA and Narcotics Anonymous (NA), may be needed.

Part of detachment is learning that you are not responsible for your loved one's drinking or drug use. It may take time to see that you do not cause someone to drink or take drugs and that you cannot control or cure the problem. While there are actions you can take and things you can stop doing that may encourage an alcoholic or drug addict to seek help, you are not responsible for curing her. The power to change is ultimately in her hands, and to succeed over time, she must have a personal desire to change.

Through detachment, families of problem drinkers and drug users learn to cope more effectively and take care of themselves. Detachment may start with taking a walk rather than getting into an argument, or engaging in a physical activity like running or cleaning the house to relieve anger or worry. Later on, family members learn to set personal boundaries when needed, to reach out to others for help, and to begin pursuing personal interests rather than being completely consumed by someone's drinking or drug use.

Over time, family members also learn to stop "enabling" the addiction by excusing and bailing out the user. If a drinker or drug user fails to show up for work because he is high or hung over, it is tempting to call his workplace to offer an excuse for his absence that keeps him out of trouble and temporarily keeps the family from experiencing negative consequences. Using detachment, family members stop doing things for others that they can and should do for themselves. Family members allow the natural consequences of the user's behavior to occur. They neither create a crisis nor prevent a crisis from happening. Experiencing negative consequences does not guarantee that a problem drinker or drug user will seek help, but not experiencing those consequences is likely to prolong problematic behavior.

The primary purpose of Al-Anon is to help family members cope with and recover from the negative effects of a loved one's drinking. However, by learning to detach from and to stop enabling the drinker's behavior, family members may make it harder for the drinker to avoid facing her problem. Often, learning these new behaviors can help motivate the drinker to enter treatment or a recovery program like AA.

Other Family Interventions

Community Reinforcement and Family Therapy (CRAFT) is a relatively new approach in which a counselor usually works with a family member who is very concerned about another's alcohol or substance abuse (called a Concerned Significant Other or CSO) to change factors that contribute to the abuse. Research shows that CRAFT is very effective at getting individuals with alcohol or substance abuse to enter treatment and also helps improve the quality of life of the CSO. Compared to Al-Anon, CRAFT similarly improves family members' well-being, but is considerably better at getting problem drinkers into treatment.

A trained counselor usually works with the CSO for ten to twelve weeks on several key tasks:

- Teaching the CSO to recognize the potential for violence and to reduce the risk of harm.
- Working with the CSO to identify the triggers and consequences of his loved one's drinking or drug use.
- Improving the CSO's ability to communicate effectively with the user.
- Improving the CSO's quality of life by reducing stress and increasing rewarding activities.
- Planning and preparing for how the CSO can suggest treatment to the drinker or drug user.
- Arranging to have treatment available, ideally within forty-eight hours, once the user decides to start treatment.

Johnson Institute Intervention Approach. If you have exhausted other avenues for communication or your loved one's problems have clearly reached a crisis level (e.g., her life is in imminent danger), you might consider the Johnson Institute Intervention approach, originally conceived by Vernon Johnson and his colleagues. In an intervention, those who have been affected by drinking or drug use (e.g., family members, employers) confront the alcoholic or addict. The goal of the intervention is to get the alcoholic or drug addict to commit to a treatment program. Alcohol and drug treatment centers often have counselors who are specially trained to help families prepare for an intervention. The intervention usually takes place in an environment where the alcoholic or addict is most likely to be receptive.

It is recommended to do the intervention under the guidance and support of an interventionist or counselor who has experience with interventions and can help facilitate the process. Prior to engaging a counselor for an intervention, find out about the counselor's background, training, and experience with substance use treatment and interventions, and whether she is licensed or certified.

It is important to know that if you opt for holding an intervention, there is always the risk that things will not go as planned. Your loved one may refuse to listen and walk out of the intervention. If this happens, you may not know what to do next, and family members may end up criticizing the intervention. It is helpful to consider this possibility and discuss it with other intervention participants ahead of time to reach an agreement on the next steps before the intervention begins. Another possibility is that the user may appear to listen to what people say, but harbor a strong resentment because he or she was "ambushed" and embarrassed. One way to reduce this possibility is to inform the user that you and others are talking with a counselor about his or her drinking or substance use several days before the intervention. A third possible pitfall is that the user agrees to seek treatment but is not committed to recovery. If this is the case, it can be helpful to remember that relapse is often part of the process of eventual recovery from alcoholism and drug addiction, and seeking treatment now may lay the groundwork for future attempts at recovery.

Johnson interventions work about as well as CRAFT in getting troubled drinkers into treatment. Unfortunately, a large number of family members may be unwilling to do the intervention, and sometimes rifts caused by an intervention can add to the family's or veteran's distress.

Interventions with the Alcohol or Drug User

Only one-fourth of people with alcohol dependence undergo formal treatment. Many people successfully quit drinking without going through a detoxification program, but it is important to remember that if someone drinks heavily or is a heavy drug user, quitting suddenly can lead to significant health problems, and in some cases withdrawal can be fatal. Thus, for safety reasons, the need for detoxification should be carefully evaluated by a health professional. Inpatient detoxification with medical supervision is typically short (between twenty-four and forty-eight hours), and is followed by Intensive Outpatient Programs (IOPs) in most states. IOPs meet daily for five to thirty days.

Patients who continue to abuse substances during IOPs may be referred to inpatient programs followed by time in halfway houses. Programs can vary in length and type of treatment, so it is important to evaluate each program and seek guidance from local health professionals on the utility of the program and feedback from others who have been through it. Talking with experienced members in AA, Al-Anon, NA, and Nar-Anon may be useful in learning about available programs in your area.

Whether a person attends AA or NA is often a matter of personal preference. AA and NA are voluntary fellowship programs that are dedicated to helping people maintain sobriety. As with Al-Anon/Nar-Anon, there are no fees to attend; the only requirement to attend is that the person wants to stop drinking or using. Additional information, including meeting locators, can be found on the Internet.

Motivation Enhancement Therapy (MET) is a relatively brief intervention aimed at enhancing the drinker's motivation to change. It can be provided by itself or as a preparation for further treatment. MET uses the drinker's own motivation to arrive at change strategies and resources. Research indicates that MET is effective in promoting change among problem drinkers. Further studies are needed to determine if MET is as effective for drug abuse and addiction.

The first two sessions of MET usually include the drinker and the drinker's spouse or significant other. The first session focuses on providing feedback from an initial assessment of alcohol consumption patterns and symptoms related to drinking. The session also aims to build motivation to change by examining the costs and benefits of current behavior and proposed new behaviors. In the second session, the counselor and patient continue to explore motivation and to strengthen commitment to change. If the patient demonstrates commitment to change, she will work with the counselor to develop a change plan. The third and fourth sessions focus on encouraging the patient and dealing with setbacks.

Several principles are used in MET. First, the therapist communicates respect, listens without judgment, and supports the client. Second, the therapist highlights the distance between where a client is and where the client wants to be. While doing this, the therapist avoids arguing with the patient and acknowledges roadblocks the patient may raise. Finally the counselor helps the client to believe he is capable of changing and that change will bring positive results.

Medication may help reduce the urge to drink. Naltrexone, a drug originally used to reduce cravings for heroin and other opioid addicts, may also be effective with alcohol. Some research indicates that taking naltrexone led to marked reductions in alcohol consumption by people with alcohol dependence because it reduced the pleasurable feelings experienced when drinking.

With respect to tobacco cessation, generally a combination of nicotine replacement therapy (e.g., nicotine patch, gum, lozenge, etc.) plus cognitive-behavioral therapy for smoking cessation has had the best results. It is not uncommon for both smokers and family members to say, "Smoking is the least of my problems. . . . I need to handle [insert other problem] first." Unfortunately, they could not be more wrong. Tobacco use is the single most preventable cause of death, and second-hand smoke causes very serious diseases and death. In addition, there is a large body of literature that indicates that tobacco use increases risk for other psychiatric disorders. With respect to PTSD, the latest evidence supports treating tobacco dependence and PTSD together at the same time. Family members can support abstinence by not smoking in front of people trying to quit and helping them to "ride the wave of urge" to resist smoking. Family members can also promote healthy behaviors (e.g., exercise, nutrition) by engaging in these activities together with their loved one.

What about "Controlled" Drinking?

Not everyone who abuses drugs or alcohol is an "addict" or an "alcoholic" or becomes one. Many people go through a period of time, perhaps when they are young or during a particular phase of life (e.g., during college, while in the military), when they binge drink or use drugs. However, many people naturally reduce their drinking and drug use over time without much effort. Although this is true, it is important not to dismiss dangerous behavior, such as drinking and driving or physical violence, by saying, "It's just a phase." This justification can be dangerous for those for whom drinking or drug use is causing problems (e.g., driving under the influence [DUI], drinking against medical advice, violent behavior). For other people, drinking and drug use continues to be a serious problem even when they change environments, and they become emotionally and physically dependent on a substance.

One question people often have is whether problem drinkers can learn to drink moderately. This continues to be a controversial subject. Some evidence suggests that younger people who are less severe drinkers and have no history of alcoholism in their family may benefit from a controlled drinking approach. Moderate drinking is not a reasonable goal for people who have repeatedly failed at attempts to drink moderately and have clear symptoms of alcohol dependence. For many people who struggle with excessive drinking, abstinence appears to be the only effective approach. Of course, there is no approach that recommends moderate use of illegal drugs or tobacco. Indeed, smoking only one cigarette per day can have negative health consequences.

How to Talk with Loved Ones about Their Drug and Alcohol Problem

Talking with a loved one about drug or alcohol use is never easy. Even if you have excellent communication skills, he may respond with anger, denial, and defensiveness. For this reason it is important to carefully consider the best time and ways to raise the subject.

Most importantly, avoid talking to a loved one about drug or alcohol use when she is under the influence. If your loved one is high or drunk, she is more likely to be argumentative, defensive, irrational, or to simply forget the conversation. It is natural that you will want to express your feelings when you are upset by someone's behavior, but it is best to wait for a time when your loved one will be more receptive to what you have to say. For example, a substance abuser may be more willing to communicate shortly after a substance-related setback, such as getting a DWI summons.

Be aware, however, that your loved one may be feeling especially guilty at these times, so avoid heaping more guilt on her. Although the user is likely to deny that her behavior is causing serious problems, she may feel quite different inside. When you lash out with criticism, you are likely pouring fuel on the fire and will make her feel defensive. To relieve feelings of guilt or shame, the drinker or user may try to deflect blame and change the focus of the conversation to anything other than substance use. The best approach is to wait for a time when you are reasonably calm so that you can do your best not to get derailed.

Do not make idle threats or empty ultimatums. If you truly can no longer handle the situation and you know that you will move out or end the relationship unless matters change, it may be valuable to express how you feel and what you are planning to do. However, it is rarely useful to make threats as a way to get someone to change. People have a way of knowing when someone is trying to manipulate their behavior and, over time, take such threats less seriously and grow to resent them.

Motivational Interviewing

An approach called Motivational Interviewing (MI), pioneered by William Miller and Stephen Rollnick, offers guidance for talking with someone who is abusing substances. MI emphasizes careful listening, and can help someone explore and resolve mixed feelings about making a change. One key principle of MI is that the person who is abusing drugs or alcohol needs to provide the reasons he should change. You cannot make him ready to change. Although we do not recommend trying to do MI on your own (there are experts who can do this in treatment), it can be helpful to understand some of the philosophy and strategies that are utilized in MI.

One way to help someone start talking about change is to *listen and express empathy*. As difficult as it might be for you, it is important to express empathy for someone who is abusing a substance. It also helps to use *reflective listening*, which involves trying to grasp where your loved one is coming from and making a guess about what she truly means. When you listen reflectively, you summarize and often deepen what someone has said. Reflective listening can help someone to feel understood and to continue exploring thoughts and feelings, including the possibility of change. For example, in a recent interview with former U.S. Secretary of Defense Robert Gates, Diane Sawyer used reflective listening to capture how American casualties were weighing on the secretary and influenced his decision to retire:

Sawyer: "How do you experience it [knowledge of war casualties] when you're
home at night?"

Gates: "Well, that's when I do the condolence letters."

Sawyer: "It's just too much." (Reflective listening)

Gates: (With sadness) "Yeah. It's time."

Do not try to convince someone to change. Instead, let your loved one voice these arguments. Generally, the more you provide reasons someone should change, the more that person will give you reasons why he should not. And the more that person argues against change, the more convinced he becomes. Instead, when someone offers reasons why he does not need to change, it's useful to acknowledge these barriers through reflective listening. Often if you acknowledge a barrier, your loved one may actually soften his statement or offer possibilities for change. Of course, you need to be genuine when communicating, and if you have always been critical in the past, it may take time for your loved one to "buy" your lack of judgment.

User: You're always exaggerating. It really hasn't been that bad.

You: There really isn't any reason I should be concerned.

User: I mean, every once in a while I might have a few too many with my
friends but I'm just blowing off steam. [Insert substance] helps me get
my mind off things.

You: A few times you've had too many, but that's your *one* way of relaxing.

User: Yeah. Pretty much. I mean, it's not the *only* way I try to relax but I like to
have a good time.

You: It's not that bad to go out drinking and have some fun.

User: No. Except I know it's dumb to drink and drive and I know you worry
about me.

Use "I" statements. Someone is more likely to listen when you talk about your own feelings than when you tell that person what he or she is feeling. Avoid labeling the person you are confronting as "uncaring," "inconsiderate," or "selfish." Your loved one is likely to react strongly to labels by becoming angry and resentful.

It can be helpful to talk concretely about one or two specific events when drinking or drug use caused a family problem (again, "I feel . . ." versus "You did . . ."). Explain what you think happened. Make it clear how, in your judgment, alcohol or drugs played a role in the events and explain how you felt at the time (e.g., hurt, scared, frustrated). Make sure you talk when you think you can be relatively calm and caring.

Remember to breathe and take your time, so you are not simply reacting to what is said. Try your best not to get sidetracked from the issue at hand. If your loved one criticizes you and draws attention to your own negative behavior, it can be helpful to say, "That may be possible" and offer to talk about that issue later. Then, calmly assert that you would like to return to the original subject.

You can certainly suggest what you think your loved one should do, such as see a drug and alcohol counselor, seek treatment, or go to an AA/NA meeting. However, it may be valuable to first ask him what he thinks he is willing to do, if anything, about the problem; generally, people are more likely to accept their own ideas.

Let go of the outcome. Ultimately you cannot control how someone will react when you bring a problem to that person's attention. It may help to realize that you are only responsible for your own actions and to know that you acted in a responsible and caring manner.

Coping with Relapse

An important part of supporting a person in recovery is recognizing that relapses are common. People with addictive behaviors may often make several attempts to quit before ultimately quitting, so it may be necessary to connect and reconnect loved ones with treatment. It is important to understand the difference between a "lapse" and "relapse." A lapse is a "slip," while relapse implies going back to where one started. It can be important for both military personnel and their families to identify in advance what would be considered a lapse, so that relapse can be prevented. For example, lapses could include not going to AA/NA meetings as frequently, or engaging in negative self-talk (e.g., the person in recovery admits saying things to herself such as, "If I only had a drink [drug], things would be better"). Family members might ask themselves: "What were the things that first led me to think [name of loved one] had a problem?" Although these factors can change over time, they might offer clues that the person is again having problems with alcohol or drugs.

It can also be helpful to identify *vulnerability points* to reduce the likelihood of or prevent a relapse. For example, being under a lot of pressure at work might be a vulnerability point for someone who previously drank to cope with work stress. The same could be true for family stress or arguments if the person avoided talking through family issues and instead went off to drink or escape problems. To reduce the likelihood that this could become a vulnerability point, families may need to re-learn, on their own or through therapy, how to communicate with one another after the person becomes sober.

Understandably, relapse is difficult for family members, often bringing back bad memories. This highlights the importance of prevention, as discussed above, but it is important for families to recognize that the person in recovery will make her own decision, good or bad, and that this is a decision that the family cannot control. Indeed, one can only control or take responsibility for one's own decisions and actions. During periods of relapse, families may need to make difficult decisions regarding setting boundaries with their loved one to avoid destructive patterns. First and foremost, children must be kept safe. Adults need to be wary of behaviors, both direct and subtle, that may be enabling the addiction. Agreements might need to be made as to what circumstances would need to be met in order to allow the loved one back into the family's life (whether in whole or in part). These can be painful times when Al-Anon or Nar-Anon can be helpful or, depending on personal preference, other support systems may need to be developed.

Summary and Conclusions

In sum, the pivotal substance use question that concerned family members face when their service member returns home is, "How much is too much?" Many American families celebrate good times and cope with setbacks by drinking alcohol or taking other mood-altering substances. For service members who have not suffered the invisible wounds of combat, such as PTSD and TBI, drinking and partying upon returning home may give way to normal drinking and responsible use of medication. In these instances, the main cause for concern is protecting everyone's immediate safety (e.g., not drinking and driving). In contrast, if a returning service member has a strong family or personal history of substance use, got his "bell rung" while deployed, or has clear signs of PTSD, very cautious use of substances or complete abstinence is advised. If a veteran's use escalates, then families need to be empowered to intervene. Good solutions are available. Veterans who survive combat should not be lost in peacetime to misguided attempts to manage their postwar symptoms through misuse of alcohol, medications, or illegal substances. It is important to remember that one of the best predictors of recovery is a strong family system that is supportive of abstinence.

References

Al-Anon Family Groups. *How Al-Anon Works for Families & Friends of Alcoholics.* From Preamble, Al-Anon Family Group Headquarters, Inc., 1995, Virginia Beach, VA.

Bray, R. M., J. A. Fairbank, and M. E. Marsden. "Stress and Substance Use among Military Women and Men." *American Journal of Drug and Alcohol Abuse* 25, no. 2 (1999): 239–256.

Brown, D. W. "Smoking Prevalence among U.S. Veterans." *Journal of General Internal Medicine* 25, no. 2 (2010): 147–149. Doi:10.1007/s11606-009-1160-0.

Bush, K., D. R. Kivlahan, M. B. McDonnell, S. D. Fihn, and K. A. Bradley. "The AUDIT Alcohol Consumption Questions (AUDIT-C): An Effective Brief Screening Test for Problem Drinking." *Ambulatory Care Quality Improvement Project (ACQUIP).*

Alcohol Use Disorders Identification Test. *Archives of Internal Medicine* 158 (1998): 1789–1795.

Carlson, S. R., W. G. Iacono, and M. McGue. "P300 Amplitude in Adolescent Twins Discordant and Concordant for Alcohol Use Disorders." *Biological Psychology* 61, nos. 1–2 (2002): 203–227.

Centers for Disease Control and Prevention. *Alcohol and Public Health Fact Sheet: Binge Drinking.* http://www.cdc.gov/alcohol/fact-sheets/binge-drinking.htm (accessed 13 October 2011).

Ewing, John A. "Detecting Alcoholism: The CAGE Questionnaire." *Journal of the American Medical Association* 252 (1984): 1905–1907.

Hasin, D. S., F. S. Stinson, E. Ogburn, and B. F. Grant. "Prevalence, Correlates, Disability, and Comorbidity of DSM-IV Alcohol Abuse and Dependence in the United States: Results from the National Epidemiologic Survey on Alcohol and Related Conditions." *Archives of General Psychiatry* 64 (2007): 830–842.

Hawkins, E. J., G. T. Lapham, D. R. Kivlahan, and K. A. Bradley. "Recognition and Management of Alcohol Misuse in OEF/OIF and Other Veterans in the VA: A Cross-sectional Study." *Drug and Alcohol Dependence* 109, nos. 1–3 (2010): 147–153. Doi:10.1016/j.drugalcdep.2009.12.025.

Hawkins, J., R. F. Catalano, and J. Y. Miller. "Risk and Protective Factors for Alcohol and Other Drug Problems in Adolescence and Early Adulthood: Implications for Substance Abuse Prevention." *Psychological Bulletin* 112, no. 1 (1992): 64–105. Doi:10.1037/0033-2909.112.1.64.

Jacobsen, L. K., S. M. Southwick, and T. R. Kosten. "Substance Use Disorders in Patients with Post-Traumatic Stress Disorder: A Review of the Literature." *American Journal of Psychiatry* 159 (2001): 1184–1190.

Johnson, V. E. *I'll Quit Tomorrow.* Oxford, England: Harper & Row, 1973.

Longabaugh, R., and M. C. Beattie. "Social Investment, Environmental Support, and Treatment Outcomes of Alcoholics." *Alcohol Health and Research World* 10, no. 4 (1986): 64–66.

McFall, M., A. J. Sazon, C. A. Malte, B. Chow, S. Bailey, D. G. Baker, J. C. Beckham, K. D. Boardman, T. P. Carmody, A. M. Joseph, M. W. Smith, M. Shih, Y. Lu, M. Holodniy, and P. W. Lavori. "Integrating Tobacco Cessation into Mental Health Care for Post-Traumatic Stress Disorder." *Journal of the American Medical Association* 304 (2010): 2485–2493. Doi:10.1080/10550490600859892.

Miller, W. R., and S. Rollnick. *Motivational Interviewing: Preparing People for Change.* 2nd ed. New York: Guilford Press, 2002.

Murray, M., and J. Wang. "Secretary of Defense Robert Gates on Why He's Ready to Retire." 6 June 2011. http://abcnews.go.com/US/time-secretary-defense-robert-gates-ready-retire/story?id=13772606.

National Institute on Alcohol Abuse and Alcoholism. *Alcohol Alert: Children of Alcoholics: Are They Different?* No. 9 PH 288, July 1990, http://pubs.niaaa.nih.gov/publications/aa09.htm.

Russell, M. A. "Prevalence of Alcoholism among Children of Alcoholics." In *Children of Alcoholics: Critical Perspectives,* ed. by M. Windle and J. S. Searles, 9–38. New York: Guilford Press, 1990.

Seal, K. H., T. J. Metzler, K. S. Gima, D. Bertenthal, S. Maguen, and C. R. Marmar. "Trends and Risk Factors for Mental Health Diagnoses among Iraq and Afghanistan Veterans using Department of Veterans Affairs Health Care, 2002–2008." *American Journal of Public Health* 99 (2009): 1651–1658.

Smith, J. E., and R. J. Meyers. *Motivating Substance Abusers to Enter Treatment: Working with Family Members.* New York: Guilford Press, 2004.

Swan, G. E., C. N. Lessov-Schlaggar, L. J. Beirut, A. E. Shields, A. W. Bergen, and M. Vanyukov. "Status of Genetic Studies of Nicotine Dependence." In *Phenotypes and Endophenotypes: Foundations for Genetic Studies of Nicotine Use and Dependence.* Tobacco Control Monograph 20, ed. by S. Marcus, G. E. Swan, T. B. Baker, L. Chassin, D. V. Conti, C. Lerman, and K. A. Perkins, 19–69. Bethesda, MD: U.S. Department of Health and Human Services, National Institutes of Health, National Cancer Institute, 2009.

Got Kids?

Parenting Tips for When Your Warrior Returns from Deployment

10

Michelle D. Sherman, Jeffrey E. Barnett

Your warrior makes it home, your children (all decked out in patriotic outfits) run into his arms, you enjoy the picnics, parades, and homecoming celebrations, and then return home to the "Welcome Home" signs. After a day or two of celebrating, everything goes back to how it was before he deployed, right? Definitely not. This is a huge transition for everyone in the family, and it takes time. To help prepare for, and assist with, your service member's transition this chapter will address:

- The benefits of military life for kids.
- The challenges of military life for kids.
- Specific tips on how to take good care of yourself as a parent
- Tips on how to help your warrior and children reconnect after deployment. (A more detailed list by age group of children's common reactions to deployment and recommendations on how to help them is available in chapter 12.)
- Resources for you, as a parent, and your children.

Military Life and Its Effect on Your Children

Being a young person in the twenty-first century can be pretty stressful. Today's youth face many challenges such as peer pressure, access to alcohol and drugs, bullying, and busy, demanding schedules. The entire family is affected by societal changes such as the difficult economy, resulting in more parents working (sometimes even two jobs). Children can be given additional responsibilities within and outside the home, decreasing their available time for socializing and relaxing. Further, with the tremendous growth in the digital age, young people face dangers involved with Internet use and social networking, issues we adults never encountered as we were growing up. Throw into the mix the joys of puberty and hormones, and being a kid can be pretty tough. It is thus not surprising that a considerable number of young people experience some depression and anxiety. For example, a recent survey by the American Psychological Association (APA) of young people ages eight to seventeen and their parents found considerable numbers of youth reporting stress due to school pressure and family finances; these problems often resulted in insomnia and headaches in these young people. According to this survey, many parents are not aware of how stressed their children are or the effects of stress on them.

Benefits of Military Life for Your Children

Fortunately, the military provides a lot of support for children, and can serve as a buffer for some of these stressors. Military kids are fortunate to have these services that their civilian counterparts generally do not have. It is true that children of active-duty families tend to have greater access to these programs than children of National Guard and Reserve families, but efforts are being made to strengthen support for all military youth. For example, in January 2011 President Barack Obama released the document *Strengthening Our Military Families: Meeting America's Commitment* focusing on our commitment to serving military families. This document was signed by the head of every department of the president's cabinet, and much of the document is focused on improving care for military children. In particular, it addresses frequent geographic moves, educational challenges, and child care. You can see that our very highest branches of government are dedicated to supporting you and your children.

Overall, it is important to remember that most military children are resilient. Although some experience difficulties, most do well. This is likely due to a combination of strong families, community support, DoD/VA services, and peer support among families. The military culture has many strengths lacking in the civilian world that can be great for children and families, including:

- A cohesive community environment, especially for those living on or near a military installation.
- A sense of duty and mission to the military and the unit.
- A focus on respect for authority.
- Predictable routines and schedules.
- Many resources available for military families and children (including health care, mental health care/support, childcare, etc.).
- Job security.
- Opportunities to see various cultures and parts of the world. With frequent moves, children get a lot of practice in making new friends and entering communities; these social skills can be useful as they mature and into adulthood.

Challenges of Military Life for Children

Military families face many unique and significant stressors. Although your family members did not sign up for military duty, you each play key roles in the success of your warrior and her military career. You may have thought you knew what you were getting into when your warrior joined the military, but repeated deployments halfway around the world were not part of your expectation. With each additional deployment, the level of distress and frustration you have experienced may have increased. In this section, we address the challenges of military family life in the twenty-first century, both for adult family members and for your children.

As a family member, your emotional support of the warrior helps make for a successful deployment. During your warrior's deployment, knowing that duties at home were being handled effectively helped him to focus attention and energies on mission-related activities. You may have had to make sure that bills were paid on time, budgets were balanced, lawns were mowed, household repairs were made, and so much more. You may have felt pressure to put on a happy face during contacts with your warrior, not wanting to complain, share bad news, or cause any additional stress or concern. Further, knowing that the deployed service member was thousands of miles away, you may have learned to take care of business and do what was needed. Yet, over time, many military families find this to be quite challenging and stressful.

What is the life of a military child in the twenty-first century like? As opposed to adults, children have no choice about their involvement in military service. They are a captive audience and have little if any say in the matter. Yet, they also may feel a pressure to put on a happy face, be emotionally supportive of their deployed parent, and not create additional stress for either parent by sharing their own challenges and difficulties. Being a military kid involves a number of unique challenges. The high operational tempo and frequent deployments may feel never-ending for children. High rates of parental exposure to trauma and resultant physical, emotional, cognitive, and spiritual injury each can have a significant impact on military children as well.

Deployed parents are likely to miss numerous important life events and milestones in their children's lives. Deployed parents cannot be a coach of their child's youth sports team, volunteer in their child's classroom, be a chaperone on school field trips, or just be there for a bicycle ride, walk around the neighborhood, or impromptu chat. As most busy parents know, it is tough to schedule appointments with our children for quality time. There is no replacement for just being there. For deployed parents and their children alike, periods of separation can be especially stressful. While interactive video communications such as Skype, telephone conversations, and the use of e-mail now make keeping in touch much easier than in past years, there is no substitute for being physically present.

Each child is different and each child will have different needs based on personality, emotional needs, developmental level, gender, age, and even role in the family. Because every child is unique, there are no set rules for how children will cope or respond to challenges and stressors in their lives. Some children are very easygoing and others are more difficult, experiencing changes in routines as stressful and upsetting. Some children are more outgoing and others are more timid and shy. Some are very independent and others seek parental approval and permission before making decisions. Some children jump right into new situations and others are more hesitant and slow to warm up. These differences in temperament are quite normal and are generally stable over time. Additionally, some children tend to be good sleepers and healthy eaters with vigorous appetites, while other children experience difficulty falling asleep, may be afraid of the dark, may fear being alone, or may be picky and finicky eaters who are difficult to please.

Typically, these differences are present independent of parenting style and parental actions. What is more important than merely the presence of any of these individual differences is if they are stable over time or if there are significant changes in them. For example, it is of greater concern if a child who has always been easygoing, a good eater, and a sound sleeper now seems much moodier, is more difficult to please, and wakes up frequently with nightmares. The child's age and developmental level can impact which changes emerge. For example, a younger child may display clingy behavior and bedwetting while an older child may display acting out behaviors such as getting in trouble at school or lying. But, again, one important thing to watch for is changes in a child's typical patterns of emotional, behavioral, academic, and social functioning.

Taking Care of Yourself Post-Deployment

While your warrior was away, you have likely been very busy, worrying about your deployed warrior and trying to be supportive of her while simultaneously taking care of your children and supporting them emotionally. You have had to ensure the smooth and efficient running of your household. (Okay, maybe smooth and efficient is just a dream, and just making sure everyone was where they needed to be, everyone was fed, homework got done, and the bills were paid before you passed out at night is more realistic.) Does that sound about right?

We hope that, in addition to caring for everyone else, you found ways to take care of yourself. In fact, perhaps the best thing you can do for your warrior and children is to take good care of yourself. Research has demonstrated that one of the best predictors of child functioning is parent functioning. Parents who are anxious, overwhelmed, stressed out, or depressed will not be able to effectively care for their children and to meet their emotional needs.

Now that your warrior is home, it is essential that you engage in ongoing self-care to promote your own psychological wellness. If you do not take adequate care of yourself, how will you be able to care for and meet the needs of others? Thus, it is not selfish to take time for yourself (within reason). It is important to strike a reasonable balance between caring for others and caring for yourself; between meeting the needs of others and taking time to get your own needs met. These needs can be physical, emotional, spiritual, and relational.

How can you do this? We recommend that you develop a personal list of self-care strategies that include:

- Different forms of relaxation such as meditation, yoga, and massage.
- Regular exercise.
- Activities you engage in solely for the enjoyment of them such as listening to or making music, making art, or reading for pleasure.
- Activities that enrich you spiritually such as prayer and attending religious services.
- Activities that meet your social and relationship needs such as talking with friends and extended family. Use others for support.
- Attending to sleep, eating a healthy diet, and maintaining physical health.

Know your personal warning signs of distress, be on the lookout for them, and do not ignore them. Each person is different, but examples may include:

- Withdrawing from others.
- Disturbed sleep.
- Moodiness.
- Increased frustration and anger.
- Striking out at others.
- Feeling resentful.
- Feeling emotionally exhausted.

Additionally, look out for negative coping strategies such as:

- Self-medicating with various substances such as alcohol, drugs, prescription medications, and food (although a little chocolate every now and then can be a part of healthy self-care).
- Trying to just work harder through all difficulties. Burning the candle at both ends only works for a short period of time.
- Denying that problems exist and "putting your head in the sand."
- Trying to do it all on your own. Shutting others out and trying to do everything yourself will not work.

Being the spouse of a recently returned warrior and the primary caregiver of your children is not like the 60-meter dash; rather, it is more like running an ultra-marathon. You must pace yourself and ensure that you are operating at a pace that can be sustained over the long run. Failure to do so can result in burnout, leaving you emotionally exhausted, unfulfilled, and losing your ability to care about others and their needs. Rather than attempt to dig out of this deep hole of despair, engaging in prevention is the best course of action. If you keep working beyond exhaustion, attending to everyone else's needs, being the strong one, and not taking time for yourself, you will eventually be unable to effectively accomplish any of this.

It is important that you develop a support network of friends and utilize them actively. Share the stresses and difficulties you are facing, openly acknowledge and discuss how hard it is for you at times, acknowledge your fears, doubts, and concerns, and accept others' support and assistance. Additionally, make good use of professional resources available to you, both for yourself and for your family. Military mental health professionals including psychologists, social workers, psychiatrists, and clergy are available to help promote your family's mental health. Family services are available for you and your children through a wide range of programs and dedicated people, such as Military OneSource, your warrior's unit/youth coordinators, Operation Military Kids and 4-H programs, the National Military Family Association's Operation Purple Camps, school personnel, and so forth. Accessing these professionals and programs is not a sign of weakness. It is actually a sign of strength. A list of these organizations and other resources appears in the appendix.

To be strong means to know your limits, to know your strengths and weaknesses, and to know when to seek assistance and support. It is also important that you not compare yourself to others who seem to you like they may be coping better, whose children seem to be better behaved, and whose spouse seems to be more emotionally supportive. When we make comparisons to others we are basing these comparisons on what the other individual is showing publically—something likely very far from the actual situation. After all, how often have you put on a brave act, held it all together during the day, and then fallen apart at home alone at night? It is possible that the person you are comparing yourself to is going through a similar process. We know everything about ourselves, what we are going through, and how we are coping (in our opinion); yet we may know very little about how the other person is really coping or actually is feeling inside. Thus, when we make these comparisons we are comparing our insides to others' outsides—a very unrealistic comparison that is likely to leave us feeling more alone, defeated, and defective.

We encourage you to be a good teammate to those in your community. Do not engage in the conspiracy of silence. If you see a friend or neighbor who may be in distress, offer a hand in support. Share information about the difficulties you have experienced, tell them about how imperfect your life is, and tell them about how actively seeking the support of others has helped you. Effective coping is a group activity and no one can go it alone.

Set realistic goals, have realistic expectations of yourself, and prioritize the tasks and challenges before you each day. Some days you may decide to postpone certain chores or housework to take time for you and your children. Making sure your children feel loved, supported, and understood can be more important than that final load of laundry or unloading the dishwasher.

Many resources have been developed for military children, and new programs are being released all the time. We encourage you to check out the appendix of this book with descriptions of a number of resources we hope you will find helpful.

As you very well know, experiencing a deployment involves sacrifice for everyone in the family. For example, your son may not have been able to participate in the soccer league, simply because you could not get him to all the practices and tournaments. Your daughter may have missed her daddy's help with tricky math homework, and she missed him a lot at the father-daughter dance at school. When your warrior returns and is not able to jump back into full-time parenthood, your children may feel resentful, confused, and sad. As your children experience these losses, encourage them to talk about their feelings; as a parent, try to listen respectfully, validate their reactions and feelings, and be supportive of what your children are going through. Encourage them to talk with their military friends about their feelings and experiences, as peer support can be very useful.

Tips on Helping Your Warrior and Children Reconnect after Deployment

Now that your warrior is home and well rested, is he ready to jump back into the same parenting role as before? Definitely no—he has changed, your children have changed, and the relationships have changed. Some at-home parents feel responsible for forcing the reconnections between their warriors and children, which can be a heavy load. We encourage you to avoid doing so, remembering that those relationships are your spouse's responsibility. However, it is great if you want to help him in reconnecting, and the following list includes some approaches that may be helpful. (For a detailed list on how you can help your children with the homecoming and transition, see chapter 12. If your service member was injured or disabled in service, chapter 11 provides guidance and suggestions to help your children understand and cope with these changes.)

- Most importantly, go slowly! Allow parents and children to reconnect at their own pace. Remember that reintegration is a process that takes time. Sometimes warriors feel hurt and sad when their children do not bond with them imme-diately; you can help a lot by urging your warrior to not take this personally. As we said above, very young children may not even remember the warrior, and teenagers usually like to spend a lot of time with their friends anyway. To help your warrior, talk about realistic expectations and have a plan for reintegration. Keep the lines of communication open, as the best-laid plans often need to be changed as time goes on.

- Remind your warrior and children that everyone in the family has changed. Even if there has been frequent contact during deployment (e-mail, telephone, Skype), everyone needs to get to know each other again. Your daughter may now be walking; your son may have hit puberty; and your stepchild may now be driving. Hang on for the exciting challenges associated with these new stages of development.

- Mutually agree upon specific things your warrior can do with your children to create or strengthen their bond. For example, perhaps he can read stories and help with pajamas at night for the bedtime ritual. But remember, this is time for you to get out of the way. You may need to even leave the room. It is OK for your warrior to do things differently than you have done. Actively give your warrior opportunities to become a part of the family again and to participate in daily routines even though you may be able to do them more efficiently.

- Structure fun, special family times to help everyone reconnect as a family. For example, you may want to have rituals of watching a family-friendly movie and having popcorn together on Sunday evenings. Or you could volunteer as a family once per month at a local homeless shelter. It is important to also create new routines that include the returning warrior, allowing him to take the lead at times in establishing them. Do not just keep repeating the old routines or get caught in the trap of saying things like "That's not how we do it" or "We do it this way." Creating such regular activities can help everyone to feel more com-fortable and reconnect as a family.

If you want more specific tips for connecting with children of different ages, we recommend you check out some free online Veteran Parenting Toolkits (http://www.ouhsc.edu/VetParenting). This Web site has five age-based toolkits (infants, toddlers, preschool, school-age, and teenagers) and provides a lot of useful infor-mation about normal development, red flags, children's reactions to homecoming, how to reconnect with a child, and resources for children of that age. Chapter 12 of this book also has recommendations on communicating with your children based on their age groups.

Children of Injured Military Parents   **11**

*Rebecca Tews, Alaina Grover, Carol Getkin,
Desiree King, Angela Schroedle*

This chapter is about cutting through the stress and uncertainty around how to best help your family adjust in a healthy way after a family member is injured or wounded during deployment. First and most importantly, an injured service member needs to know that his family is really glad to have him back, even if he does not feel like himself. He has returned and that is what matters. Second, you need to know that your whole family will have to work together to help each other. Ordinary deployment takes a toll and deployment that ends in injury carries many additional challenges. The third thing you need to know is that your family is not alone even after your family member separates from the military.

Scope of the Problem, to Put Injuries into Perspective

It is important for you to know what we mean when we say that you are not alone. Injuries can be isolating and many spouses report that time stands still after the service member comes home. Kids wonder if things will ever be better. Deployment is not easy but strong families can handle it. In the same way injuries can often be traumatizing but strong families can cope. Tired, overwhelmed families are still strong families. Help is out there—many families are coping and even succeeding with their family member's reintegration with wounds. Yours can too.

More than 2 million service members have been deployed to Afghanistan or Iraq as part of Operation Enduring Freedom or Operation Iraqi Freedom over the past decade. Research has found that emotional difficulties among military children (i.e., anger, increased anxiety, and grief) are often associated with the impact of multiple deployments that their service member parent faces. According to a 2011 study from the Department of Defense (DoD) there are approximately 700,000 active-duty military spouses and 400,000 Reserve spouses. Additionally, 220,000 children have a parent who is deployed overseas, according to the research by

Sogomonyan and Cooper. Currently, there are approximately 1.76 million children and youth in military families. Of those children, at least 19,000 have had a parent wounded in action and approximately 2,200 children have lost their parent in Iraq or Afghanistan. These numbers do not include those injured in training accidents and those injured while in the United States, and we want to acknowledge that these families often have just as many challenges and are not excluded from our suggestions for positive coping.

As of 17 October 2011, the DoD reported that 1,738,547 military service members had been wounded in action. This number only includes injuries sustained in Iraq and Afghanistan. According to the Office of the Surgeon General (as mentioned in the Congressional Research Service report written by Fischer), between 11 September 2001 and 7 September 2010 there were 1,621 amputations, including 935 major limb amputations and 351 minor amputations. As of 7 September 2010, approximately 66,935 deployed soldiers were officially diagnosed with post-traumatic stress disorder (PTSD). An estimated $63.8 million had been spent on care for individuals with PTSD.

The majority of casualties of Operation Enduring Freedom and Operation Iraqi Freedom—an average of 65 percent—are attributed to explosive blasts and improvised explosive devices (IEDs). These explosions leave distinctive injuries, including traumatic brain injuries (TBI), blindness, spinal cord injuries, burns, and limb damage. Many service members suffer more than one of these injuries, resulting in what is known as polytrauma to the body. With regard to amputations, two times as many soldiers required an amputation in 2011 than in the two previous years and three times as many lost more than one limb. In 2009, 7 percent of soldiers received amputations—this number rose to 11 percent in 2010.

While these numbers are already very large, it is important to remember that the Global War on Terror has lasted more than ten years. In addition to the children of currently deploying and separating service members, there are an additional 1 million children who have spent the majority of their childhoods coping with parental military service and service-connected disabilities. The number of children in these families is growing as many of these younger families grow their families and give birth to more children. The bottom line is that there are a lot of children and their families coping with service-connected loss and disability on a daily basis. You are not alone!

Before addressing the scope of challenges and suggesting approaches and resources that can help you, we must acknowledge how your family differs from the typical family in your community who is seeking mental health support and other resources. Military families across the board are frequently strong, motivated to wellness, and frequently seek out active means of coping to become stronger. They usually appreciate support that acknowledges their strength and inherent wisdom and supports their cultural uniqueness. One of the main reasons that we find military and veteran families do not access support resources is that they feel as though doctors and mental health workers think there is something "wrong" with them. They report feeling talked down to or criticized for their experiences and coping strategies.

Coupled with the old, and often still unspoken, military code of not admitting weakness, it can be very difficult for service members and veterans to admit that their household is in need of support. Helpful doctors and mental health workers will acknowledge the power within your family and should support solution-focused intervention and a clearly outlined process of normalizing rather than criticizing your family's experience. The concept of honoring the courage to ask for help and supporting this with insightful, meaningful help draws the best response. Asking for support before problems are out of control (called early intervention) is the best indicator for long-term health and wellness. This approach forms the foundation of benefits to children by helping to de-stress and re-anchor parents, so that they can begin to address the often unseen needs of their children.

Risk Factors That Could Intensify Injuries

Like most things in life, timing is critical in coping when unexpected or traumatic experiences come your way. There are things that can make managing an injury or traumatic event very challenging. If you find your family is dealing with substance abuse, alcoholism, marital distress, domestic violence, financial problems, or lack of support you will need to seek extra support right from the beginning to cope with these issues as they will make it ever more difficult to deal with the injuries of your service member. Your family can succeed, but you will need to deal with these issues at the same time as you are managing the new experiences that are coming your way.

Domestic Violence

We know that families that have been dealing with seen or unseen domestic violence prior to an injury will experience more distress in managing the transitions and role changes that come with those injuries. It may be harder for these families to adjust because anger and frustration may have been running under the surface for a long time. Families with past domestic violence may already be tired from coping with other crises, distress, and unmet needs. Violence can become a way of life in these families and an injury increases the tension and anger in a family. Being honest about the need for help with these issues is critical to everyone's wellness as the family adjusts. If domestic violence begins after an injury or new medication, seek help immediately. Do not let this become a pattern or way of dealing with newfound stressors.

Substance Abuse and Alcoholism

Substance abuse and alcoholism can also be risk factors for difficult transitions. If you had a tendency to manage stress, anxiety, unhappiness, or anger with drugs or alcohol prior to the injury this tendency is not going to go away just because an injury occurs. In fact, families that use this method of coping often isolate more, and have increased coping problems because the drugs and alcohol cause other problems within the community. They are also more at risk for domestic violence, problems with prescription medication, and financial distress. No matter what anyone tells you, illegal substances and alcohol do not make your life easier or help you heal faster. Pot is not a solution for PTSD, chronic pain, or post-TBI irritability. The sooner this method of coping is out of your life, the more effective other therapies will be in your family.

Financial Problems

We know that nobody gets rich as a member of our armed services. Some families are better off than others while some military spouses can work while others cannot. Choices you made in the past may now be causing you financial problems. Frequent deployments, economic downturns, and investment instability may also be impacting your family. Financial distress prior to an injury generally gets worse during the recovery. You will need to seek out sound financial advice, make use of community resources, and possibly even utilize welfare resources before you can achieve a balanced budget and financial security. We want you to know that while this distress can be a risk factor for a poor post-injury outcome, it is not a permanent condition. We have seen many families come out of financial challenges stronger and more able to make their reformulated dreams come true. Having more severe injuries and having younger children will make the challenges you face ever more difficult. Working together, and utilizing as many resources as you can, will help you overcome this risk factor.

Marriage Problems

Repeated deployments will also take a toll on a marriage. Infidelity, communication problems, money problems, parenting challenges—all of it takes a toll. When the call comes regarding an injury these issues do not disappear. They may go underground for a while or they may prompt a spouse to decide they are not up for the challenge. Being able to work as a team is really important and it may not be for everyone. The families that come out of injury transition with strength are the ones that remember the "Golden Rule"—treat other people the way you would want to be treated. Be careful not to make life decisions during a crisis—take the time to think things through until after the crisis has passed. Make sure you involve mental health support people in the process during the crisis—if not for yourself then for your partner and children.

Lack of Social Support

The lack of social support for meeting the challenges of your life is also a risk factor. We know that not everyone has a great family or belongs to a responsive house of worship or congregation or extended community. It is important, though, to take inventory of whom you do have and what resources exist and then seek out additional resources to fill the gaps. By the time you have survived deployment you will be very aware that "it takes a village." Remember to call on this village during the transition period and during the long-term recovery period whenever you need their help.

How Injuries Can Impact Your Children

There are numerous disabling physical, cognitive, and psychological changes that can be a result of war-related injuries. While some of the symptoms may appear to improve over time, it is likely that there will be at least some lasting impairments. Behavioral changes that occur as a result of brain injuries may include problems with remembering (i.e., loss of short-term memory, long-term memory, or both), problem solving may be impaired, impulsivity may increase, emotional control may disappear, and a marked increase in irritability or aggression can occur. The changes that are a result of the TBI may present as a change in personality, and if these changes are pervasive the personality change that is a result of the injury will be permanent. Significant personality changes may leave loved ones feeling as though the injured person is a stranger.

Those with physical limitations may have to relearn skills of independent living or may need assistance for the long haul. Families may grieve the loss of limbs or the disfigurement caused by burns and infections. Chronic pain can change the feeling of joyful living. These injuries can also affect children's school performance, obedience, and emotional and behavioral health. Often for those with obvious physical injuries the road to recovery is very long, with multiple surgeries, intense physical therapy, and widely variable outcomes. Chronic loss of health can also cause a sense of loss and require families to reconfigure in ways they never dreamed imaginable in order to cope.

For more information on how injuries can impact your children and how you can help them cope with these injuries (including a list of responses and recommendations based on your children's age) see chapter 12.

Post-Traumatic Stress Disorder (PTSD)

According to the National Academy of Sciences, approximately 19 percent of returning veterans screened positive for PTSD. Symptoms of a parent's PTSD that may be seen in a child include depression, anxiety, increased emotional problems, and behavioral problems. Also, a parent's hyperarousal symptoms such as irritability, impaired concentration, and restlessness can be detrimental to their interaction with their child. One study found that children often pick up on a parent's low frustration tolerance and therefore further question their parent's love and ability to care for them. Increased irritability and restlessness can also be interpreted by the child as a sign that their environment is not safe.

Traumatic Brain Injury (TBI)

According to the Defense Centers of Excellence, an estimated 202,281 service members sustained a TBI between the years 2000 and 2010. Approximately 20 percent of returning soldiers sustained mild TBI that has been associated with long-term health outcomes. The study by Sogomonyan and Cooper estimated that 85 percent of veterans with TBI also have psychiatric issues.

The prevalence of Americans living with TBI is likely to continue to rise as medical technologies continue to advance, and as more and more military men and women return from combat. Sustaining TBI is clearly a health risk for military personnel in active duty; however, TBI is not unique to the military population. TBI, in fact, is an epidemic in the general public as well. Each year more than 1.5 million people sustain TBIs, but of that number only about 50,000 of those people die from the injury. Although the incidence rates of TBI remained alarming over the past few decades, the death rate from TBI has been declining. High incidence rates and low fatality rates mean that there are an astounding number of people living with TBIs. In the United States, the number of people living with TBI is exceeding 5 million people. While there are cases in which people who have sustained a TBI show no significant or pervasive impairments, there are many people who experience devastating effects as a result of the injury. Moreover, the effects of TBI are not isolated to the person who has sustained the injury. Family members and loved ones may be also greatly impacted.

TBI often results in drastic changes in personality or identifying characteristics of the injured person. Although the injured person is not dead, the personality or characteristics that defined the person may be different as a result of the injury.

Despite your injured service member physically surviving a TBI, your family may feel a sense of loss as though that person has passed away. This psychological death of a loved one with a TBI injury is one of the most difficult aspects of these kinds of injury—it is called "ambiguous loss" and is described later in this chapter.

TBI and Families

Spouses may experience a dramatic role change as a result of a TBI brain-injured spouse's personality change. In many cases, in addition to obtaining a new role as the primary caretaker of the injured spouse, the non-injured spouse also takes on the domestic duties and responsibilities as well as economic burdens that were normally split between them. The non-injured spouse may find the behavior of their injured spouses to be embarrassing (especially in social situations) and consequently they may abstain from socializing with the injured spouse. Non-injured spouses also report feeling as if they are more of a parental figure instead of a spouse and describe themselves as "married widows." It is common for spouses to experience increased anxiety, depression, and isolation, especially when the perception of role and personality changes has been drastic.

All transitioning families need to address their grieving over what has been lost and what has changed. One of the best ways to do this is by creating a special photo album or scrapbook that celebrates the pre-injury activities and events that are meaningful to the family. Soliciting children's input and participation in completing this activity allows them to fully express the memories that matter to them and ultimately allows them to express their unique sense of the most dramatic changes to them. These may or may not be the things that adults grieve and they may not even be the things that adults would perceive to be important. This can be a positive whole-family activity because it allows parents to contribute what they value and now miss as well. It can become a very concrete way to plan for the future by allowing families to find adaptive ways to keep doing what they used to enjoy together. Bringing these losses out into the open allows the adults to be more insightful about what they want to include in their "new normal."

In order to manage brain injury over the long haul families must be prepared to focus on acquiring support and getting educated about their loved one's health condition. Involvement in beneficial activities outside of the home also helps to provide respite for everyone. Beneficial activities include involvement in work, religion or spirituality, recreational activities, and ongoing participation in support groups as well as maintaining a healthy and optimistic outlook. Research shows that one of the best practices in brain injury management is community-based peer support. Peer programs are not available in every community but it is worth the time and effort to seek them out. See the resources section in the appendix of this book for suggestions for community-based peer support, and contact the veterans' service organizations (VSOs) and other groups dedicated to helping individuals with TBI in your area for more recommendations of peer programs that can help your family.

It is important for families of military-related TBI survivors to connect with community resources for brain injury. In many communities these resources can fill in the gaps for transitioning families and help them understand their long-term needs, including how to save money while meeting medical needs, how to ask for help, where to ask for help, and how to find resources for respite care. It is important to remember that no two brain injuries are the same. This means that your service member's needs and your family's needs are unique. Nevertheless, it is a very good coping strategy to connect with people who are finding their way through similar challenges and may have more experience than you with caring for someone with TBI.

The take-away message is to understand that there are stages to coping with all TBIs. Those with unseen injuries or whose personality and sense of self have been dramatically transformed by their experiences affect their families in ways that many within the community may not expect. Visible injuries tend to be less surprising for people within your community because most people can more readily imagine what it means to face a life with a missing body part than they can imagine what life can be like with an invisible injury. That does not mean that they actually understand. It means that they think if they see the injury then they understand it. Families coping with unseen injuries like TBI often express great frustration when well-meaning people say, "He looks OK to me." This is the difference between seen and unseen injuries and it can create additional issues for children and other family members.

For teenagers, a parent with a TBI has different spiritual and religious implications for each individual, but many report using this as a way to help them comprehend or explain the circumstances. Teens often express frustration that non-injured parents and medical professionals often neglect to share information regarding the injured parent with them and say this makes them feel anxious. Guilt and anxiety are often accompanied in them with the desire to move away from the family home. Those feelings can be increased by your teen's concern for the injured parent as well as the non-injured parent and siblings. Changes in family relationships come about in various ways, and in some cases the teens can experience "parentification" in which they perceive themselves as having duties or the role of caring for their families and injured parent. Some teens share that their perception of the injured parent had transformed into them seeing the parent as more child-like. Loneliness and isolation are often reported, both on an individual and family level, and this appears to have the potential to increase the vulnerabilities and may be self-perpetuating (both accidentally and by choice). Loneliness and isolation seem to increase through teens thinking that others could not empathize with their situation, shame, or a feeling of rejection.

The rigors of meeting the ongoing need for medical appointments over the long haul, struggling with a parent who is injured and having the other parent preoccupied with helping the injured parent, poverty due to unemployment or partial employment, and delays in compensation and access to services can all raise the tension level within families to unacceptably high levels. Children often respond unexpectedly to the intensity of these situations and it can be challenging initially to find a system that works and keeps everyone's needs met. Sometimes, just when you think you have the situation handled, a secondary injury or deterioration of the current condition occurs and you have to start all over again. The best recommendation is to make an extra effort to help your family stay in the loop from the first notification call of the injury and then throughout each stage of the reintegration.

Families in the early stages of coping are often not yet fully coming to terms with their reality. Spouses and children alike may be frightened by all that is happening but still focused on having it change for the good. They may experience intense frustration as improvement in the injured parent's condition slows down or even stops. Hopelessness may replace hope long before they reach the point where resources, compensation, and community support are readily available to them. Intertwined with these difficulties is that they must slowly come to terms with the loss of who the injured person was and the way in which he previously functioned inside of the family. It is really critical to remember that all of those reactions are completely normal and part of the learning and adapting curve. Just because these reactions are normal does not mean that you should skip the seeking of support. In fact, those who get support cope better and find their new normal much more efficiently and with fewer long-term negative consequences. Bottom line: Take all the help you can get. Seek it out. Look for what works. Cooperate with the process. Your whole family will benefit.

Although the effects of TBI may impact the family as a whole, the emotional bond between the injured person and each family member will individually be affected. Parent-child bonds are the most basic foundation of healthy child development and have a unique influence on the overall adjustment and development of children. Impairments due to TBI are often identified as contributing factors to negative parent-child interactions. Parents with brain injuries may be less able to be nurturing, may be less involved or responsive, less encouraging on skill development, and less encouraging of obedience than non-injured parents. There are numerous factors that contribute to this phenomenon. If a child is uncomfortable with the symptoms of the impairments, he may respond with behavioral problems or develop poor responses as coping methods. Children learn the skills necessary for coping and problem solving from observing and interacting with their parents. A child may see the injured parent's impairments in executive functioning and learn from these behaviors how to cope with her own difficulties. The parent-child relationship may also be impacted if the child begins to purposefully avoid interaction with the injured parent because the child finds the symptoms of the impairments to be unpleasant.

Recommendations and Suggestions

Children of military parents with injuries are at greater risk of psychological problems. The research by Sogomonyan and Cooper reported that outpatient mental health visits for children of active-duty parents doubled from 1 to 2 million from 2003 to 2008. One study points out that inpatient psychiatric stays for children of active-duty parents age fourteen and under increased by 50 percent between 2003 to 2008 (from 35,000 to 55,000). Another study notes that half to three-quarters of children with a parent diagnosed with a psychiatric illness were reported to be at serious risk for developing their own personality disorders.

Our goal in this chapter is to offer prevention and early intervention strategies that can help your family prevent some of the more serious mental health fallout issues. This is a tough path yet families do survive and thrive. We do know that the need for such services is not just about the first few weeks or months. In fact, oftentimes the greatest need for support is when reality really starts to sink in between six months and two years post-deployment. By being alert to the signs that more support is needed, families can meet their challenges as they evolve. Every family has its own process and needs. Families of services members injured early in the conflict report still needing support five to eight years after the injury. Even if the kinds of support you might need may be different from the support you needed in the early stages, you should continue to seek help each and every time you need it. Hoping for problems to disappear on their own usually results in bigger problems and more stress. This downward spiral is not necessary. Remember that you need to advocate for your family to make sure that anyone who needs it gets supportive mental health care. A detailed list (by age groups) of children's reactions to war-related injuries and disabilities (as well as their reactions to deployment and reintegration) and recommendations to address these reactions and their concerns is available in the next chapter.

The Initial Injury and Impact

Your family's reaction to the initial news of injury is going to depend on severity level and resources. This period can be a whirlwind for spouses, who may need to quickly place children with relatives or friends in order to rush to an injured partner's side. If you get the news, it is absolutely essential to take time to calm down.

A calm, composed presentation will help your children cope best. You should seek support for yourself while talking about this with children. It is absolutely normal to be scared, uncertain, and emotional. Having a trusted friend or family member on hand for moral support during the conversation may help. If several children or very young children will need to be told together, having an extra adult on hand can help with meeting the developmental needs of each child. Even where time may appear very short, telling children directly and taking the time to answer their questions and reassure them is an essential first coping step.

Even if the injury is less severe, there may be an intense period of anxiety and distress for your service member. Children feel and experience this even more intensely. They may not know how to ask questions and they may misunderstand what the grown-ups are discussing around them. The attachment anxiety that they experienced when their parent deployed may become very intense as their remaining parent becomes focused on helping their partner. As much as possible, keep your children with someone who is briefed on how to support them at an age-appropriate level.

Returning Home

The first few days after returning home with injuries often seem like a dream. Once the adrenalin rush of homecoming wears off everyone in the home may be irritable, stressed, and short-tempered. Roles still need to be renegotiated. Coming to terms with what the injuries mean and how the family will cope begins to sink in. These first few weeks at home are often a challenge. Normal post-deployment strategies of taking time to reintegrate, staying on a familiar schedule, and taking time to talk things through are extremely important. Early contact with mental health professionals may provide a safe space for everyone to debrief, normalize their experiences, and develop solid coping strategies that address the family's specific concerns. This early contact with resources helps families learn about those resources, which can ease their initial burdens and provide a healthy setting for healing.

Parents can expect that their children will go through emotional reactions during the deployment phase that are similar to what the parents went through and should be ready to provide a similar level of support for their children's emotional reactions. If the injury or trauma has left both parents unable to help the children, additional time may be required for support resources or the involvement of a supplemental caregiver or support person. Be prepared to be as clear as possible with that person about what you need from them, their level of involvement in decisions, financial considerations, and exit strategies. This will help prevent misunderstandings and unexpected distress.

Tips on Preparing for a Health Care Provider Visit

There are several things your family can do to be proactive about the health care for the injured or disabled service member in your family. When going in for treatment, make sure you are prepared to record important information.

- Be prepared with a checklist of questions for your health care provider regarding your service member's physical or mental health condition.
- Be able to provide your physician with information about your service member's medications or special diets and dietary supplements.
- You may request health care literature from your provider or ask for recommended Internet sites to help further educate yourself on the condition.
- Ask your medical provider for a way to follow up with any additional questions you may have in the future either through them or their staff. If the family member is agreeable, it is often helpful to be accompanied by someone to take notes and help capture all necessary information.
- Openly communicate with your provider about any health care concerns, and ask for clarification if you do not understand some of the information provided. If you do not feel you are getting the service or care you need, ask your provider how to go about getting a second opinion.
- Parents can use this opportunity to serve as good role models for children and youth regarding health care–related behavior and responsibilities such as nutrition, exercise, and stress management.

Addressing Grief, Loss, and Depression in Children

Grief is a natural process that accompanies death and dying. It is part of the human experience since everyone will experience a loss or the death of a loved one. It is a process that no two people experience in the same way. Over the decade that the wars in Iraq and Afghanistan have been waged, many service members have been faced with grieving the death of a fallen comrade and having to continue on with their mission. Many families also have had to deal with the death of a service member that they hold dear to them. Even if a death has not occurred close to you, life has changed because of war and quite possibly a lot has changed depending on the type(s) of injury sustained.

The Five Stages of Grief

Understanding the five stages of grief (listed below) is often helpful when service members or their families have to face death or other losses. These stages of grief have often been applied to many other aspects of life including relationship break-ups, miscarriage, loss of financial stability, loss of health, loss of a dream, and loss of a friendship. Examples are provided with reference to females experiencing the loss of their husbands. We want to acknowledge, however, that while the majority of spouse loss fits this model, many women have served in uniform and left behind partners and husbands for whom this experience has been no less traumatic and for whom the coping has been equally challenging.

The five stages are: 1) denial, 2) anger, 3) bargaining, 4) depression, and 5) acceptance. The stages were derived from Elisabeth Kübler-Ross' work with terminally ill patients, and are described in her book *On Death and Dying*. They were later modified to help individuals cope with the death of a family member, friend, or other loved one. Knowing these stages helps individuals understand the emotions they may encounter while in the grieving process. Dr. Kübler-Ross also stipulated that individuals may not go through all five of these stages or do them in any specific sequence. While the model is mostly utilized for those dealing with death, its stages are also useful for studying other types of loss such as a member of your family experiencing a serious injury.

Denial

Denial is used as a defense mechanism and is a way to buffer against dealing with uncomfortable situations that arise when one is confronted with death. This occurs when one denies that the death of a cherished person occurred. The length of time denial lasts may depend on how much time an individual has to acknowledge the inevitable death and how well an individual is able to cope with stressful situations.

The wife of a service member who has just been told by the casualty assistance officer that her husband was killed overseas may demonstrate denial by stating, "This can't be happening to me. My husband can't be dead."

Anger

Anger is often displaced in all directions and projected onto the environment at seemingly random times. It may be aimed at inanimate objects, strangers, friends, family, or the dying or deceased loved one. It is possible for the grieving person to find grievances everywhere she looks. Rationally, the angry person knows that these things or people are not to blame for her loss, but emotionally she may resent a person for causing her pain or for leaving her. At the same time she may feel guilty for being angry, which often increases her anger. Anger is more likely to arise as a result of an unexpected death or the death of a child or young adult.

The same wife of a dead service member may then blame the service branch (Army, Navy, Marines, or Air Force) for her husband's death because they deployed him, which resulted in his death. She may begin to yell at anyone she then associates with this branch of service or that she believes is to blame for her loss, such as fellow squad members.

Bargaining

As a result of feeling helpless and vulnerable and needing to regain control, many individuals facing the death of a loved one may try bargaining. When a person passes away the family members may feel that if they had done something differ-ent then the outcome would have changed and their loved one might not have been taken from them. Family members often barter with whatever deity or higher power that they believe will help them in an attempt to postpone the inevitable. They may offer to exhibit "good behavior" in exchange for some prize (i.e., more time with their loved one) and additionally make the promise not to ask for any-thing else if their wanted postponement is granted.

The military wife may pray to God, "If you bring my husband back I will promise not to distract him from his mission by complaining to him about how much I miss him or how badly things are going at home without him here."

Depression

There is a multifaceted sense of great loss that often coincides with the death of a close friend or family member. It is normal and appropriate to feel depressed when you lose someone close to you. Kübler-Ross identified two types of depres-sion (reaction depression and preparatory depression) that exist among those who are grieving. *Reaction depression* includes the feelings of sadness and regret that accompany the realization that a loved one is dying or has died. Worry may also play a role in terms of individuals having concerns over the cost of burial expenses. Withdrawal from others is also sometimes observed. *Preparatory depres-sion* is a tool to help facilitate the next stage in the process, acceptance. The person who is grieving may feel the need to discuss death and any fears that he has about death and dying.

In our example, friends and family members may try to reach out to the widow to cheer her up, get her out of the house, and be supportive only to be rebuffed in their attempts to do so and are told by her that she "just wants to be left alone."

Acceptance

Not every individual is able to reach this last stage since many find it difficult to make peace with death. It is sometimes viewed as a stage void of feelings. The individual is able to face the reality that the loved one is physically no longer pres-ent and will never be returning. The person in this stage can start to adapt to life without the loved one, can grow from the experience with the death, and start liv-ing again.

In our example, the widow is able to start picking up the pieces of her shattered life and start putting them back together. She understands that there is nothing she can do to bring back her deceased husband and no longer believes the military or her husband's comrades are responsible for his death.

Symptoms of Grief for Kids

If your children are going through the grieving process their grief may manifest itself in the following ways:

- Sadness, sorrow, depression, fears, anxieties.
- Ambivalence, loneliness, longing, jealousy.
- Hypersensitivity to other's comments, emotional reactivity, lack of enjoyment, emotional flatness.
- Guilt, shame, regret, shock.
- Anger.
- Stress symptoms like nightmares, teeth grinding, shortness of breath, stomach trouble, a feeling of heaviness, headaches, and other unusual body sensations like tingling, numbness, and muscle tension. Menstrual changes in teens or adults can also be signs of intense grief.

Ambiguous Loss

Although the Kübler-Ross model can be beneficial to help your family understand death and other serious losses, it is not one that appears suitable to handle other uncertainties that arise in military families, such as in families who have a service member who is missing in action (MIA) or a prisoner of war (POW). These family members are often unable to find acceptance because the status of their beloved service member is unknown. The family is left not knowing if their loved one is alive or dead and whether or not he will return. The same is true for the circumstances facing the families of service members who return from war having suffered either a visible or non-visible war wound. This ambiguous loss framework may be more adequate in dealing with these kinds of grief.

Ambiguous loss is unclear, uncertain, vague, and indeterminate. It is externally caused (e.g., by war, illness) and can be confusing and incomprehensible to the individual(s) who experience it. The typical stages of grief do not apply to this type of loss. The grief process is complicated in ambiguous loss due to the ambiguity of the situation, and the grief in the person can become frozen. This leads to the immobilization and isolation of the sufferer from his usual support system. Because the situation is out of the sufferer's control the bereavement process is blocked. Concerns arise in families who are left not knowing about their service member or her condition and injuries. They wonder how to cope, how to grieve, and how they can move forward.

There are two types of ambiguous loss. The first type is *physical absence with psychological presence*. This is similar to the loss experienced by families of service members who are POW and MIA. The second type is *physical presence with psychological absence*. This is similar to the loss resulting from changes that occur in the service member's personality, behavior, or emotional reaction as a result of a war injury such as a TBI or PTSD. These two types of ambiguous loss may also occur simultaneously in a family.

Families who suffer from physical absence with psychological presence are never able to gain closure, often due to the fact that there is no body or body part for them to bury. People often need to see a body and participate in the burial ritual to help them break down denial and cognitively cope and grieve. Human beings have a need to say good-bye to a person they cherished. It may be impossible to let go of a loved one without being able to participate in rituals that honor her and bid her farewell.

Because there is so much uncertainty in military families, the feeling of ambiguous loss can begin as soon as they know that their service member's unit is being mobilized to deploy. Even though a date of deployment is often given to family members of a deploying troop, this date has been known to change. A family may accompany their service member to the send-off point only to be told that there has been a change of plans and the date has changed, forcing the family to have to repeat their good-byes. It is not uncommon to have the date of deployment moved ahead unexpectedly and not have enough time for the family to prepare and say good-bye.

The ambiguity in military families continues on several different levels. On a practical level, a military family is forced to reorganize their typical routine so they can continue to function without the presence of the deployed member. This is somewhat easier for family members of an active-duty service member than for those family members of a National Guard or Reserve member. Emotionally, ambiguity persists throughout the deployment because of concerns over the deployed member's safety. Family members are aware that their loved one is in harm's way while on deployment but often have no idea how close their family member may actually come to being harmed. As a result of today's technologies, deployed service members have better communication with their families than ever before, thus allowing the family members of the deployed to presume they are safe, at least during the time of communication, helping to reduce the uncertainty of the situation until the contact ends and safety becomes unknown again. By the way they cover the war's daily developments, members of the mass media also play a role in reinforcing the uncertainty of the safety of the service member. Families of deployed service members also have the daily uncertainty of not knowing when a loved one will return home. Even though return dates are often provided, deployments are often extended, adding to the rollercoaster of emotions that military families often face.

The second type of ambiguous loss can be seen most often in service members who have returned from deployment and have suffered an injury. Service members with TBI or PTSD may require a family member to care for them, depending on the severity of the injury or disorder. The shift in personality or loss of memory (which can be the result of TBI) may cause anxiety and depression in the caregiver because the person they once knew is slipping away. Unlike with death, the loved one is still physically present but may not be the same person the family knew prior to deployment. We recommend that you grieve the loss of your living loved one's previous presence through new rituals (e.g., releasing a balloon into the air, lighting a remembrance candle) rather than waiting to grieve at her funeral after her death.

Building Resiliency in Your Family

Here is a list of six ways that you and your children can help build resiliency and learn to adapt to ambiguous loss. (For more information on building resiliency, see chapter 7.)

Finding Meaning

Finding meaning and being able to make sense out of what is happening is very difficult when dealing with ambiguous loss. Families may not be able to celebrate special occasions and holidays the way they did before the loss, but they should continue to celebrate special days and holidays. Kids can surprise us with their insight about meaning. One nine-year-old told us that all of this happened so her daddy would be able to be around more to play with her more and so that they would not miss each other so much. Advocacy and raising community awareness can be a great way for your family to cope. Sharing your story with others and seeing how it helps them can be a source of meaning. One veteran told us that his TBI transformed his life by teaching him what he valued most.

Tempering Mastery

Individuals who are able to live well even in the face of ambiguous loss are often able to do so by "tempering mastery" or holding two opposing ideas in their minds at the same time. They are able to move into a both/and mindset. Their loved one is both here and not here. The wife of a deployed soldier may feel both married and not married. A veteran's caregiver and spouse may feel her redeployed service member is both her husband and a stranger to her. This thinking allows individuals facing ambiguous loss to become more comfortable with ambiguity.

Reconstructing Identity

When your service member deploys, you and your family members must change who you are and your daily routine. Family members need to be able to become more flexible about societally prescribed gender roles and gradually broaden their individual roles to maintain the household. Undoubtedly everyone in the household has to do more and function more independently. This is the reality of one-parent households. Take great care not to "parentify" your children: While it is common to look at the oldest child of the same gender as the absent parent and ask him to be the man of the house till your service member returns, this actually places a great deal of pressure on the child to perform at a level that is impossible to fulfill. It is better to enlist the child as a helper in the process and to continue to look at all your roles flexibly.

Talk with children about what is working and what is not working, and about how they are feeling about their changing roles and challenges. You should also seek outside adult support to ensure that children have a chance to be children. Encourage children to write in their journals about their experiences and to be honest about their feelings. Making up silly stories that tell the tale of their challenges can also help them organize their feelings and sense of self. Be prepared to hear these stories non-judgmentally and have a good laugh with your child.

Normalizing Ambivalence

Unresolved loss feelings can lead to ambivalence or a feeling of not caring about what happens, or feelings of being withdrawn. This often occurs because of difficulty in holding both a feeling of frustration and loss with a feeling of relief and acceptance. Having a non-judgmental environment where those experiencing this kind of loss can discuss their negative feelings and emotions helps individuals see that others are also facing similar emotional conflicts. Once these feelings are acknowledged and brought to light ambivalence is more easily managed and minimized. Opportunities to discuss these conflicts are important for children, for the injured or recovering service member, and for caregivers. Kids can be very fluid in their acceptance. What may seem resolved one day may not be resolved the next day. Be prepared to revisit concerns with children as needed and remember that at each new developmental milestone they may need to revisit these feelings again and each time they gain a little more clarity.

Some children display traits of withdrawal and avoidance in ways that are hard for busy parents to understand. We have seen kids who hide behind their video games and just flat out refuse to engage while working through their ambivalence.

If they act like this, it is important for you to physically be with your children: Sit quietly by them, make opportunities for one-on-one time (even to do ordinary activities), or try a new hobby or sport together. Send the message loud and clear: "Your feelings are normal and I am here to support you."

Revising Attachment

Revising attachment means that your family is able to accept rather than resist the ambiguity that surrounds their relationships when your service member returns from war with an injury, and is able to acknowledge the changes and accept them as a normal part of the process. It is important that your family is able to celebrate what your service member is still able to do or remember and grieve the connections that have been lost. The goal of this is to balance human connections and social activities with whatever is fading away and to find a new normal.

No matter how hard we try to go back to the old ways that worked before deployment or the injury or loss of a loved one, the fact is that we are all indelibly changed by these life experiences. Things are going to be different to at least some degree. How much things will be different will vary by family since each family is unique. Learning to be flexible and take things as they come, and to accept that the family may need to function more as a team than as a top-down unit, are both associated with better mental health and attachment for everyone. Kids can do their share as team members with support. Being a teammate allows for collaborating to get things done and keeps family connections healthy.

This approach takes the focus off of the person with the injury and what he cannot do and focuses on what he can do and what the family can do as a team. Kids can take an active role in describing what they can do, what they would like to be able to do, and how they can help out. Be prepared for imperfection, age-appropriate attention spans, and the need to be flexible while skills develop. Children tend to be more positive about their families when they can see how they can contribute. They feel more securely connected to their parents (even injured parents) when they are able to actively participate in family life and receive recognition for their efforts.

Discovering Hope

People are able to discover hope in many ways. Some find hope in religion, others in nature and meditation, and still others find it in exercise and the arts (music, theater, poetry, and dance). Some find it in a mixture of some or all of these things. Some find it in creating new community programs to assist other families in their journey toward a stable post-service life. New hope is more easily found when one is able to make meaningful human connections.

Make an effort to help your children find unique ways to participate in their community. Developing new skills and hobbies with their injured parent can instill a sense of hope. The camaraderie of facing new challenges together helps parents and children bond. Adaptive sports can be a great way for injured parents to get active again. Their families can often participate with them. Participating in the support of other families coping with similar experiences can instill a sense of hope and community interaction. Taking time to pray or meditate or worship as a family each week can also provide emotional relief and a sense of hopefulness that comes with a sense of inner support and purpose. It can be hard to find just the right program or support in some communities. Be prepared to try a few things before you find what really connects for your family. Be open to the new experiences and try to talk openly about fears or PTSD triggers as they occur. The right setting and activities will support the entire family and your service member.

Sleep and Sleep Hygiene

When families are under stress, sleep may be seriously affected. Maintaining a healthy sleep/wake rhythm is associated with healing, mental health, and positive coping skills. Nearly all war-related injuries come with some level of sleep disruption and this can heavily impact the household. Children with disrupted sleep patterns have more mental health issues, lower grades in school, appear to have ADHD/ADD, and display more behavioral disturbances.

War veterans today are four times more likely to experience sleep-disorder problems (based on data from the U.S. Department of Veterans Affairs). In addition, according to the National Sleep Foundation the number of veterans that are disabled due to sleep problems has increased by 61 percent in the last two years. Common sleep complaints in war veterans include recurrent nightmares, distressed awakenings, and difficulty returning to sleep. The nature of training and combat in the military today is such that a continual disruption of the sleep/wake cycle is present. This occurs because service members must sustain a high degree of readiness such that they can engage in combat at any time of the day or night. However, to do so naturally disrupts the sleep cycle and, in turn, physiological functioning. The experience of sleep disruption when changing time zones and reintegrating into home life is to be expected over the first one to two months of returning home. Decompressing from these habits can take time.

Returning home to a distressed family with young children also experiencing sleep disruptions can create a cycle of sleep challenges. These challenges can become chronic. Individuals who had been diagnosed with post-traumatic stress disorder (PTSD) experienced more sleep problems than a control group, though the reason behind these disturbances is largely unknown. Individuals with PTSD tend to report an increase in the amount of arousals and this may account for the sleep problems. This "hyperarousal" has been shown in many studies to exist in individuals with PTSD and is thought to be a central component that corresponds to the increase in sleep problems and an increase in sleep deprivation.

Since the primary function of sleep is restorative, it is reasonable to think that disruptions in this restorative purpose and the physiological stress that co-occurs with insomnia could potentially impact the individual's health and his ability to actually recover from PTSD. If sleep problems persist it can actually extend and aggravate the symptoms of PTSD. In addition, individuals who have more severe sleep complaints one month after a traumatic event occurs are more likely to develop PTSD within six to twelve months. If sleep symptoms persist for more than eight weeks after returning home seek help from medical providers.

While it is clear that military personnel are often sleep-deprived for numerous reasons, what may be less clear is the effect this loss of sleep may have on their family's physical, cognitive, and psychological health. Cognitive slowing is even greater for chronically sleep-deprived veterans who are required to perform critical tasks and make quick and complex decisions every day.

When the veteran experiences loss of sleep or disturbances in sleep, such as thrashing or violent nightmares, it is inevitable that a spouse or partner will also be awakened by this. It often falls on the spouse to try and calm the veteran down after a sleep disruption, and they may also experience problems falling back to sleep due to worry caused by knowing their partner is having problems sleeping. Erratic and impulsive behaviors following sleep awakenings may also ensue due to PTSD symptoms. The strain and stress of having a spouse or parent who suffers from PTSD may disrupt sleep in the spouse and family members, causing them to become sleep deprived and affecting their everyday performance.

Sleep deprivation in the family can lead to a host of problems, including increased irritability, decreased alertness and performance, sleepiness throughout the day, and memory and cognitive impairments. Chronic sleep deprivation can also lead to an increase in blood pressure, heart disease, stroke, cancer, and diabetes. This not only exacerbates other problems already experienced by the families of veterans but places additional stress on their relationships. Veterans and families with sleep problems may become especially moody and multiple fights may ensue due to sleep deprivation. Their sleep difficulties may also lead to attempts to self-medicate, by using prescription pills or through substance use. These endeavors can cause disruptions in the family unit, both with the partner and children, and can lead to measures being taken such as sleeping in separate bedrooms or even living separate lives, which undermines total family strength.

Sleep Hygiene Tips (Adapted from the American Sleep Association)

Do:

- Make a set sleep schedule, including a set time every day to go to bed and wake up.
- Try to exercise regularly but not too close to bedtime. It is preferable to exercise in the morning.
- Make your bedroom as comfortable as possible, by keeping it at a comfortable temperature, keeping the noise level down, and making it dark enough so sleep will come more easily.
- Use your bed in your bedroom only for sleeping and for sexual activity.
- Try to relax yourself at least thirty minutes before going to bed, by taking a warm bath, having a massage, doing deep breathing, using imagery, using relaxation techniques, reading, and so forth.
- Make and keep a nightly routine before bed to signal your mind that it is time to go to sleep.
- Shut off electronic devices (such as cell phones and TV) that could potentially disrupt sleep. If you need noise, use "white noise," such as a fan or soothing nature sounds.
- If you are sitting in bed for twenty to thirty minutes and cannot get to sleep, get up and do something relaxing and quiet, such as reading a relaxing book, until you feel you are able to fall asleep.
- Take all medications as directed.

Don't:

- Exercise right before going to bed.
- Eat a large meal right before going to bed.
- Use any caffeine products or drink alcohol right before bed.
- Engage in any activities that would be stimulating, such as playing a stressful game (including video games), doing homework, or having an important conversation with someone close to you, directly before going to bed.
- Take naps throughout the day.
- Have the TV on while trying to fall asleep.
- Try to fall asleep. The harder you try to make yourself fall asleep, the less likely it is that you actually will fall asleep.
- Turn on any bright lights if you get up in the middle of the night. Light triggers to the brain that it is daytime, and thus time to wake up.

- Take any medications that have not been prescribed to you or use over-the-counter sleeping pills without first consulting your health physician.

Goals for Healthy Family Functioning

Your goal for healthy family functioning is to make your home a place where family members can find support, love, and acceptance. Home should be a place that is free of domestic violence of all kinds. That includes between the adult partners, between adults and kids, and between kids. The family is empowered to access the resources they need, and to know how to do this and where to start on their own. They also know who to ask when they are stumped.

Healthy families should receive appropriate medical care, rehabilitation, and family support services. They know how to access this care and how to appeal the process if they feel something important is missing. They have clearly identified advocates to help them navigate the complex government systems to get these needs met. They are also able to access community resources for long-term emotional and peer support.

All members of the household should have their pressing needs met and their long-term health and wellness on the radar. Kids who are able to connect with a parent or mentor for meaningful support are better able to navigate in school and have hopes and dreams for the future. Caregivers should have adequate support and opportunities for their own health and wellness, with adequate respite services so that they can look forward to a break from their caregiving responsibilities. They are able to have hopes and dreams for their futures as well. Marital distress is handled proactively when both partners are able to feel comfortable with their commitment level and ability to work through the inevitable tough times. As parents, the adults have peace of mind that they are working together in support of their children. Veterans have a place of recognition and value within their homes, families, and communities and are able to contribute at their ability level. They feel supported and connected and appreciated for their service.

Is this a dream? No! It is an achievable goal. Many families have been able to overcome their traumas and challenges and do make these goals into reality. You can do so too.

Military kids and their families are amazing. They can and do find ways to get their needs met. Many times resources are available in the community that, when combined with the military and VA treatment resources, can create a real, functional support network. It does take time and energy. There is hope!

References

Betz, G., and J. Thorngen. "Ambiguous Loss and the Family Grieving Process." *The Family Journal: Counseling and Therapy for Couples and Families* 14, no. 4 (2006): 359–365.

Boss, P. *Ambiguous Loss: Learning to Live with Unresolved Grief.* Cambridge, MA: Harvard University Press, 1999.

———. "Ambiguous Loss in Families of the Missing." *The Lancet* 36 (2002): S39–40.

———. *Loss, Trauma, and Resilience: Therapeutic Work with Ambiguous Loss.* New York: Norton, 2006.

———. "The Trauma and Complicated Grief of Ambiguous Loss." *Pastoral Psychology* 59 (2010): 137–145.

Brain Injury Association of America (BIAA). *Traumatic Brain Injury in the United States: A Call for Public/Private Cooperation.* 2007. http://www..biausa.org/ (accessed 11 January 2011).

Brett Gordon, A. *All About Me: While You Were Away Keeping America Safe!* Coral Springs, FL: Families Facing Solutions, Inc., 2009.

Butera-Prinzi, F., and A. Perlesz. "Through Children's Eyes: Children's Experience of Living with a Parent with an Acquired Brain Injury." *Brain Injury* 18 (2004): 83–101.

Carnes, S., and W. Quinn. "Family Adaptation to Brain Injury: Coping And Psychological Distress." *Families, Systems, and Health* 23, no. 2 (2005): 186–203.

Center for Disease Control and Prevention (CDC). "Traumatic Brain Injury in the United States: A Report to Congress." 1999. http://www.cdc.gov/traumaticbraininjury/tbi_report_to_congress.html (accessed 11 January 2011).

Cozza, S., R. Chun, and J. Polo. "Military Families and Children during Operation Iraqi Freedom." *Psychiatric Quarterly* 76 (2005): 371–378.

Cozza, S. J., et al. "Combat-Injured Service Members and Their Families: The Relationship of Child Distress and Spouse-Perceived Family Distress and Disruption." *Journal of Traumatic Stress* 23 (2010): 112–115.

Degeneffe, C., and R. Lynch. "Correlates of Depression in Adult Siblings of Persons with Traumatic Brain Injury." *Rehabilitation Counseling Bulletin* 49, no. 3 (2006): 130–142.

Ducharme, J., A. Davidson, and N. Rushford. "Treatment of Oppositional Behavior in Children of Parents with Brain Injury and Chronic Pain." *Journal of Emotional and Behavioral Disorders* 10 (2002): 241–247.

Eaton, K., C. Hoge, S. Messer, A. Whitt, O. Cabrera, D. McGurk, A. Cox, and C. Castro. "Prevalence of Mental Health Problems, Treatment Needs, and Barriers to Care among Primary-Care-Seeking Spouses of Military Service Members Involved in Iraq and Afghanistan Deployment." *Military Medicine* 173, no. 11 (2008): 1051–1056.

Emswiler, M. A., and J. P. Emswiler. *Guiding Your Child through Grief.* New York: Bantam Trade, 2000.

Fischer, H. *United States Military Casualty Statistics: Operation Iraqi Freedom and Operation Enduring Freedom.* Congressional Research Service Report for Congress (7-57000//RS22452). http://www.fas.org/sgp/crs/natsec/RS22452.pdf, and http://www.defenselink.mil/news/casualty.pdf (accessed 11 January 2011).

Frain, M., M. Bishop, and M. Bethal. "A Roadmap for Rehabilitation Counseling to Serve Military Veterans with Disabilities." *Journal of Rehabilitation* 76 (2010): 13–21.

Gorman, L., H. Fitzgerald, et al. "Parental Combat Injury and Early Child Development: A Conceptual Model for Differentiating Effects of Visible and Invisible Injuries." *Psychiatric Quarterly* 81 (2010): 1–21.

Grieger, T., et al. "Post-Traumatic Stress Disorder and Depression in Battle-Injured Soldiers." *American Journal of Psychiatry* 163 (2006): 1777–1783.

Griffin, J., et al. "Communicating Information to Families of Polytrauma Patients: A Narrative Literature Review." *Rehabilitation Nursing* 33, no. 5 (2008): 206–214.

Harris, D., and A. D. Stuart. "Adolescents' Experience of a Parental Traumatic Brain Injury." *Health SA Gesondheid* 11, no. 4 (2006): 46–56.

Hart, T., et al. "Executive Function and Self-Awareness of Real-World Behavior and Attention Deficits Following Traumatic Brain Injury." *Journal of Head Trauma Rehabilitation* 20 (2005): 333–347.

Huebner, A., J. Mancini, R. Wilcox, S. Grass, and G. Grass. "Parental Deployment and Youth in Military Families Exploring Uncertainty and Ambiguous Loss." *Family Relations* 56, no. 2 (2007): 112–122.

Klonoff, P., et al. "A Family Experiential Model of Recovery after Brain Injury." *Bulletin of the Menninger Clinic* 72, no. 2 (2008): 109–129.

Kobayashi, I., J. M. Boarts, and D. K. Delahanty. "Polysomnographically Measured Sleep Abnormalities in PTSD: A Meta-Analytic Review." *Psychophysiology* 44, no. 4 (2007): 660–669.

Kübler-Ross, E. *On Death and Dying.* New York: Routledge, 1973.

Lagarde, D., and D. Batejat. "Disrupted Sleep-Wake Rhythm and Performance: Advantages of Modafinil." *Military Psychology* 7, no. 3 (1995): 165–191.

Landau, J., and J. Hissett. "Mild Traumatic Brain Injury: Impact on Identity and Ambiguous Loss in the Family." *Families, Systems, & Health* 26, no. 2 (2008): 69–85.

MacDermid, S., R. Samper, et al. *Understanding and Promoting Resilience in Military Families,* 1–28. West Lafayette, IN: The Military Family Research Institute at Purdue University, 2008.

Maher, M. J., S. A. Rego, and G. M. Asnis. "Sleep Disturbances in Patients with Post-Traumatic Stress Disorder: Epidemiology, Impact, and Approaches to Management." *CNS Drugs* 20, no. 7 (2006): 567–590.

Makin-Byrd, K., E. Gifford, S. McCutcheon, and S. Glynn. "Family and Couples Treatment for Newly Returning Veterans." *Professional Psychology: Research and Practice* 42, no. 1 (2011): 47–55.

Mansfield, A., J. Kaufman, S. Marshall, B. Gaynes, J. Morrissey, and C. Engel. "Deployment and the Use of Mental Health Services among U.S. Army Wives." *The New England Journal of Medicine* 362, no. 2 (2010): 101–109.

Mellman, T. A., D. David, B. Bustamante, J. Torres, and A. Fins. "Dreams in the Acute Aftermath of Trauma and Their Relationship to PTSD." *Journal of Traumatic Stress* 14, no. 1 (2001): 241–247.

National Institute of Neurological Disorders and Stroke (NINDS). "Traumatic Brain Injury: Hope through Research." http://www.ninds.nih.gov/disorders/tbi/detail_tbi.htm (accessed on 11 January 2011).

National Sleep Foundation. *More Veterans Suffer from Sleep Apnea*. (2010) http://www.sleep foundation.org/ (accessed 11 January 2011).

Pessar, L. F., et al. "The Effects of Parental Traumatic Brain Injury on the Behavior of Parents and Children." *Brain Injury* 7 (1991): 231–240.

Schnyer, D. M., D. Zeithamova, and V. Williams. "Decision-Making under Conditions of Sleep Deprivation: Cognitive and Neural Consequences." *Military Psychology* 21 (2009): S36–S45.

Smith, M., et al. "Who's Teaching Whom? A Study of Family Education in Brain Injury." *Rehabilitation Nursing* 27, no. 6 (2002): 209–214.

Sogomonyan, F., and J. L. Cooper. *Trauma Faced by Children of Military Families: What Every Policymaker Should Know*. New York: National Center for Children in Poverty, 2010. http://nccp.org/publications/pdf/text_938.pdf (accessed 11 January 2011).

Stein, R. "Scientists Finding Out What Losing Sleep Does to a Body." *Washington Post*, 9 October 2005, http://www.washingtonpost.com/wp-dyn/content/article/2005/10/08/AR2005100801405.html (accessed 11 January 2011).

Tanielian, T., and L. Jaycox. *Invisible Wounds of War: Psychological and Cognitive Injuries, Their Consequences, and Services to Assist Recovery*. Santa Monica, CA: RAND Corporation Monographs, 2008.

Thompson, C. E., F. B. Taylor, M. E. McFall, R. F. Barnes, and M. A. Raskind. "Non-nightmare Distressed Awakenings in Veterans with Post-Traumatic Stress Disorder: Response to Prazosin." *Journal of Traumatic Stress* 21 (2008): 417–420.

Urbach, J. "The Impact of Parental Head Trauma on Families with Children." *Psychiatric Medicine* 7 (1989): 17–36.

Uysal, S., et al. "The Effect of Parental Traumatic Brain Injury on Parenting and Child Behavior." *Journal of Head Trauma Rehabilitation* 13 (1998): 57–71.

Wade, S., et al. "An Online Family Intervention to Reduce Parental Distress following Pediatric Brain Injury." *Journal of Consulting and Clinical Psychology* 74, no. 3 (2006): 445–454.

Williamson, V., and E. Mulhall. *Invisible Wounds: Psychological and Neurological Injuries Confront a New Generation of Veterans*. Washington, DC: Iraq and Afghanistan Veterans of America, 2009. http://iava.org/files/IAVA_invisible_wounds_0.pdf (accessed 11 January 2011).

Zeigler, E. A. "Psychosocial Issues for Spouses of Brain Injury Survivors." *Journal of Neuroscience Nursing* 31, no. 2 (1999): 106–109.

Children's Reactions to Deployment, Reintegration, and Injuries by Age Groups, with Recommendations on How to Help Them

12

Jeffrey E. Barnett, Carol Getkin, Alaina Grover,
Desiree King, Angela Schroedle,
Michelle D. Sherman, Rebecca Tews

This chapter looks at how children of different ages respond to reintegration (with information listed for each age group) and offers suggestions for how you can communicate with your children. We also offer information on how you can help your children cope with the new disabilities or injuries of your wounded warrior. The suggestions in this chapter are based in part on training from the VA National Center for PTSD, research from others, the experience and knowledge of teachers from all branches of the military, and practical clinical experiences from clinicians who work with military and veteran families. Remember that there is no "one size fits all" approach and parents of multiple children may find it especially challenging as each child may have different needs. Also, how your child experiences one deployment may be quite different from how she handles a deployment a couple of years later. You know your child best, so we encourage you to use what works.

Of note is that regardless of your child's age or developmental level, there may be times when all your best efforts prove insufficient. Some children (and families) will need and benefit from receiving professional assistance. If you find negative or unhealthy reactions to your warrior's return occurring despite your best efforts, and if they are worsening over time, seek professional assistance. Do not worry about overreacting or wasting the professional's time. It is much better to have a session or two than to feel that "if you would have come in sooner we could have prevented many of these problems." Research shows that up to one-third of military children experience some type of emotional difficulty; getting them the help they need is essential for their emotional health and well-being.

General Tips for Parents to Help Children Cope with Deployment

- During the service member's absence, plan and engage in normal family activities, such as watching movies, hiking, or having a picnic together.
- Allow children to ask all questions regarding deployment and give them open and honest (age-appropriate) answers.
- Talk about changes that occur during deployment. Some children may not want to talk, but may want to express themselves through playing or drawing.
- Involve children in the communication process (e.g., videos, telephone calls) to keep the deployed parent abreast of events and accomplishments..
- Ensure that children are involved in age-appropriate activities in school, camps, and recreational activities. Enroll your children in a military youth program, if available.
- The deployed parent can voice-record books that the child can read during the parent's deployment; this will help the child feel connected to the deployed parent and continue family routines, such as reading before bed.
- Kids do not understand time frames as well as adults (depending on age), but continuing to reinforce plans during and after their parent's return will help them deal with the separation.
- Spouses should try to refer to the service member's deployment as work instead of just saying that she is gone. This will help children realize that the service member did not simply choose to leave them and may make for a better reunion. Before your service member returns, communicate about what activities you can do and what issues to address after she returns. This will help maintain a relationship with children and spouses.
- If needed, participate with your children in group counseling sessions; it can be a helpful forum where everyone can discuss their experiences, feelings, and thoughts.

Infants and Toddlers

Infant Responses (twelve months or younger)

- The infant may experience a "stranger reaction" to his returning parent, seeming afraid of this parent, and being very clingy with the other parent.
- The infant may become more sensitive and react emotionally to physical environment changes, to changes in schedules, or when her caregiver's mood changes.
- Common reactions may include refusal to eat, apathy, and even weight loss.

- Excessive crying, clinginess, and a disrupted schedule (sleep, eat, wake) may also occur.
- Developmental milestones may be delayed until attachment is once again secure between the infant and each parent.
- The infant may say the missing parent's name (if the parent is still away or in the hospital) as a question or use two-word questions (e.g., "Dada? "Where Dada?" "Mommy?").

How to Help Infants

- Help your returning warrior have realistic expectations about reintegrating into the family. This takes time and cannot be forced.
- Provide lots of direct contact between the warrior and the infant. For very young children extra skin-to-skin contact time could be beneficial and help foster an emotional bond, as well as potentially calming both parent and child.
- Take time each day to read a story, sing together, or go for a walk. Make it a dependable opportunity to connect. Children thrive in consistency.
- Keep talking to the baby in a reassuring tone of voice even if he seems not to understand. Explain to infants that the absent parent loves him, misses him, and that one day the parent will come home.
- Have photos of your warrior in your home. Prior to your warrior's return be sure to speak with your young child about her other parent and speak about the warrior's impending return.
- Have the absent parent make a recording singing a favorite lullaby or reading a favorite story. Use this as part of your bedtime ritual. It can be continued if the parent is hospitalized or emotionally unavailable on his return home.
- Have your warrior send letters or e-mails intended for the young child that you can read aloud to him. Include your young child in video calls with your warrior. Keep the calls positive and loving.
- Spend time together as a family upon your warrior's return. Physical expressions of affection between parents and saying "I love you" can help the young child.
- Have the returning warrior join in daily routines such as mealtime, bath time, reading stories at bedtime, and the like. Begin these as a couple and then shift to having the returning warrior doing them independently.
- Give your little one a t-shirt with the scent of the missing parent to sleep with, to aid in remembering the parent.

- Take care to use good sleep practices and stick to a schedule to minimize irritation and distress. This will help a great deal when the parent returns as well.
- Seek out early intervention home services if development seems to not be progressing well. In many communities social workers services are available to help children.
- Respond to questions from your child in simple terms. Say, "Yes, daddy is gone on a long bye-bye. He loves you and will be home as soon as he can," or "Mommy's arm does have an owie. It hurts. It's getting better every day."
- Try to be focused on your child when you are home. Avoid being preoccupied by phone calls, computer time, social media, or TV. Make lots of eye contact and spend time on the floor with your child.
- When an absent parent returns, follow the baby's social cues. Babies who are uncomfortable cry, withdraw, arch their backs and go to sleep to avoid overstimulation. Take it slow with children.
- When your baby is comfortable find small things for the returning parent to do (e.g., share a snack, sit at the child's level and play with a toy, or offer a bottle or cup). Save baths and diaper changes with the returning parent warrior for when your baby is more comfortable and making eye contact.

Toddler Responses (one to three years old)

- He may react if he can sense that his caregiver is not available or if he sees the caregiver experiencing emotional difficulties.
- Common reactions include frequent or increased temper tantrums, sulking, crying, or difficulties with sleep.
- The toddler may bite the parent if angry or frustrated.
- The toddler may misbehave to draw attention if feeling neglected or uncertain.
- The toddler may ask more fully formed questions about the missing parent or the parent's injury.
- The toddler may experience vivid nightmares about monsters or other dark forms threatening the toddler or its loved ones.
- The toddler may demonstrate play themes containing issues she is trying to work through.
- During high stress he may become regressed in potty training or self-care.
- She may become unusually tearful and clingy.
- An age-inappropriate resurgence in separation anxiety may reappear in the toddler.

- He may show a decrease in developmental milestones during high-stress periods.
- The toddler is aware of what is happening and can form long-term memories, even if he is not able to express these experiences and feelings to you.

How to Help Toddlers

- Make use of the strategies recommended for younger children (listed above) to ease transitions as well.
- Try to keep intense emotions out of your toddler's awareness, verbally reassuring her that you are not upset with her.
- Try not to personalize tantrums and difficult behavior. Some of these outbursts are developmentally normal. It can be hard to differentiate when an outburst is a reaction to life events versus normal toddler behavior. Be compassionate. Do not yell. Use time-outs for yourself if you feel you are going to lose it. Put your toddler in a safe room or crib and take a bathroom break.
- If you are stressed by the behavior, change your environment. If you are at home, head out for a walk or a ride. If you are out, head home for a rest.
- Keep trying to stick to a schedule. If your toddler challenges the schedule, flex a little bit on time but stick to sequence. This reassures toddlers that their world is orderly and predictable.
- Have daycare providers, teachers, and family help you look and listen for themes during play that can help you understand how your toddler is coping.
- Expect regression during high-stress periods and respond with reassurance that you know that he they will do better next time. Be sure to be consistent in your expectations and support.
- If you feel resentment about single parenting or parenting and caregiving for a spouse building up in you, talk to someone right away, and seek support and respite.
- Remember that even negative attention (responding to naughty, daring, or tantrum behavior by giving attention) increases the child's behavior. Do not just respond to negative behaviors: Try to focus on behaviors that you like and encourage your little one to do more of these good behaviors.
- Do respond in a soothing way to nightmares. Do not change sleeping arrangements based on nightmares. You may find it is very hard to get a child back to her bed if you do. This can lead to more stress for you now (since it can be hard to sleep with a toddler) and even more distress when

your partner returns or is having a bad night and needs space to manage her own sleep issues.

- Follow your toddler's cues during reintegration. Take things slowly. Allow your children to re-establish the relationship on their own terms.

- Use simple sentences to explain feelings and changes.

- Use art items like markers, finger paint, chalk, and play dough to express feelings.

- Find a "something" that the returning parent and child can do together that is just for them such as a new daily or weekly ritual.

Preschoolers (three to six years old)

Preschooler Responses

- At this age, your child can generally understand the family dynamics by reading her caregiver's emotions.

- Your child may personalize the stress in the household and believe that her parent is upset because of something she did wrong.

- Children at this age may regress in their skills, such as thumb sucking and difficulty with potty training.

- Your child may be more irritable, clingy, depressed, aggressive, and may feel guilty about the separation or injury.

How to Help Preschoolers

- Be honest about what is happening but keep the explanations short and simple.

- Reassure your children that any stress that is happening or emotions that they may observe adults experiencing are not about them.

- Try to ignore regressive behaviors and offer support for emotions by focusing on what is going right and offering good coping options (e.g., when you see the child sucking her thumb offer an alternative soothing activity that competes with the behavior, like "washing" dishes or digging in the sandbox).

- Praise self-reliance and big-boy or big-girl behaviors but offer lots of extra hugs, cuddles, and one-on-one time with a trusted adult.

- Many of the toddler recommendations listed above can also be effectively used with preschoolers, particularly finding a special activity for the returning parent to do with the child on a consistent basis.

- Reassure your children that they can ask any question they want and you will do your best to answer their questions.

- Be sure to discuss these issues with your children's teachers and enlist them as your allies in supporting your family.

- Preschoolers can be demanding. When you are worried and distracted these demands may escalate and you may feel pressured, disconnected, and unloving. This is a time to stop. Try to manage your own emotions, breathe deeply and refocus on what matters. Nothing is as important as meeting the emotional needs of your children. The tantrum or demand could be about your focus. In some ways your child's demands can be a good reminder that the stress level is rising and it is time for you to take a break. If you can respond to your child by taking that break you both will benefit.

School-Age Children (six to twelve years old)

Experience of Deployment

As children become older, their ability to think abstractly and understand their parent's absence develops markedly. Children may withdraw emotionally, become fearful, experience disturbed sleep and appetite, and engage in regressive behaviors such as becoming clingier, engaging in thumb sucking, or even soiling their bed. Each child is different and expresses emotional distress differently. Some will act out their emotional distress through anger, impulsive behaviors, teasing or picking on others, and misbehaving. Others will internalize their distress, withdrawing and become more closed off to others.

As children enter middle school there may be an expectation to take on increasing amounts of responsibility at home, to behave perfectly at school, and to be a top student. The message they may perceive (or think on their own) is that they must not create any additional stress or difficulties for either parent. During deployment, the parent at home may seem overwhelmed and may be going through his own emotional struggles; efforts to avoid adding to this may be on the child's mind. Additionally, caring for younger siblings and feeling responsible for others' behavior and emotional functioning may prove to be too much pressure for the young person. A range of acting-out behaviors may occur as a result, and the young person may seek support from peers, at times closing parents out emotionally.

Some middle-school-aged children may be resentful of the returning parent's efforts to enter into ongoing routines and may seek to spend more time with friends than with family. Others may want to be with their returning parent all the time and be fearful of something bad happening to that parent. Some may deny having any feelings and may withdraw emotionally, at least initially.

School-Age Children Responses

A wide range of reactions to the returning warrior's homecoming are possible, ranging from fearfulness and avoidance, anger and resentment, being very emotionally needy and clingy, to wanting to be with the returning warrior constantly.

- Your school age child may express somatic complaints such as stomach aches, headaches, and so forth.
- Your child may also appear more whiny, aggressive, or irritable.
- Children at this age may be able to directly express fears about the service member's safety.
- Your child may need more time to talk about his feelings.
- Your child may demand more physical attention than usual.
- Your child may have lots of questions but be afraid to ask them for fear of causing people to be sad or upset.
- Your child may feel alone and like the only kid who ever went through this.
- Your child's moods may shift rapidly while trying to understand and cope with frustrating or scary events.

How to Help School-Age Children

- Include your child in the preparations for the homecoming, making your child an active participant in both the planning and the activities.
- Help your child develop a plan for family activities and individual activities with the returning parent. For example, if the child has always wanted to go camping, planning a camping trip with the returning warrior (after a reasonable amount of time at home) can be a special activity for both child and parent.
- Slowly transition roles and responsibilities at home while addressing the needs of each family member as well as the family as a whole.
- Let children know they are loved unconditionally, while providing clear expectations and boundaries.
- Brainstorm a list of fun activities to do as a family.
- Children grow up and go through different events that service members miss; they grow and change over the course of a deployment. Devoting individual time with each child upon return home could help the returning warrior get to know the children again during reintegration.
- Since children learn from watching their parents, model healthy coping strategies in front of them. Work on having conversations rather than arguments with each other so that your children will see and copy these strategies.

- Use age-appropriate emotion management strategies. For example, children can be taught emotion management techniques such as a feeling thermometer where you list how you are feeling on a thermometer scale. Family members can help monitor and regulate their feelings along the thermometer so that stress management strategies can be employed when the temperature is too high.

- Encourage your returning warrior to participate in daily routines such as drop-off and pickup from school, homework, and the like. Sharing chores such as raking leaves together, taking materials to the recycling center together, and so on can be great as well.

- Plan for one-on-one time every week with each parent separately. School-age children can report feeling disconnected from both parents upon reintegration—particularly if their returning parent is dealing with a combat injury. The child may be shy about reunification and feel isolated if the caregiving parent or the service member is preoccupied.

- Respond to outbursts and aggression calmly. Try to create a coping plan that includes walking away, taking deep breaths, physical movement, writing out feelings, and coming back to discuss calmly what the problem is.

- Remember that it can be hard for kids this age to explain how they feel, or why they did something. Your child may need to be active doing a project with you before he finds the words to explain. Think about whether shared hobbies like planting and tending a celebration garden, working on a woodworking project, packing boxes for troops, or training for fund-raisers for a cause may help you and your child stay connected and talking.

- Connect, connect, connect! Utilize resources in your community that connect veterans and injured service members' families to others (see the appendix to this book). Children of all ages report how meaningful it is to meet other kids in their age group or grade who have service member parents.

- Children can be easily embarrassed and may need to be debriefed several times if an embarrassing event occurs out in the community with their injured parent or family. Children may say, "Why does my mom or dad have to be different?" There is no good answer to this question. With love and support your child will appreciate the difference and understand that it is part of the injury and part of the cost of war. They do not have to like it. Try to help support the child to not take the difference or events personally.

- This is the age of questions. Be ready and let children this age know that you are not going to be upset if they ask questions.

- If your children see you upset, let them know that emotions are normal, and if you do cry, tears are OK.

- For children of injured parents, this age group might enjoy reading about the science behind the injuries and the rehab process. It can help children understand if there are pictures to look at (such as a science textbook or encyclopedia). They may or may not be ready for long explanations and technical reading, but they may like having diagrams and pictures that help them understand.

- Support your child in forging a new relationship with the returning parent. They may find new hobbies with the parent and new ways to support each other.

- Protect your children from graphic stories of violence, deployment photographs, and violent video games. These are associated with vicarious trauma in all ages but children ages three to fifteen seem particularly affected.

- If your child tends to externalize feelings (by slamming doors, running around the house, standing on furniture, hitting others, etc.) you can create an alternative nonverbal action that is acceptable. This might include putting on an angry mask, wrapping up in a favorite soothing blanket, or putting on a particular shirt that serves as a sign to the family that he is angry, upset, and hurting. Kids who act out may be trying to communicate what they are feeling. Try to find a coping action that works. Enlisting professional help for brainstorming ideas that might work could be helpful.

- Find a physical activity that is suited to your child. This does not need to be competition style. Children report that swimming, running, golf, baseball, tai chi, art, dance, kayaking, biking, and basketball have helped them through tough times. Injured parents can often join their children in adaptive recreation activities.

- Even the strongest of families need additional support at times. Be sure to seek mental health support for children who are extremely quiet and withdrawn *and* for those who act out frequently. Both types of behavior can be calls for help.

- This age group really benefits from support group programs like Project Trust, Camp Cope, or online support groups.

- Work to create open communication and discussion of age-appropriate feelings and responses. Normalizing how your child may be feeling is especially important. Encouraging free and open expression of feelings is very helpful.

- Be patient and give your child time. Be patient and give your returning warrior time. Be patient and give yourself time. Strive to encourage and support both of them while taking care of your own needs.

• Give your returning warrior opportunities for greater involvement in family routines, activities, and chores. Have your child assist the returning parent when possible. For example: "Honey, show Daddy where we put the leaves and how we compost them. He hasn't seen us do this before."

High-School-Age Children (Teenagers)

Experience of Deployment

By now military youth may have learned what life with a deployed parent is like. However, each deployment is different and may garner different reactions, depending on the effects from the last deployment as well as the developmental stage the teenager is in. Many may have become independent and unwilling to let their parents "in" emotionally. Being emotionally guarded or detached, and denying feelings, may be some teenagers' way of protecting themselves emotionally from additional disappointment and hurt. They may have numerous responsibilities and obligations, and may see themselves as the glue that holds the family together. At times, this pressure and responsibility may prove to be too much. Anger, acting-out behaviors, emotional withdrawal from parents, and emotional support and closeness from their peer group are common responses. You may also see lower grades, avoidance of homework or other responsibilities, and perhaps even lying.

Tips for Parents to Help Teenagers Cope with Deployment:

• The most important strategy for working with your teenagers is to maintain open communication among all family members about concerns, emotions, and questions. Youth can be encouraged to express their thoughts and feelings to their loved ones as a way to manage their emotions while simultaneously fostering cohesive family relationships.

• The adjustment of military teenagers can be fostered by parents communicating what the deployed parent is doing while deployed and discussing with their teen their own feelings related to the deployment.

• Communication between the deployed parent and the teenager, especially using the technology the youth frequently uses (e.g., Twitter or Facebook), can help maintain the relationship bond.

• Allowing teens to establish the frequency and mode of communication can also be a way to reinforce their growing autonomy while maintaining the relationship in new and flexible ways during deployment as well as upon the service member's return.

• View deployment as a chance for the whole family to grow.

Teenagers' Responses to the Homecoming

In addition to the possible responses discussed above, upon your warrior's return, high-school-age children may be resentful of the returning parent, seeing him or her as an intruder who will alter or disrupt existing family routines. Feelings of relief at the return of the warrior can be complicated by anger, resentment, and even fear of an additional deployment.

- Your teenager may act more rebellious or irritable, fight, or participate in maladaptive attention-seeking behaviors.
- Your teenager may participate in more risky behaviors such as substance use and sexual promiscuity in order to self-medicate the pain.
- Your teenager may express dislike toward new family roles and responsibilities after the deployed parent returns home.
- Your teenager may be hypercritical of what has changed or of mistakes made by parents who are trying to cope.
- Your teenager may feel extremely isolated, particularly if she refuses to join community events that would help her connect with other teens going through similar experiences.
- Your teenager may prefer to talk to someone other than a parent about experiences and how he is feeling.
- Teens can be very vulnerable to transitions and distress.

Tips for Parents to Help Teens Cope with Reintegration:

- Teen moods can fluctuate on a day-to-day basis. Remember that this is a function of their biology, and do not take it personally. Do monitor how things are going on a weekly or monthly basis so that you are aware of trends.
- Help your teenager learn about the deployment cycle and the emotions that can be associated with it (e.g., depression, anger, anxiety).
- If needed, participate in counseling with your teen; it can be a helpful forum for additional support where everyone can discuss their experiences, feelings, and thoughts.
- Deployment and reintegration can also be a time of family strength and growth—reframing the deployment and reintegration period as a way of practicing new roles and routines can sometimes help families adapt as necessary to the challenges of this period.
- Continue to be vigilant about your teen's friends, connecting with your teen's friend's parents, and enforcing your house rules and values. Deployment and the return home (particularly after injury) are very much times of transition

during which teens may test limits. Just as with toddlers and preschoolers, teens are often looking for the security of consistency.

- Self-medicating through alcohol, substance abuse, and unsafe behavior is a big worry for most parents. Talk with your teen about your values and concerns. Listen to her views respectfully. Forge an agreement ahead of time when things are calm.

- If the returning parent is self-medicating, address this immediately. A role model making poor choices can quickly appear to be permission for a teen's own bad behavior. This is a danger sign for both the injured member and the rest of the family. Seek help immediately. Do not hope it will improve on its own.

- Continue to keep one-on-one time opportunities with both parents available. At times your teen will not want this and at other times he may want it a lot. The point is that it needs to be consistently available and parents need to realize that it is not personal if their teen chooses another activity instead.

- Interpret hypercritical behavior as a request for information. Just as with school-age children, always be prepared with materials that explain what is going on to help your teen understand what you are dealing with.

- Give plenty of time for adjustment to new family roles and changed expectations. Try not to go head-to-head on conflict items. Better progress comes from a more democratic style that acknowledges a teen's growing sense of fairness and justice. It is OK to make the bottom line clear but include your teen's input up to that point.

- Try not to treat your teenager like another adult in terms of helping out. Some teens report feeling like they are required to be an adult in the house not just during deployment but after the parent returns home injured.

- Encourage your teen to give community events a try. Teens we know have really enjoyed Wounded Warrior Project events, Project Sanctuary, Camp Cope, and other programming aimed at supporting teens in wounded warrior families. This helps to combat isolation.

- Teens may really benefit from one-on-one mental health support as well as group support because they learn how to manage their family's needs and express their uniquely teen perspectives about what has happened. Teens sometimes tell us they did not want to tell their parents how gross they thought the injury was or how mad they were that the parent was injured. They may feel very hopeless about marriage or incredibly angry and vengeful. In most cases they may be afraid to say what they really feel directly to their parents for fear of making it worse.

- In addition to the points made above, keep in mind that no matter how big your teenager is, inside your teen is still a child. Regardless of any tough exterior, he may have many mixed emotions. Encouraging open discussion of these reactions and feelings is important.

- Realize that your teenager may want to spend more time with friends. Be supportive of this (within reason) and try to make your home the place where the kids hang out (e.g., movie night, barbecues, etc.).

- If there are special activities your teen is looking forward to such as learning to drive, rock climbing classes, and so forth, speak about the things she will be able to do with the returning warrior upon the return. Then make sure these events happen.

- Encourage both your teen and your returning warrior to take the time to be together so they can get to know each other again. Each has changed a lot during the time of the deployment.

- Encourage your returning warrior to initially focus more on reconnecting with your children emotionally and less on parenting and disciplining. There will be plenty of opportunities for discipline later.

Hints for Working with Your Children's Teachers and School Staff

- Children spend up to eight hours per day with teachers and school staff. Communication with your children's schools and teachers regarding what your family is experiencing during reintegration or coping with injuries is essential.

- Teachers are often willing to provide extra support, timely feedback, and a partnership that can be a valuable asset for your children during the initial difficulties.

- Try to connect via e-mail and in person with teachers as often as you can.

- Let teachers and guidance counselors know about what is changing in your children and in your family, about new behaviors or concerns that you are seeing at home, and how you observe your child to be coping.

- Share educational materials with your children's teachers and schools about the types and nature of the injury in your family and how it affects your family's functioning.

- Provide educational materials to your children's teachers and schools about how kids cope with these types of family experiences.

- Encourage your school's staff to provide your children with a consistent environment and opportunities to meet with counselors.

- Encourage your school's staff to provide your children with a short break as needed during high intensity periods in your family.
- Let your children's teachers know that you appreciate their partnership and that you will be seeking extra support for your family from other community resources—this reassures them that you do not expect them to overstep their roles.
- Be sure to sign communication consent forms if another adult will care for your child in your absence.
- Be clear about any changes in your consent for communication, pickup/drop-off, and so forth as the situation changes.
- Speak with teachers and staff privately in the event that the injured service member may need special accommodations in order to participate in your child's education.
- Military-base schools may offer more support depending on the community but during transition access to these programs may change. Offer to help your school create a program for injured service members and veterans' children. This may be beyond what you can commit to initially but often schools are happy to create these small groups and just need a few requests and supportive materials to get started.
- Look for articles and stories that clearly show experiences similar to your family's and bring copies for teachers and staff to add to their resource files. This helps them understand your child's experience but may also help them reach out to others.
- Remember that there is a balance between TMI ("too much information") and just the right amount of information. Ask yourself, "How will it help my child for my children's teachers to know this about the situation?"

Tips for the Families of Injured Service Members with Children

In the event of a combat injury, the non-injured spouse must focus on childcare needs during the service member's treatment and rehabilitation process. Here are some tips on how to handle children of injured service members. For additional information, see chapter 11.

- Consistent routines can give a child a sense of safety. Continuing to meet the needs of children during this difficult time is important for ensuring family strength in the long run.
- Children will feel the stress caused by the absence and subsequent injury of the service member. They may display it differently. In babies, the stress

may manifest itself as a disruption in feeding and sleeping patterns. Slightly older children may be more prone to temper tantrums or complain of physical ailments, which are representative of their internal emotional ailments. Teenagers may lash out, confused by their feelings and torn by their growing desire for independence and their need for a connection to their family due to their parent's combat injuries.

- Adults can strive to be good role models for children by discussing the children's feelings with them, helping them express their feelings, and modeling healthy behavior for children.

What You Can Do Daily to Support Healthy Child Coping

- Protect children from stories, images, and memorabilia with a graphic or violent depiction of war.
  - Remember that kids can be vicariously traumatized.
  - Remember that kids do not benefit from seeing actual or graphic images of war material.
  - Remember that children do not understand their parents' experience better for seeing it.
- Use simple, age-appropriate explanations for medical, physical, and emotional changes occurring in the family. Pictures and diagrams help.
- Help children understand that the adults will take care of the adults *and* the children.
- Give your children permission to be children rather than installing them in a more adult role.
- Find positive ways to involve children in the family team and encourage them to help in age-appropriate ways.
  - Seek out opportunities to have fun together, explore adaptive sports, travel, and attend local events.
  - Create a family memory book to celebrate the new experiences that the family shares post-injury.
  - Create new rituals and holidays to celebrate the family. Make a memory or scrapbook to honor these events.
  - Find time to do healthy activities as a family each week if not daily (e.g., walking, biking, or other relaxing activities).
  - Ask your children for input about how things are going and what they think needs to be improved, changed, or supported.

- Take family time to reconnect and cocoon regularly and in response to increased stress or behavior problems.

- Remember that children use play and activity to try to work through their emotional concerns and fears. Give them space to do this.

- Be alert to themes and stories inside of your child's play. Take the time to ask about what you see and hear and join them on the floor for playtime. Encourage those caring for your child to do this as well.

- Limit zoning out in front of the TV, computer, and video games. This zoning out is a form of self-anesthetic and avoidance. It has a purpose but too much (more than five to ten hours per week or 50 percent or more of recreation time) is associated with longer term coping problems and withdrawal.

- Remember that kids of all ages need to talk. We have seen kids as young as eleven months asking questions about a missing family member.

- Remember that kids talk best when their hands are busy.

- Physical movement helps children of all ages release physical stress. Understand that children copy both the behavior and the speech and thinking styles of their parents. Children will need support to develop healthy skills in this area—particularly if one parent is unable to present a solid role model. Children learn to solve problems by copying parents. Children may copy cognition and self-regulation deficits (e.g., poor problem solving, memory impairment, mood swings, and problems) if they see the injured parent acting that way.

- Teach children about the parent's need for self-regulation, self-modification, behavioral adjustments, and self-awareness so that kids can understand a parent's limitations but focus on what the injured parent *can do* as opposed to what they cannot do or need extra help with. Every activity the parent formerly did now has an adaptive alternative that lets them be involved. (For information on making adaptations to injuries and disabilities, check out the resources in the appendix.)

- Challenge the family and treatment team to find adaptive solutions.

- Keep trying new things.

- For the children of injured parents, prepare children for reunification by asking your treatment team for injury-specific family support materials. Tell children what to expect. Even children as young as nine months old benefit from a simple explanation for example: "We are going to see daddy today. He has a big bandage." Show the child where the bandage is on the body. Practice putting one on a doll or yourself. Let the child play with it. Older children can handle more information. Children as young as five to seven enjoy seeing simple diagrams of brains, skin layers, or other internal body parts and having a simple explanation of what is hurt.

- Remember that telling is not experiencing and there will be emotional responses during reunification. Take it slow. Keep the schedule as normal as possible with meals, school, naps if appropriate, and so forth. Answer questions honestly but simply.

- Try to limit things to one transition at a time. It is usually best not to try to adjust to an injury, reunification, and a move all in the same three- to six-month period. Do your best to manage things in smaller stages to allow time for family members to adapt.

- Keep your answers to questions succinct and remember: "I don't know; I'm still learning too" is an OK answer.

- During the reunification period (which may last for months and may also reoccur after each hospitalization) meet the child's needs with extra warmth, attention, and playtime.

- Try to keep established routines to provide a sense of security and normalcy.

- Remember that each child in a family will have different needs and express them in very different ways (e.g., one child may cling or be weepy, another may yell and pretend to be a superhero jumping off of the furniture, another may withdraw, yet another may become super-responsible. These should all be interpreted as requests for support, extra love, reassurance, and warm structure.)

- Allow your children to maintain a relationship with the people who provided support during the traumatic transition period. These are important adults in the child's life and though you may not have a connection, your child does. Respect that.

- Develop an injury contingency plan with materials to support the person who may care for your child in a worst-case scenario. Like a will, you hope you will not need to use this plan but you have peace of mind for "just in case." Be sure to keep this resource up-to-date.

- Make sure that this person has access to resources ahead of need so they are prepared to support your children in the event of an emergency.

- Make sure that all adults helping children during this phase are aware of age-appropriate emotional support.

- Keep yourself healthy and take care of yourself so you can help your children when needed.

Coping with Sudden Loss for Children and Families

Losing a loved one or a really significant person in one's life is very difficult. When the event has been sudden, such as in an accident or due to an event where there is little to no warning, the shock is often the first and most overwhelming experience of the death.

- Be honest about what has happened. Tell the child in age-appropriate words what has occurred.

- If the situation was particularly gruesome, give only the most important facts without adding in details that might be overwhelming—again this is based on what is age-appropriate.

- Do not be afraid to answer questions. Again: honest, simple answers. "I don't know" is a fair answer.

- Allow your child to attend the wake or funeral if they want to. Even very young children of two or three years old appreciate the ritual and the coming together of people to remember the person's life. Children need to see us grieve and to understand that death is part of life. Encourage but do not force the conversation.

- If the viewing of the body is attended, children should be prepared for what they will see. This does not have to be a traumatic experience. In many cases it helps you to explain to the child that the person is no longer living and is not asleep but that their spirit has separated from the shell of their body.

- Young children are often afraid that the person is buried, and afraid because they are in a box in the ground. To a child there would be nothing more frightening than to be locked in a box underground away from family and friends. Reassurance that the person's spirit or "knowing part" is not there is very important.

- Cremation is best explained to older children as part of an understanding of cultural practices. Children under nine years old can have difficulty with this idea unless they have been exposed to it prior to the death and cremation of the person close to them.

- Children of all ages may seek reassurance that they or their family will not suffer a similar tragedy. This may take the form of bad dreams, direct questions, or death themes in play. It is important to reassure them that they will always be cared for. Care should be taken not to make promises that are not in your or their control (e.g., "I won't die until you are all grown up," or "Nothing is going to hurt you").

- Children grieve in intense but brief episodes and these may come and go over time. There is no time limit on grief.

Conclusion

As we have mentioned throughout this chapter the children in military families can be remarkably resilient. But every child is unique and will respond in different ways to each situation. When it comes to your children, trust your instincts: You know your own children better than anybody and know what they need and when they need it. You will also know when you feel overwhelmed or when something does not seem right with your children. Please remember that there are many people and resources out there that can provide help. Do not hesitate, be ashamed, or be bashful in reaching out and seeking this help. Consider these resources as part of the debt that the American people owe you for your family's service to our nation. Our nation owes you the best we can provide to support your family. For all that you have done as a military family your children deserve nothing less.

Family Assistance for Service Members Seeking Employment or Education

13

Nathan D. Ainspan, Walter E. Penk, Alexa Smith-Osborne

I s the transitioning service member in your family looking to get a job or go back to school after leaving the military? This chapter will provide you with information and suggestions to help your service member and your family go through this process. We will describe what it feels like to transition from the military into working in the civilian world or going back to school, help you better understand what your service member is going through, describe the educational and employment options available to your family, and describe how you can help your service member look for a job in the civilian world. We also discuss how injuries obtained in service can impact his job search or his chance to go back to school and what programs and resources are available to make it possible for him to work or to go back to school.

"What Do I Do Next With My Life?"—and How You Can Help

In order to determine what to do after the military, your family member must determine what she likes to do and wants to do. This can be difficult for someone who has been in the armed forces for many years since members of the military are usually ordered around and are rarely given an opportunity to explore what interests them. The very idea of learning about yourself can be exciting to some people but could fill others with dread or even paralysis. It is not uncommon for a job searcher to "freeze up" at the thought of being overwhelmed by this process and to stop looking for a job even before she begins to get involved in the search—or to take the first job that comes along even if it is a bad fit. Work does not have to be a four-letter word, and going through this process can ensure that your family member can find a job that can be motivating and interesting and possibly even enjoyable. Most members of the military have found a sense of purpose and more than a job while they were in uniform. Their next job out of uniform should not be an exception.

A number of resources are available to help your family member answer the question of what he wants to do after he leaves the military. You can help the process by alerting him to these resources and encouraging him to use them. Do not hesitate to use these services—your family member has earned them just as he earned his paycheck while in uniform, and to not draw upon them now would be like leaving money behind in the bank.

Although we want you to encourage your family member to use these resources we insert a word of caution here: Be encouraging, but be careful not to become a "nag." If your family member feels overwhelmed by the process, hearing constant reminders from you and others may increase negative feelings and draw him further away from engaging in the job search process. If you think he really feels overwhelmed and seems reluctant to start the process, he may benefit from speaking with counselors in the military, military chaplains, or even buddies from the service that have been through the process and can advise him on what to do. If the reluctance to look for a job seems to be a small part of a general lack of energy it may be indicative of a mental illness like depression or post-traumatic stress disorder (PTSD) or a sign of traumatic brain injury (TBI). If you think that this might be the case it may be worthwhile to seek medical advice. Depression, PTSD, TBI, and other psychological conditions can be treated. Access to the military's and VA's counselors, therapists, and doctors is another one of those benefits earned along with the paycheck while in uniform, so feel free to draw upon them.

Another word of caution: This chapter describes a number of programs and resources that are available to help your service member find a job or go to school. We emphasize that these resources are tools that can help you in your search. None of these tools is guaranteed to find a job or gain admission into a school, nor will they do all the work. Your service member must take the initiative to locate these resources, contact them, ask questions, and utilize them. He will also need to supplement any information we provide in this chapter with whatever else he finds and thinks might be useful. No government program or non-profit organization can or will do this work for you.

Transition Assistance Program

The main resource available to service members to help with their transition out of the service (and to figure out what to do next) is the military's Transition Assistance Program (TAP). TAP is a three-day workshop that is mandatory for all transitioning service members, and it is also available to spouses. Each service member is expected to go through the TAP on their base before they leave the service. Every military base has a transition office that provides the TAP as well as other resources. The quality of resources available and the counseling provided by each

TAP office will vary based on the size and location. The online TAP (http://www.taonline.com) provides the *TAP Manual* as well as teleconferences, informational sessions, links to other Web sites, and other useful resources. The military has also recently begun to offer "reverse boot camp" programs to help transition service members out of uniform and into civilian employment.

Other Transition Resources

In addition to the TAP, there are a number of other great resources that can advise your family member on the transition out of the military and on how to figure out what to do with her life:

What Color Is Your Parachute?

What Color Is Your Parachute? is regarded as the bible for job searchers. The book is revised every year and is available at most bookstores and online stores. It walks you through exercises to figure out what you enjoy doing and how you can find it in your next job.

Corporate Gray Books

From Army Green to Corporate Gray, From Air Force Blue to Corporate Gray, and *From Navy Blue to Corporate Gray* are available through the TAP and can be purchased at a bookstore or online. The books walk you through the job search process and also describe which employers are interested in hiring employees with military experience. They also offer other suggestions and recommendations to make the transition smoother and easier.

Other Books

Information on the process of looking for a job or applying to a school has filled a number of books. For detailed information about the transition process we recommend *Military Transition to Civilian Success: The Complete Guide for Veterans and Their Families,* and *Military to Civilian Career Transition Guide: The Essential Job Search Handbook for Service Members.* Libraries on military bases should have them available (or can obtain them through inter-library loans) or you can purchase the books at stores or online. We list these and other useful ones in the references section at the end of this chapter.

Skills Assessment Tests

A number of tests can help your family member figure out her interests and translate these into civilian jobs. Internet searches can provide you with details about the following: the ASVAB (Armed Services Vocational Aptitude Battery), the Myers-Briggs Type Indication (MBTI), the Campbell Interest and Skills Survey (CISS), the

Career Assessment Inventory (CAI), Holland's Self-Directed Search, Kuder Career Search with Person Match, the Strong Confidence Inventory, the DISCOVER career planning online program, the ISEEK Skills Assessment, and the Vocational Preference Inventory. The transition centers on many military bases may be able to offer these tests. Service members interested in advancing their education can also use these tests to determine what major and courses they want to pursue. Many of these same assessment tools are available at low cost or free through college career counseling departments once a service member becomes a student. Many are available on the Internet and can be accessed (for a fee) along with counseling about their findings from career job counseling professionals. If you do decide to use a counselor, utilize caution when choosing one since some might not be properly qualified and may try to use the testing to sell you more services. VA facilities typically do not provide educational testing services unless they are part of a cognitive functional clinical evaluation for which your family member has been referred by a primary provider or through a DoD/VA polytrauma center.

Military-Civilian Crosswalk

One difficulty faced by many service members is translating their military skills into something comparable in the civilian world of employment. One tool that can help you do this is the military-to-civilian skills crosswalk search engine available at http://www.onetonline.org/crosswalk/. Enter in your family member's Military Occupational Classification (MOC) and the system will suggest jobs that match the MOC's skills. The crosswalk contains links and information about these career fields. Other crosswalk programs are in development to improve and speed up this process.

Educational Tests for Counseling

Standardized aptitude and achievement tests, intellectual level performance (so-called IQ, or intelligence quotient) tests, and neuropsychological tests of cognitive functions such as memory and processing speed are all available and can be interpreted by a trained counselor. Learning-style inventories are available for free online, while other types of educational testing may be obtained through university health service centers or career centers (for enrolled students) or through private testing providers for a fee.

Veterans' Service Organizations (VSOs)

These organizations were created by veterans to help other service members through the transition process. Many can also provide you with advice on locating and filling out paperwork, lobby our elected representatives to represent your interests, and even provide you with someone who can listen to your concerns, answer your questions, and provide support from someone who has been through similar experiences. Some of the larger VSOs include the American Legion, the Veterans of Foreign Wars (VFW), the Disabled American Veterans (DAV), Iraq and Afghanistan Veterans of America (IAVA), the Wounded Warrior Project (WWP), Paralyzed Veterans of America (PVA), and the Military Officers Association of America (MOAA). Each branch of the military has its own organizations as well, such as the Association of the United States Army (AUSA) and the United States Naval Institute (USNI—the publisher of this book). One word of caution—a number of groups that sound like legitimate VSOs have been created to take advantage of service members and those who want to support them. You can trust the VSOs listed above but be cautious, conduct due diligence, and closely investigate other groups that might sound too good to be true.

State and Local Organizations

In addition to the VA and its state offices, every state has its own office and programs to help veterans with the transition process (including recommendations to veteran-friendly employers in that area). A list of state programs is available at the VA's Web site: http://www.va.gov/statedva.htm.

Tax Credits

The federal government offers private-sector employers tax credits if they hire veterans—and additional credits for hiring wounded warriors. Conduct research to learn more about these credits so that you can share information about them during interviews with potential employers.

Relocation Costs

Another under-utilized benefit that many service members do not even know about is that the government will pay most and possibly all of the costs for your family to transition to your new home after serving in the military. When you leave the service, the government will pay all of the costs to move you back to your listed home of record. If you want to move somewhere else to start a job the government will pay the amount equal to the costs of a move to your listed home of record. If you are retiring from military service, your move anywhere in CONUS (the continental United States) will be covered. This can be a good incentive to an employer interested in hiring you, since the company will not have to cover your moving costs. Contact the transition or transportation office at your service member's base for more information.

What Transition Feels Like—and How to Help Your Family Member

The transition to civilian life can be psychologically difficult—especially if your service member engaged in recent combat. The change in pace, lifestyle, and the interactions that the military provided will be missing in the civilian sector and service members may have a rough time making this transition. After facing life-and-death decisions every day in uniform it may be difficult to come back home and interact around people whose conversations center around the latest episode of a reality show. Every service member usually had a strong sense of direction and purpose while in the military and may have difficulty in the civilian world now that that sense is no longer present. In the military (and especially during deployment) service members were surrounded by loyal and dedicated comrades. Not only would these colleagues do anything to save and protect each other but they also provided a group of friends who knew what each was experiencing and provided a safe place to talk about experiences. The civilian sector does not offer the same advantages: Unless your service member finds a company or school with a large population of veterans she may feel isolated and unable to connect and talk with others. And after taking fire in Fallujah, a member may have difficulty connecting with other employees complaining about the trauma of a bad commute or a fellow student's difficult life during the all-night kegger party at the fraternity house.

Getting a job or going to school can also offer psychological benefits to your family member. As Ernest Hemingway long ago phrased it, "Work could cure almost anything, I believed then, and I believe now." And so it is for service members now returning home from war, as they search for new ways to define themselves through changes made in their career from the military to transitioning home—changes within themselves, for their family, and for their community. For the service member, work fulfills many needs within the person, such as the need to achieve something, the need to be productive, the need to contribute, the need to collaborate, the need to end social isolation that many times results from reactions against the memories of trauma experienced in war, the need to control emotions, the need to master the environments at home and in the community, the need to be with one's family, and the need to find groups that are like units on a mission. By working, service members find ways to belong to a new unit, to master feelings such as anger and aggression, to control feelings, to feel excitement, to relate to others, to test new forms of coping with new stresses, and, perhaps, even ways to cope with new traumas. And work defines one's self and contributes to defining one's family.

Getting a new job in the community means transitioning from a prior career in the military to a career as a civilian. Leading a career as a civilian may mean something different than pursuing a career in the military. It is possible that some civilian jobs have features similar to work in one's military career, especially jobs in law enforcement, some jobs in federal agencies, and other jobs contracting for civilian work that overlap with what one did in the military. Although there are differences, similarities remain between work in the military and in civilian life. Getting a civilian job brings service members together with new co-workers in the civilian community, which, in turn, enhances relationships with family members, as well as leads the family in demonstrating capacities to cope with demands of everyday living. Some civilian jobs can even open up new opportunities to form new relationships not only for your service member but also for your family. A major difference between military and civilian work is that the service member, along with your family, must find the new missions that are central to working as a civilian, central to one's character and the characters of the family.

The major contribution of civilian jobs is that work assuages the tragedies of war within the mind and the body. Working usually decreases the social isolation that is a hallmark of PTSD. Your service member working continues her sense of personal mission to protect and to support your family. Working reinforces one's abilities to master old and newly learned skills, which, in turn, lessens the learned sense of helplessness that is sometimes an aftermath of having endured combat traumas. Civilian work continues to provide opportunities to improve aspects of character that are central in leading your family.

One helpful resource to achieve this objective is the book *Flourish: A Visionary New Understanding of Happiness and Well-Being* by Martin Seligman. Dr. Seligman continues to develop his ideas for members of the military and includes in the book exercises that can be used to develop growth and maturity in your service member and your family. These exercises and other resources are available for free, with instructions and directions, at http://www.authentichappiness.com.

Helping the Job Search, and the Emotions Involved

Transitioning to a private-sector job can be a long, demoralizing process. The transition may bring out painful emotions in your service member. As with other parts of the process, you may not fully understand what happened to your family member during his time in service but you can still provide help and emotional support to him. If he wants to talk about it, be prepared to listen. If he does not want to talk about it (and this is frequently the case), do not put pressure on him to talk before he is ready. He may be silent to keep the pain away from you. Let him know that you will be there when he is ready to share. You can also encourage him to seek out others who have been through this process by contacting some of his war buddies, the VSOs, or some of the national programs run by the VA or other organizations.

The longer a job search takes, the more demoralizing it can become. That is why some veterans join up with job-hunting groups of veterans in their communities for support with the challenges of job-hunting. The emotional toll of the job search can also become a negative spiral: If the job search starts to take too long and becomes too depressing, your family member may lose interest in devoting time to it and may even give up looking for a job. The best job search approach is a continuous, daily effort, but it can be difficult to find the daily energy if the search process itself becomes depressing and feels like it will never end. A lengthy job search process may be especially demoralizing to a veteran because it can emphasize the lack of purpose and mission she used to feel while in uniform and could lead to feelings of helplessness. Be supportive and encouraging of your family member, and be willing to listen. If the depression seems particularly severe do what you can to encourage your family member to seek professional counseling or help. Veteran suicides are increasing to the point that more veterans died by their own hands in recent years than those killed in battle. If your service member seems particularly depressed, do not hesitate to contact local chaplains, call the suicide prevention hotline at 1-800-273-TALK, and read the suicide chapter in this book.

The Practical Side of Job Searching—and Surviving the Search

In addition to the emotional impact that being unemployed can have on your family there is also the financial toll as well: Without a job your family will have reduced income or even no income. It can take months to find a job (during good times the standard estimate is one month for each $10,000 of salary you plan to make but it will probably take longer during the current financial situation), and it can take months to apply to college programs and gain acceptance. We recommend that you take any action and utilize all resources you can to support your family during this period. Many military families will go on welfare or Medicaid during the job search process to keep their heads above financial waters. Do not let a feeling of pride prevent you from applying for these programs. They were created to help Americans in situations like yours. As with other military benefits (i.e., the GI Bill or TRICARE insurance), consider this another form of the paycheck that your family member earned while in uniform. These programs could mean the difference between a comfortable existence while waiting for a job or a precarious one with large debts to pay off once the job is obtained. State veterans' commissions and Veteran and Family Resource Centers can also provide financial assistance or suggestions of other useful programs that can help. The latter also provide job training, navigation resources, short-term counseling, and money for food and emergency payments.

Benefits Your Family Member Can Bring to Her New Job

One way you can help your family member in the job search process when she becomes frustrated is to remind her of the benefits that she can bring to a private-sector employer. In addition to learning technical skills that private-sector employers appreciate, the military is also effective in developing a number of character traits. These include loyalty, selflessness, respect for rank and authority, discipline, leadership, teamwork, working with diversity, respect for procedures, integrity, and working under enormous pressure to triumph over adversity. Your family member may not be aware that she possesses these traits—to a person serving in the military it seems like everyone has these traits. But in the civilian world these traits are relatively rare and highly desired. Encourage your family member to notice these traits within her, appreciate that she possesses these skills, and mention them frequently in communications with schools and employers and in interviews. One way to learn about character of self and family is to complete such tests as the VIA Classification of Strengths Survey (http://www.authentichappiness.com).

How to Help Find a Job

After going through the assessments listed above, how can you help your family member find a job after the military? Most people look for jobs by searching the "help wanted" sections of newspapers and online job sites, or submit applications where they see "help wanted" signs. When you apply for an advertised job you end up competing against many people (one advertisement or sign brings in hundreds of applicants for one job), so the odds of finding a job this way can be rather slim. When you use this passive job approach your application can easily get lost in the pile of hundreds of other passive job searchers who applied, and you run a great risk of being screened out and not getting the job if your background is not exactly what the human resources person thinks they need in that position. Instead of this passive approach, the most effective way to find a job is to take the active technique of networking. This technique is described in detail in the *Parachute* book, the TAP, and the *Corporate Gray* books, so we only will summarize it here.

Job networking starts by helping your family member figure out what she wants to do and the type of place where she wants to do it. She then needs to find people in these places doing this kind of work. She would do this either through research (going online or going through books) to get names or by asking people your family knows to suggest contacts in these places. It is called networking because you network out—if one of the contacts does not know anyone in a place of interest, you and your service member can ask people to see if they might know someone who knows someone. Your family's network expands by asking each person if they know other people, and the network keeps expanding out until your family can locate the person in the organization who has the ability to make a hiring decision.

Where can you find people for this network? Your family already has a network in place but may not yet realize it. Help your service member to realize the network he may already have in place and to connect with the people that can form your network. You, your service member, and your family can then expand from the inner connections out to a wider network. Start with your family members and friends and see who they know. The members of your house of worship can provide contacts. Any religious, volunteer, or social club can also provide contacts that can be utilized in your family member's job search. The USOs mentioned above can also provide contacts for a network. Your network and the resources listed above can also help you find employers that appreciate and understand the military—and avoid the places that might have issues with your time in uniform. Do not be shy about asking someone for help in the job search: Most people want to help others out and a polite and respectful request for help will usually receive a positive response. No one place may be as helpful for networking as your local library. The library in your town is supported by your taxes, has computers, and employs specialists who are experts in teaching citizens how to use the computer and how to access resources about education and employment.

As an example of how your network of friends can help you get a job, the first author of this chapter got his first job because his friend's mother was on an airplane flight sitting next to a woman who ran a company that was having trouble finding employees. His friend's mother mentioned that her son's friend was looking for a job in that area. They exchanged cards and his friend's mother passed it along to him. He interviewed with the company and got the job. As this example suggests it is hard to network from the computer or while sitting at home. The best connections are made in person and are frequently spontaneous interactions. We recommend turning off the computer and the TV and getting out and meeting people as the best way to network for a job. Two hours spent at a social event meeting people who could lead you to someone looking to hire will be more productive for your job search than sitting at home for those two hours sending résumés to places that advertised for positions.

Creating Your Own Job—Entrepreneurship

Many service members utilize the initiative and self-determination that they drew upon in uniform to create their own jobs through entrepreneurial activities. For those with the determination and the temperament, there is nothing like being your own boss and determining your own destiny. Self-employment is not for everyone so we present the following warnings to consider before your family takes the plunge into self-employment:

- Do not go into self-employment just to avoid the difficulty of the job search. While you will avoid the necessity of having to sell yourself to an employer in an interview you will now have to sell yourself to clients every day.

- Make sure that someone in the family has health insurance (through TRICARE, the VA, or through a spouse) since an employer will not be providing it and no family should have to face major medical expenses without health insurance.

- Someone in your family will also need a job. Most small businesses expect to lose money for at least the first year as they become established and known by clients. Make sure that your family has a source of income to cover the family's expenses during this first year.

- Do not think that self-employment is an easier way out of getting a job. One line I heard from a self-employed business owner summarizes the difficulties involved with being an entrepreneur: "I love being self-employed. I get to only work half days. And I get to choose which twelve hours a day I work."

If your service member does choose to go the self-employment route there are a number of resources available that can provide help, information, and assistance. The Small Business Administration (SBA) has numerous programs for veterans including the "Patriot Express" loan program, Veterans Business Outreach Centers, and SCORE chapters (Service Corps of Retired Executives—volunteer small-business owners who consult with new owners). If your family member was a Reservist the SBA has special Military Reservist Economic Injury Disaster Loans available. A Veterans Business Development Officer is stationed at every SBA District Office. Check out the SBA Web site at http://www.sba.gov/vets. The VA also has a Center for Veterans Enterprise located at http://www.vetbiz.gov.

Education after the Military

For most veterans, initiating or completing a college education is a prime objective after military service. Department of Defense surveys since the ending of the draft have documented this objective as the most common reason enlistees give for their decision to enter the All-Volunteer Force (AVF) military service. Current forms of military financial aid include the Montgomery GI Bill, VA Vocational Rehabilitation college funding, the Post-9/11 GI Bill, and state-specific veteran aid. All of these programs provide tuition and fee assistance, and some even provide books, tutoring, and living stipends. Eligibility and application requirements for this aid are described on the federal VA Web site (http://www.va.gov) and state veterans' commission Web sites.

Most veterans who utilize any form of military financial aid will usually do so in order to obtain an undergraduate degree. However, available data suggest that the average educational attainment of veterans has not improved significantly from the draft era to the Gulf War era. A possible contributor has been the previously insufficient support provided by the government to veterans. The enactment of the new Post-9/11 GI Bill in 2009 is intended to help reduce this by providing sufficient support for completion of a four-year undergraduate degree at the tuition level of a public university. Other contributors to this educational shortfall may include the following:

- A lack of informational social support to prepare for the transition to the classroom.
- Unrealistic family and veteran expectations about the cultural and lifestyle shift involved as the service member transitions to being a student.
- Challenges in navigating academic structures.
- A lack of, or insufficient access to, appropriate educational testing, academic support, and health services needed to facilitate the transition from combat to classroom.

We will provide tips on how to overcome these challenges and suggest innovative programs that are becoming increasingly available.

Considering Going to College

While on active duty, many military members take advantage of opportunities to take courses offered on military installations by military training commands, community colleges, universities, or for-profit institutions that design curricula specifically for the military. Some of these course credits may transfer to colleges in the military member's home community, to which he will return after military service or transition to Reserve status. Others may not, depending on the accreditation status of the educational institution from which the credit was earned, the range of comparable courses offered in the home-front college selected by the service member, and the academic major chosen.

If you are thinking about going to school after serving in the military, we highly recommend that you contact the Student Veteran Project at the University of Texas at Arlington, at studentveteranproject@uta.edu, 817-272-2165, or online at http://www.uta.edu/ssw/research/veterans-project.php. The people at this project will act as your "personal trainers," providing advice and information to guide you, as a transitioning service member, through the college decision and application processes, and provide you with an understanding of how the transition will impact you and your family.

The educational experience is likely to be very different in a civilian community-based higher education institution than in the military environment, since their institutional missions are different. It is important to be prepared with realistic expectations about these differences when college is being considered. Here are some of the most common differences:

**Table 13.1 Comparison of Academic Experiences
in the Military and Civilian Environments**

In the Military Environment	In the Community Environment
All courses are scheduled in a uniform manner to fit duty shifts at the particular installation	Courses are scheduled to fit classroom space, available faculty, registered student cohorts, priorities of academic departments and their community constituents, and the accreditation requirements of curricular centers and degree programs
Military personnel are often directed to a limited number of courses available in the time permitted by their unit's mission or to a designated course required for promotion within their MOS (Military Occupational Specialties) and command	College students must meet their core liberal arts requirements in the first two years and then pick their major and follow the degree plan for that major. Much more self-direction and flexible scheduling is required. It will not be possible generally to obtain a bachelor's degree fully online or at night in many majors
Paperwork to register and pay for a course tends to be uniform and highly structured	College students are responsible for completing the college application and the Free Application for Federal Student Aid (FAFSA) for the college of their choice, with no direction about these decisions, unless there is a supported education program available to them.
Paperwork may be pre-completed for the student; if the student deploys before completing an on-post/base course, course withdrawal will be expedited by the unit through agreements with the sponsoring educational institution	It is the student's responsibility to find out the paperwork required to transfer credits, to select a major, to meet the prerequisites for the major, and to withdraw or arrange an incomplete in the event of deployment or health events.

continued

In the Military Environment	In the Community Environment
Academic work is completed primarily in class	For every hour of class time, three or more hours of additional outside work is assumed. If the class meets more than once a week, outside assignments must be done throughout the week, not be deferred to weekends or when not doing paid work
Instructors are often facilitators of concrete course assignments targeted to an occupational skill	Faculty are developing students' general fund of knowledge and higher-level cognitive skills in addition to teaching specific content
Classes are passed by satisfactory final test grades, attendance, and brief in-class assignments	Classes are passed by satisfactory outside assignment completion (often submitted online) and satisfactory completion of experiential assignments (e.g., attending a lecture, play, art exhibit, political event, agency meeting), reading, quizzes, essays, tests, papers, and class participation
Accommodations, academic support services, and career assessment and exploration are generally not available	Accommodations for students with documented disabilities, academic support services, and career assessment and exploration are available in "bricks and mortar" colleges, but generally not in for-profit, online institutions
Courses are freestanding and often taken one or two at a time, based on convenience	Full-time students, who are more likely to complete a degree on time, usually take at least four or five classes each semester continuously; classes build on each other through a planned sequence of prerequisites in the declared major and minor, or specialty and sub-specialty; required classes will not be offered every semester nor at a consistent time slot

Your returning service member should discuss with you how your family may need to adapt to the student lifestyle and academic pace if he decides to go to college. For example, the discipline and time management acquired in military service will be very useful in completing a degree when adapted for application to self-initiated intellectual tasks. Since career services and advising on the selection of a major are not available until a student is registered, and colleges offer different curricula and services, veterans interested in going to college often find it useful to explore the Web sites of a range of colleges carefully. Veterans with disabilities should also enroll in a supported education program, if available, to guide the initial decision-making process. (See the section on disabled service members below for information on supported education programs.)

One Army Reservist veteran now in graduate school commented, "I was not prepared for the uphill battle of grad school. Nobody warned me how difficult reentry into the battlefield of academia could be. I had earned a master's degree over twenty years ago with high honors. I had never had any trouble taking tests or writing essays or position papers before. I had done all the right things after I got back from the war zone. Yes, I had been diagnosed with PTSD, but I had sought help at the VA and got excellent treatment. The VA gave me a 30 percent service-connected disability rating for PTSD. The PTSD eventually went into remission and I was symptom-free for several years. I still saw a therapist on a regular basis and took maintenance meds. I was managing life and work and doing reasonably well before I started school."

For-Profit Educational Companies

One recent change in American higher education has been the increase in for-profit educational companies enrolling non-traditional college students. In the past, these companies primarily enrolled managers whose employers paid their tuition when their positions or promotions required a bachelor's degree or other specialized higher education. Now these programs draw 90 percent of these revenues from the federal government in the form of federal financial aid. Active-duty personnel and veterans have been attracted by the ease of an admission process facilitated by a large cadre of recruiters and by the convenience of well-packaged and efficiently delivered online courses. The for-profit institutions are businesses whose primary mission is to maximize profit for their shareholders, so their tuition is often higher than that of community colleges and public universities, and their graduation rates often no higher.

This was the experience of an Army Reservist now in graduate school: "Most of the veterans I have talked to say they want to earn a college degree as fast as possible so they can have a chance for a better, higher paying job. They have been led by recruiters and online universities to believe all the courses they took, plus many of their military education courses, would transfer to any school and put them on a fast track to an early graduation. This is rarely the case. The first-time freshmen get excited about getting some dependable cash from the new GI Bill housing stipend, but fail to realize how expensive it is to go to school full-time and not be able to work and bring in money at the same time. I have seen them dropping courses to keep up the pace, which leads to getting less of a stipend to pay expenses, so they end up having to get a low-paying job, which eats up their study time and leaves them too exhausted to study when they get home. My advice to these first-timers is this: Before you sign on the dotted line, find out how veteran-friendly the campus is. Do your 'recon.' Make it your new mission: does your chosen institution have a student vet center? If not, do they have upper-class student vets who are willing to help incoming students navigate this whole new system they know little about? Does the school have a vet mentorship program for new student veterans [with mentors] who can show them the ropes, tell them from a veteran's perspective which professors are sensitive to veterans' issues and which ones to avoid?"

The Department of Education, the VA, and the DoD have all expressed concern that the combination of high tuition and low graduation rates puts students at the for-profit institutions at risk for quickly expending their GI Bill and other aid and then being left with an unmanageable debt load and no academic degree. Another concern has been expressed about the lack of student support services and accommodations available at the for-profit institutions, many of whom provide primarily online courses with limited faculty and advisor contact. The standardization of the online curricula design and delivery, while efficient, makes it difficult to individualize for students with special needs. Here are some tips for veterans and active-duty service members who are considering enrolling in a for-profit program:

- Check the level of the program's accreditation to make sure your course credits can transfer to a traditional non-profit college.
- Check course descriptions if you want to enroll in a professional major, such as nursing, to make sure the clinical skills will be delivered.
- Consider whether you will be able to pay back the larger loans you may acquire.
- Compare different programs in your area that offer the same degree or courses. Studies conducted by the government found differences in prices for the same type of education—sometimes non-profit schools offered the lowest price but sometimes the for-profit schools were cheaper.
- Check the level of support services and disability accommodations provided (if you have disabilities that require them), and the balance between face-to-face and remote access of such services.
- Consider whether taking primarily online courses fits your learning style and needs, including the need to transition to civilian culture and community.
- If you enroll, test out services (such as tutoring) early in the semester to see how available and extensive they are in your college.

Some Yellow Ribbon Army Reserve Reintegration events, military TAP programs, and VA clinics sponsor college information fairs, which offer an opportunity to speak to college recruiters from many different institutions in a specific geographic region. Other sources of information commonly used by college-bound high school students include guidebooks available at public libraries, and their companion Web sites (e.g., *Peterson's Guide*, at http://www.petersons.com, and *The Fiske Guide to Colleges*, http://www.fiskeguide.com), and the national college rankings done by the magazine *U.S. News and World Report* (http://www.usnews.com/rankings). The Educational Testing Service (which administers the SAT, or Standardized Admission Test, for college entry) also provides extensive free college planning, preparation, and search guidance on its Web site (http://www.college-board.org). You can access and benefit from this information even if you do not plan to take the SAT.

When considering going to college, your family will need to consider not only your family member's career goals, your family's finances, and desired college characteristics, but also your family member's strengths and weaknesses, prior educational experience, learning style and aptitudes, any pre-existing conditions that may affect learning, any service-connected conditions that may affect learning, family and cultural values related to educational attainment, and what related preparation may be necessary prior to engaging in a successful pursuit of higher education.

How to Select and Apply to a College

When looking for a veteran-friendly college, you may want to start with identifying the colleges that have a memorandum of agreement with the Department of Defense for active-duty military, known as Defense Activity for Non-traditional Education Support or DANTES (http://www.dantes.doded.mil). These colleges are military-oriented and often also participate in special financial aid and degree programs for student veterans, such as the Troops to Teachers program (http://www.dantes.doded.mil/dantes_web/library/docs/TTT/RegistrationForms.pdf). If you are interested in attending a private college, you can identify those that have a special matching tuition agreement with the VA to supplement the GI Bill coverage, known as the Yellow Ribbon Program (http://www.gibill.va.gov/gi_bill_info/ch33/yellow_ribbon.htm).

In addition to looking for colleges with these partnerships, consider the types of financial assistance (scholarships, discounts, and waivers) specifically for veterans, the school's policy on acceptance of military learning and subject tests, campus culture for veterans (e.g., the percentage of veterans in the student body and faculty, special events for student veterans, a student veteran interest organization), and support services (e.g., number and kind of staff designated to work with veterans, range of tutoring and assistive services, and availability of career counseling, educational testing, and study skills training). Be aware that all colleges will have an office called "Veterans Affairs" or "Veterans Services," but that these often have the duty primarily to certify and process veterans' educational benefits and financial aid, and may not have specialized academic advisers or counselors on staff other than those financial aid staff. Colleges are generally receptive to diverse student groups, but some have more experience with diversity in general, and military students specifically, than others. The objective indicators listed above will give you the best overall assessment of a particular college's preparedness and goodness of fit to educate student veterans.

Prospective college students are responsible for completing the college application and the Free Application for Federal Student Aid (FAFSA; http://www.fafsa. ed.gov) for the college of their choice. In the American educational system specific direction about these decisions is given at the secondary level through high schools' college counseling departments, but many service members did not receive such direction when they were in high school. Although designated military personnel may offer some general guidance, their role is generally limited to processing tuition assistance payments for military members who are taking college courses while on active duty and to identifying Web sites and general information about the GI Bill. These personnel are not trained to provide specific college selection, entrance testing, and application guidance as are high school college counselors. Support in the college selection, entrance application, and FAFSA or other non-VA financial aid application processes is available to veterans through supported education programs for veterans. Be prepared to spend several consecutive sessions working with your supported education staff on these tasks, and on any recommended college preparation tasks, to complete this initial process. If you decide to go to college and want to finish in a reasonable time, do not delay or drag out accomplishing these preliminary steps. Alternatively, once you have selected a college, that college's admissions and financial aid staffs are available to assist you in the remaining steps.

Be sure to complete the FAFSA online or by mail. You may be eligible for non-VA financial aid that is helpful to pay for non-credit courses and living expenses during semester breaks or delays in GI Bill processing. You must complete the FAFSA in order to be considered for such aid. Completing the FAFSA is also necessary to be eligible for non-VA federal work-study jobs. These jobs are plentiful on many campuses, and offer a very convenient and often résumé-enhancing work setting for college students.

After selecting a college, you can apply for admission and pay application fees online. Many states now use a common application for all public universities in that state, and an alternate application for all private universities in that state. Be sure to review the college Web site carefully to determine what admission tests or placement tests may be required. Extended time and quiet locations for testing are available for applicants with documented disabilities, as is personal assistance in completing admission forms. Placement testing may indicate that some non-credit "refresher" courses will be necessary to prepare your family member for college-level mathematics, reading, or writing. Some colleges have Veterans Upward Bound programs (http:/www2.ed.gov/programs/triovub/resources.html), which offer these refresher courses for free to veterans. If your family is eligible for the Post-9/11 GI Bill, the fees for the admissions test will be reimbursed to you when you provide appropriate documentation either directly to the Veterans Benefits Administration (VBA) or to your college VA certifying official that you have taken the test.

Also check the Web site or call the college's Student Affairs Department to find out what face-to-face and online orientations are available. Some colleges convene designated orientation sessions for veterans and for transfer students, and combine them with a campus tour, advising, and class registration opportunities. You can locate the college's free and fee-based tutoring and supplemental instruction services at the same time; they are often spread over the campus in different departments and in the college library. The VA can reimburse you for fee-based tutoring services upon application to the college's VA certifying official, if you are GI Bill–eligible.

Transitioning for Service Members with Disabilities and Injuries

Hundreds of thousands of service members have had to think about employment and educational options sooner than they expected because the injuries that they sustained while in service have forced them out of active duty. If your family member is one of these wounded warriors this next section will provide a brief overview of options and resources that can help him make the transition to a job or to school. For a more detailed description we can refer you to the book *Returning Wars' Wounded, Injured, and Ill: A Reference Handbook*, edited by two of the authors of this chapter.

Disabilities and injuries will add additional steps and complications to the job search and educational assessment processes described above, but they will not make them insurmountable. In the past most people with disabilities would not have thought that they could have been able to get a job or go back to school. But thanks to rapidly improving accommodation technology, changes in thinking about disabilities, and new laws (including the Americans with Disabilities Act) people with all types of disabilities—including potentially restrictive ones like PTSD and TBI—are going back to school and working at jobs every day. Be prepared to remind your injured family member of this if she becomes frustrated, depressed, or overwhelmed while looking for a job or a school. Remind her that the only disabled organ that prevents someone from working is the brain that only sees limitations and not opportunities. A person who thinks that she cannot work will not be able to find a job, while someone else with injuries or a disability who believes that she will work will usually be successful in finding a job. One of the authors of this chapter knows of blind doctors succeeding in their jobs (because they were better listeners than their colleagues) and quadriplegics creating their own businesses because no one else thought that they were capable of working. Employment and education opportunities are out there for service members with disabilities—you just need to find them and pursue them.

You can also remind your family member that he is not a disabled veteran but is rather a veteran with a disability. The word order may seem minor but it is important: The disability is only one small part of your family member's identity and is not even the most important part. Every strength, character trait, and attribute your family member drew upon in the service still exists in him. Everything that the military taught him and everything that he learned and gained in uniform (review the list of common veteran character traits earlier in this chapter) were not erased by the injury. In many cases your family member's injury may have intensified many of these positive traits. He needs to understand this so that he can highlight it during his interviews.

Unfortunately many people—including bosses, hiring managers, teachers, and admissions officers—are afraid of disabilities and will (consciously or unconsciously) try to avoid people with disabilities at work or in the classroom. This has been called FUD—fear, uncertainty, and doubt. Research from psychologists suggests that people with disabilities remind us about our own mortality so we thus try to avoid interacting with them by finding reasons not to hire them or admit them to schools. This is unfortunate, but on the other hand many people will have no issue with disabilities. As you will need to locate employers who appreciate your family member's military background you will also need to find employers that are not afraid of disabilities and see the value of hiring someone with disabilities. Many families find it helpful to have an advocate to help them with the negotiations for accommodations in the workplace or in the classroom. The VSOs listed in the appendix can provide suggestions for advocates in your area. To qualify for accommodations at work or in the classroom you will probably need to be evaluated by a physician to be certified as disabled. If you find that it takes too long to get an appointment with a VA or DoD physician you may want to schedule a visit with a doctor not affiliated with the VA or DoD to get the evaluation.

Employment with a Disability

How Employment Can Help Your Family Member

What are the benefits of civilian employment for those leaving the military and returning home with injuries and disabilities? All jobs can bring stress, sometimes even trauma, to the family. Work complicates lives for families by competing for time. There are also difficulties in some jobs that require long hours and others that do not pay reasonable wages. Finally, there are civilian jobs that are less satisfying than work in the military, where the same type of work in the military may have been more exciting when you were taking risks in war zones defending our nation.

Despite possibilities that civilian work may be more difficult at times (such as being less stressful and lowering risks for mental and physical trauma), there are positive benefits to working in the civilian world for the wounded warrior. First, as a wounded warrior your family member has learned how to understand stress and learned to cope with trauma. A person trained to cope with stress and trauma will be a more effective worker for jobs that are challenging. Those who have learned to face death as warriors in the military also bring important stress-resistant skills to confronting challenges in civilian work. The consequences of surviving the training to fight in a war, and of overcoming wounds, creates a person who has the skills for leading in the community and for guiding others in civilian work. Wounded warriors also have had access to training through both DoD and VA resources.

To prevent physical and mental wounds from disrupting the family, this means that your wounded warrior must learn with your family members how to re-create caring attachments and caring environments. Activities that promote caring by reducing social isolation are essential, for the warrior and the warrior's family. Both work and school provide one of the most important features critical to recovery from trauma for the disabled veteran, namely a meaningful purpose to life. Just as achieving goals and objectives was critical to performance in the military, so is having goals and objectives based upon meaningful purposes in living life as a civilian, and especially as a wounded warrior

Self-Evaluation of Employment with Disabilities

Your family member will not only need to go through the self-evaluation process in the sections described above to determine what she wants to do after the military but she will also have to figure out what she can realistically do now that she is disabled. For instance, a person who wants to be a driver may need to reconsider that career choice if she is blind. But before your family member crosses too many things off the list of activities, she will need to realize the number of accommodations out there that allow people with disabilities to do more things than they ever could in the past. The Job Accommodation Network (JAN), at http://www.jan.wvu.edu and 1-800-526-7234, can provide you with information on how to accommodate all types of disabilities in the workplace. Most of these accommodations can be made for no or very little cost. Call JAN and let them know what your family member wants to do and what injuries and disability she has and JAN will provide ideas on how to accommodate the injuries on the job.

Your family member's injuries may have changed some of the things that she could do in the past, but they did not change her character, her loyalty, and the other traits mentioned in the list at the beginning of this chapter. If your family member ever starts to get down because of her injuries and loses hope in finding a job remind her of this—and that she has many skills that some employer will find useful. Remember that everyone in the workforce has some types of disabilities and abilities—some people are not good with math while others may need to use a wheelchair to get around. We all provide "accommodations" every day on the job to help us perform the tasks that are difficult for us, and we all look for jobs that allow us to utilize the areas where we are capable and proficient.

One accommodation program that your family member can access is the Pentagon's Computer Assistance Program (CAP; http://www.cap.mil). This program provides technology to wounded warriors for free to use on the job or at home. This can be a major benefit and can save you a lot of money. However, note that the program only provides technology to service members still in the service. It is therefore critical that your family member applies for the program while he is still in uniform. Once he transitions out he will no longer have access to the CAP equipment (unless he gets a job with the federal government, but then he will lose the equipment if he leaves the government job). Almost all of the military hospitals have people trained in CAP to advise patients on equipment, so your family member should hear about the program. If he does not learn about it, make sure you ask about it and utilize it before he leaves the military. As with the other benefits mentioned in this chapter, he earned the CAP technology and to not collect on it would be like leaving money behind on the table.

The author of the *Parachute* book mentioned above co-authored another book geared for job-searchers with disabilities. It is called *Job-Hunting for the So-Called Handicapped or People Who Have Disabilities* and we recommend looking through it. It describes some of the hurdles that a job searcher with a disability might face, how to overcome them, and how to network for a job with a disability.

This book lists the advantages that employees with disabilities can bring to an employer. Many employers may not be aware of these advantages, so it may be necessary for your family member to educate herself about them so that she can explain them to a potential employer. Some of the benefits include tax credits that companies can earn by hiring veterans with disabilities or making modifications to their structures. Research has also shown that employees with disabilities can be quite determined and loyal to their employer. Most people with disabilities have been forced to think "outside the box" to get by in the world for so long that it is now second nature for them. This is a positive trait that many employers admire.

Networking for a job becomes even more critical for someone with disabilities. As mentioned above, many employers will have FUD about hiring a person with a disability. Your network will be able to help you get to know who might have this FUD so you can avoid them and find those without FUD who will be happy to hire you.

One question that will come up during the job search is when you should disclose your disability to a potential employer. Reveal it too soon and the employer might lose interest but reveal it too late and it might feel like a "bait and switch" to the employer. This is one benefit of networking for a job when you have a disability: As you speak with the people you meet through your networking they will learn of your disability as soon as they meet you so there will not be any surprises or questions about what you can or cannot do on the job.

Kendra Duckworth, a counselor at JAN who has worked with many returning disabled veterans advises, "The Americans with Disabilities Act prohibits potential employers from asking medical- or disability-related questions, so the choice to disclose is clearly up to the individual. If you decide to disclose, remember to talk about your abilities, not your disabilities. Employers need qualified, capable individuals to fill positions. Find a way to show that you are that person. Sell them on what you can do, not on what you cannot do and the interview will go better than you expect. Be positive about yourself and be honest."

Dale Brown, the co-author of the *Job-Hunting for the So-Called Handicapped* book with Richard Bolles (mentioned above), has dealt with this issue because she has a learning disability and has also advised other individuals. She explains that bringing up the disability while you are still competing for a job is "like tying a weight around your leg before you run a race." She adds, "In order to be covered by the Americans with Disabilities Act, you must disclose your disability. This is because the law covers only the 'known' disability of the applicant or the employee. If you need a specific accommodation, such as extended time on a pre-employment test, disclosure will often be the only way to receive it. However, disclosure opens you up to discrimination. When applying for a job, it is usually impossible to prove that you were rejected because of a disability; it can be risky to mention it in the application, résumé, or job interview. After you are offered the job, it is safer to disclose, since the discrimination would be more obvious. A good time to request an accommodation is after the employer has selected you. This is the period where your leverage will be the highest. You can negotiate your accommodations along with issues such as salaries, benefits, and work hours. It may not be necessary to label your needs as accommodations. Flexible hours, extra clerical help, the ability to work at home at times, a quiet work station, and selection of your supervisor are often requested for reasons having nothing to do with a disability. If you negotiate a high enough salary, you may be able to pay for some of your accommodations yourself. Consider asking for an offer letter that puts important matters in writing."

Here are some of the recommendations offered about how to discuss your disability with potential employers:

- Raise the issue before the employer brings it up. Even though the law prohibits the employer from asking about disabilities, there is nothing that stops a candidate from talking about the issue and it allows a candidate to resolve concerns immediately and to frame the discussion about the disability.
- Provide hard facts and specifics of how your disability limits you and what accommodations are available. Be knowledgeable about the accommodations needed and costs involved.
- Ask the employer to break the job down into tasks and describe how you can address each of these tasks.
- Emphasize the benefits that people with disabilities and people with military experience can bring to an employer.
- Remind potential employers that they can fire people with disabilities if they are not adequately performing on the job.
- Practice these arguments so that they come easily during interviews, or work with a career counselor with disability experience to learn how to make these arguments.

Customized Employment and Compensated Work Therapy

A number of service members with severe disabilities utilize programs called Compensated Work Therapy (CWT) or customized employment. CWT provides short-term employment for pay for veterans admitted to VA clinics and medical centers, as well as vocational assessment, job-hunting services, case management, and consultations on assistive technology. One CWT program called VetSuccess offers determination of eligibility of vocational rehabilitation services for service-connected (20 percent or more) veterans with an honorable discharge, and provides vocational rehabilitation counselors and vocational and training services. See http://www.cwt.va.gov for detailed information about eligibility and location of CWT services.

Under a customized employment approach a person with a disability works with an employer to craft a job that eliminates the parts of the job that he cannot perform and to emphasize the tasks that he can do. As an example, an individual who is not able to lift heavy objects can have a job on a production line redesigned so that he will not have to engage in heavy lifting. In a real-life example, one of the authors of this chapter met a job counselor who approached a chemical manufacturing company for his client, who is a man with severe learning disabilities. The counselor noticed that the highly paid research scientists at the firm were cleaning their own test tubes and other supplies. After calculating the percentage of time the scientists spent cleaning the tools (and the percentage of their expensive salaries devoted to this task), the counselor approached the chief executive officer (CEO) of the company and suggested hiring his client to clean the equipment. The CEO saw the logic, created the position, and hired the man. You can see that customized employment takes some creative, out-of-the-box thinking and could be difficult to sell to most managers (who may prefer just to hire someone who fits the job description as it appears), but if you find the right person at the right company and make the right argument it can create a great opportunity for your family member with an almost perfect match between job and skills.

Education and Disabilities

Public colleges and universities now have considerable experience educating students with disabilities due to long-standing federal civil rights policies being extended to the post-secondary level. All two-year, four-year, and university educational institutions that receive federal funding have designated offices for students with disabilities (OSD), which function to ensure compliance with the federal laws. These offices receive documentation provided by students to certify that students with disabilities that affect their education enough to require accommodations have equal access to resources to obtain their education. Equal access applies not only to physical access to college buildings and facilities, but also to instructional modalities necessary for learning tailored to the student's disability. Therefore, OSDs authorize faculty to make modifications to instruction, and also deliver special services and assistive technology directly to students at no cost. Students submit an application form to their OSD to start the accommodation process.

These services and equipment have been most widely used by traditional students with mobility and sensory impairments and least used by non-traditional students and students with impairments affecting cognition and learning. However, research with both civilians and veterans suggests that these accommodations can make an important difference in the educational performance of students with cognitive and learning impairments, and so need to be more widely used.

Accommodations in the Classroom

Typical accommodations include interpreters and captioning transcribers for persons with hearing loss, Braille textbook transcribers and voice recognition software for persons with visual impairments, and note-takers, voice recognition software, digital organizers, electronic worksheet software, text-to-speech processors, and aural textbook transcribers for persons with conditions that affect cognition. Students with a wide range of conditions can also use extended-time testing, assignment modifications, oral testing, and testing in a quiet, non-classroom environment. Disability and supported education counselors may also be able to work with the student to develop cognitive remediation (e.g., memory enhancement), study strategies, and paper-writing strategies that fit individual learning needs in order to support performance.

One Army officer student veteran with PTSD described his experiences this way: "By the middle of the first semester I was in trouble, taken completely by surprise at how PTSD had rewired my brain. I was behind in all my classes, overwhelmed by the continual writing assignments and papers due almost every week. My cognitive processing was slow. I could not handle the pressure. My reading pace was slower. I could not get my mind around the new material. I found myself staying up late at nights and getting nowhere. My mind wandered in class. My notes made no sense to me. Thankfully I sought help from [the college's] disability services. Hiring a tutor helped somewhat, but by the end of the first semester I had one A- and three incompletes for the four courses I had taken. I felt isolated, totally alone and very afraid I would have to drop out of grad school. I began having nightmares and became depressed. Fortunately, I reached out for more help, cut down on my course load for the second semester, and ended in a much better place. Before starting last fall, I knew absolutely nothing about the Americans with Disabilities Act, or that PTSD is now a recognized disability, or that I qualified for "reasonable accommodations," such as a note-taker, extended time for tests, or assistive technologies. Now I know that I have to slow down my rate of pursuit, even if it means I don't get the full-time financial benefits from the GI Bill. I am finally learning to advocate for myself, that it is OK to go slower and take better care of myself. It is not easy, but I am learning how to live with the invisible wounds of PTSD. I will not quit. I will eventually graduate, but not the way I had originally expected."

Digital and computer-based assistive technologies for education are proliferating and improving rapidly, and the most common barrier to getting them is often the first step: knowing to register with your college's OSD and asking what they have available. You can apply for funds through Chapter 31 (i.e., VA Vocational Rehabilitation) if you have selected that form of aid to pay for any assistive technology that is not available through your college. The Web sites of disability advocacy organizations such as the National Center for Learning Disabilities (http://www .ncld.org) and government disability departments have lists of assistive technology and useful accommodations to consider (e.g., http://www.nsnet.org/atc/tools/con tents.html; http://www.disability.gov; http://www.techmatrix.org/; http://www.vats .org/ATEduPortal.htm; others are listed in the appendix). Some colleges have learning centers dedicated to serving students with mild traumatic brain injury (e.g., http://www.worksupport.com/VETS/index.cfm; http://www.richlandcollege. edu/dso/triprogram.php). JAN can also provide information on making accommodations in the classroom.

Another "low-tech" resource available on most college campuses, but often overlooked by students with disabilities, is a relaxation-oriented class or group, such as yoga, tai chi, or mindfulness meditation. Research suggests that relaxation practices may help sharpen attention, focus, and problem solving, and are a non-invasive, non-addictive way to manage performance demands. Mentorship and peer-support programs are also an important resource for student veterans with disabilities as much as for other student veterans. So be sure to check out the college's student veteran organization, learning communities (sometimes called interest groups), and student-to-student mentoring options, as well as the national American Corporate Partners veteran mentor program (http://www.acp-usa.org).

Supported Education

Supported education programs originated as state or local health department sponsored psychosocial rehabilitation programs developed to assist civilians with mental health diagnoses to return to college after onset and initial treatment of these conditions. Currently some colleges have developed supported education programs and have expanded them to serve their own admitted student-veterans with mental health/neurological diagnoses with varying eligibility criteria (e.g., the University of Kansas at http://www.socwel.ku.edu/mentalhealth/projects/promis ing/supported.shtml, Virginia Commonwealth University at http://www.worksup port.com/VETS/index.cfm, Arkansas State University at http://www2.astate.edu/cpi/ beckpride/).

It is important for your service member with disabilities to prepare for student success by working on any health conditions that may affect thinking and learning, from allergies to learning disabilities to PTSD. Prior research shows that veterans who obtain appropriate treatment the year before entering college (as well as continuing treatment while in college) are more likely to graduate and meet their academic goals. Any health issue that could affect attendance or concentration needs to be anticipated and addressed. Make sure you locate your university health center and know how to use it, as well as plan to take advantage of any other health benefits available to you.

Conclusion

Your service member and your family made many sacrifices to help protect our nation. We thank you for your service and dedication and hope that this chapter can help you help your family member begin the process of transitioning into a new job that provides for your family and challenges and excites him, or allows him the chance to go back to school to expand his skills and open up new opportunities. As we mentioned throughout the chapter, your service member earned all of the educational and employment benefits, networks, and access to programs as part of his service and we encourage you to pursue and maximize all of the options that were earned during the years in service. The skills, attributes, and talents he displayed in uniform will be assets on the job or in the classroom. We hope these assets will be recognized and utilized in your service member's future endeavors. We thank you and wish you the best of luck in these endeavors.

References

Ainspan, N. D., and W. E. Penk, eds. *Returning Wars' Wounded, Injured, and Ill: A Reference Handbook*. Westport, CT: Praeger Security International, 2008.

Bolles, R. N. *What Color Is Your Parachute? 2012: A Practical Manual for Job-hunters and Career-changers*. Berkeley, CA: Ten Speed Press, 2011.

Bolles, R. N., and D. S. Brown. *Job-Hunting for the So-called Handicapped or People Who Have Disabilities*. Berkeley, CA: Ten Speed Press, 2001.

Brown, D. S. *Learning a Living: A Guide to Planning Your Career and Finding a Job for People with Learning Disabilities, Attention Deficit Disorder, and Dyslexia*. Bethesda, MD: Woodbine House, 2000.

Chapman, J. *Negotiating Your Salary: How to Make $1,000 a Minute*. 5th ed. Berkeley, CA: Ten Speed Press, 2006.

Dawson, R. *Secrets of Power Salary Negotiating: Inside Secrets from a Master Negotiator*. Franklin Lakes, NJ: Career Press, 2006.

Farley, J. I. *The Military to Civilian Career Transition Guide: The Essential Job Search Handbook for Service Members*. 2nd ed. Indianapolis, IN: JIST Works, 2010.

Hay, M. T., L. H. Rorrer, J. R. Rivera, R. Krannich, and C. Krannich. *Military Transition to Civilian Success: The Complete Guide for Veterans and Their Families*. Manassas Park, VA: Impact Publications, 2006.

Hill, J., C. Lawhorne, and D. Philpott. *The Wounded Warrior Handbook: A Resource Guide for Returning Veterans*. 2nd ed. Lanham, MD: Government Institutes, 2012.

Hoge, C. W. *Once a Warrior, Always a Warrior: Navigating the Transition from Combat to Home—Including Combat Stress, PTSD, and mTBI*. Guilford, CT: GPP Life, 2010.

Kador, J. *201 Best Questions to Ask on Your Interview*. Columbus, OH: McGraw-Hill, 2002.

Krannich, C. R. *Nail the Job Interview!: 101 Dynamite Answers to Interview Questions*. 6th ed. Manassas Park, VA: Impact Publications, 2007.

Krannich, R., and C. Krannich. *Dynamite Salary Negotiations: Know What You're Worth and Get It*. 4th ed. Manassas Park, VA: Impact Publications, 2000.

Krannich, R. L., and C. S. Savino. *Military to Civilian Resumes and Letters: How to Best Communicate your Strengths to Employers*. Manassas Park, VA: Impact Publications, 2007.

Oliver, V. *301 Smart Answers to Tough Interview Questions*. Naperville, IL: Sourcebooks, Inc., 2005.

Moore, B. A., and W. E. Penk, eds. *Treating PTSD in Military Personnel: A Clinical Handbook*. New York: Guilford Press, 2011.

Renza, D., and E. Lizotte. *Military Education Benefits for College: A Comprehensive Guide for Military Members, Veterans and Their Dependents.* El Dorado Hills, CA: Savas Beaite, 2010.

Ryan, R. *Job Search Handbook for People with Disabilities.* St. Paul, MN: JIST Publishing, 2004.

Savino, C. S., and R. L. Krannich. *From Air Force Blue to Corporate Gray.* Fairfax Station, VA: Competitive Edge Services, 2007.

———. *From Army Green to Corporate Gray.* Fairfax Station, VA: Competitive Edge Services, 2007.

———. *From Navy Blue to Corporate Gray.* Fairfax Station, VA: Competitive Edge Services, 2007.

Seligman, M. E. P. *Flourish: A Visionary New Understanding of Happiness and Well-Being.* New York: Free Press/Simon and Schuster, 2011.

———. *Authentic Happiness: Using the New Positive Psychology to Realize Your Potential for Lasting Fulfillment.* New York: Free Press/Simon and Schuster, 2002.

———. *Learned Optimism: How to Change Your Mind and Your Life.* New York: Pocket Books, 1998.

Slone, L. B., and M. J. Friedman. *After the War Zone: A Practical Guide for Returning Troops and Their Families.* Philadelphia, PA: Da Capo Press, 2008.

Yate, M. J. *Great Answers to Tough Interview Questions.* 7th ed. Philadelphia, PA: Kogan Page, 2008.

14 | Sex and Intimacy after Combat

Sharon Wills, Matthew King

T here is little doubt that the warriors returning from deployments to combat zones often bear little resemblance to the men and women known to the families they left behind. As Judith Herman notes in *Trauma and Recovery*, "Traumatic events shatter the construction of the self that is formed and sustained in relation to others" and "undermine the belief systems that give meaning to human experience." This chapter will explore the ways in which the bonds of connection often referred to as "intimacy" are compromised and often destroyed by the warrior's combat experiences. Two perspectives will be integrated—that of a clinician who works with combat veterans and that of a combat veteran with multiple deployments in service of the current conflicts in Iraq and Afghanistan.

The term "intimate" is often used euphemistically to describe a sexual relationship, but it is probably more useful to think in terms of sexual intimacy as the physical component of an intensely close relationship. The emotional component of intimacy is more complex, and probably more profoundly affected by traumatic experiences. As previously noted, traumatic stress can undermine the very foundations of psychological well-being, which are critical to the ability to form significant connections with other people.

Authors Lisa McCann and Laurie Perlman conceptualize the development of psychological well-being in terms of a hierarchy of needs that must be resolved from the base up. "Trauma," according to them, "disrupts one's central needs and alters, disrupts, or disconfirms one's beliefs, assumptions, and expectations in those central need areas. For some, this disruption is equivalent to driving on unknown roads without a map and perhaps without control over the steering." The experience of combat can thus disrupt every level of psychological well-being and leave the warrior feeling like a rabbit wandering the forest without its skin—scared, vulnerable, helpless, and alone.

Hierarchy of Basic Psychological Needs

Every human being has basic psychological needs that need to be addressed throughout their life. These needs are organized into a hierarchy with the most basic ones at the bottom and the needs increasing in complexity as you move up the list. Here is the hierarchy of basic psychological needs:

- Intimacy
- Identity/Self-Soothing
- Power/Competence
- Independence and Autonomy
- Self/Other Esteem, Validation
- Trust, Need for Support of Others
- Safety and Invulnerability to Harm
- Frame of Reference for Understanding Experience

At the top of the hierarchy is Intimacy, or more specifically Emotional Intimacy. Attainment of this level of psychological well-being involves making oneself fully known, short-comings and all, to another. In other words, to make yourself vulnerable with another and to be able to trust that your vulnerability will not be used against you. From this perspective, if your frame of reference is severely disrupted, as frequently happens in combat trauma, the prerequisites for the ability to engage in emotionally intimate relationships will not be met, and your service member may have extreme difficulty sustaining anything other than superficial or distant relationships. One of the prerequisites to attainment of emotional intimacy is having a stable identity, which refers to how an individual views herself, both as a person and in relation to other people, ideas, and nature. Identity requires exploration of various different roles a person might take on, such as student, warrior, spouse, and so forth, and eventually making a commitment to a particular role or value.

If the existential conflict between the service member's identity as a deployed warrior and as a combat veteran returning to the home front is not explored and resolved, it will likely result in *Identity Diffusion*. Identity Diffusion results when there has been no exploration of possible alternative roles and no commitment to a particular role, and the individual is often rather vague and unclear about who she is and how she fits in the world. Resolving this conflict is integral to healing the invisible wounds of war and inevitably leads to *Identity Consolidation*.

Identity Consolidation is when the individual has integrated different facets of self (e.g., the smart self, the kind self, the selfish self, etc.) into one stable personality.

The disruption of central needs in the combat veteran can also manifest itself in some, but not necessarily all, of the following ways in relationships:

- Seeing things as either black or white, with little tolerance of the "gray areas." (A difficulty with *Frame of Reference*.)

- Being overly pessimistic about human nature in general. (A difficulty with *Frame of Reference*.)

- General uneasiness about being safe and concern about others' safety. (A disrupted sense of *Safety*.)

- Being generally unreliable in providing emotional support to others and in honoring time commitments made to significant others. (Problems forming bonds of *Trust*.)

- Habitually not showing up for scheduled appointments then failing to understand why others are annoyed. (Problems forming bonds of *Trust*.)

- Having difficulty giving or receiving compliments and validation of or by others. (Deficits with *Self/Other Esteem* and *Validation*.)

- Being unreasonably jealous in one moment and appearing almost uncaring in another. (Deficits with *Self/Other Esteem* and *Validation*.)

- Impulsivity without responsibility. (Failure to attain *Independence/Autonomy*.)

- Overreacting when significant others do not do things "the right way." (Struggles with a sense of *Power/Competence*.)

- Insisting that loved ones share their extreme adherence to meticulous details. (Problems with *Power/Competence*.)

- Feeling uncomfortably threatened by closeness with a significant other, alternating between fears of engulfment and fears of abandonment. (A failure to consolidate the elements of self into a stable sense of *Identity*.)

- Feeling love for a significant other in one moment and in the next wanting to be completely rid of them. (Problems with *Identity*.)

- Difficulty experiencing strong emotions and appearing uncaring and unreachable. (Problems with *Identity* and *Intimacy*.)

- Having difficulty merging sex with emotional intimacy may result in sex as an intense physical exercise, blurring the boundaries of identity. This, in turn, momentarily staves off the depression of identity diffusion, or the inability to establish a stable identity. (Problems with *Identity* and *Intimacy*.)

- Like the little girl with the curl in the middle of her forehead (as mentioned in the old song), "when she was good she was very, very good, but when she was bad she was horrid." (Problems with *Identity Diffusion*.)

Impact on the Spouse

How does this play out for you as the spouse and lover of a combat veteran? It will at once be the most wonderful and the most painful experience of your life.

- You will always be off-balance, feeling intensely loved in one moment, and reviled in the next.
- Your spouse will place you on a pedestal one day and break your heart the next, and will not even notice your tears.
- Loving your spouse will sometimes feel like riding on a fast-moving roller coaster that jumps the track—unbelievably exhilarating but inevitably harmful.
- Your spouse is easy to love and so hard to leave, and so destructive in the middle.
- If you stay long enough, your heart will be broken many times over.

What Can Help the Spouse?

Only after coming to terms with traumatic memories can your warrior begin to make meaning of his experiences during deployment. Regaining intimacy through trauma-focused therapy has to involve rebuilding the basic needs, from correcting distortions in one's Frame of Reference to restoration of Safety, learning to develop trust, on up the hierarchy to Identity Consolidation and Intimacy. Once there is sufficient resolution of traumatic memories, your warrior can begin to resolve the issues underlying the eventual attainment of stable identity and hence, the ability to participate in intimacy. For younger warriors, especially those with childhood trauma histories, identity development prior to combat deployment may be (to varying degrees) incomplete, thus leaving the warrior particularly susceptible to Identity Diffusion. Such warriors may be at risk for over-identification with the military and the combat experience. The effects of combat trauma on the development of stable adult identity in young men in their late teens and early twenties cannot be ignored. The younger the warrior is, the more profound this disruption can become.

The result of this disruption may lead to a warrior who has difficulty seeing himself in any other role than that of the warrior. This is the warrior who is uncomfortable unless he is fully armed, who still plays war games, loves violent video games, has a collection of war movies and pornography, and feels like a fish out of water back in a civilian environment. This warrior's road to recovery is likely to be longer and more complex. These types of warriors are often erratic consumers of mental health treatment, more likely to rely on alcohol and drugs for symptom management, and frequently will drop out of treatment, returning only after some crisis in their lives. On the other hand, warriors without prior trauma histories who first deploy to combat zones in their late twenties or thirties are more likely to have already developed stable adult identities, and may suffer less disruption in the basic needs underlying identity and intimacy. Regardless of the warrior, eventually he will have to face the issue of "Who am I now?" and "Am I who I was in the war?" (the "False Self"), or "Must I be the person I think I should be?" (the "Ideal Self"). The "Real Self" is likely to be somewhere in the middle—someone who has grown from past experience, but is able to live in the present. Finding the Real Self can be viewed simply as Identity Consolidation. The person who can achieve this is the best candidate for success in achieving true intimacy in relationships.

Direct Impact of War Zone Deployment

Being deployed to a war zone undeniably has a profound and often intractable effect on service members, regardless of whether they are assigned to the infantry, artillery, tanks, vehicle repair, rear support, convoy security, or other areas. All service members are placed, to varying degrees, in life-threatening situations, and the survivors will all return home with memories of both good experiences and of horrific and indescribable experiences. They may or may not choose to share these experiences with loved ones at home, and it is important for families and loved ones to respect the choices a warrior makes and refrain from intrusive questioning. Particularly offensive questions relate to whether or not the warrior "killed any people" and other similar questions. It is more important for the warrior to be able to share her *feelings* about certain experiences than to relate specific details of horrific experiences. The non-warrior is not likely to understand the latter anyway, or may be vicariously traumatized by hearing about them.

Long Time Periods Away from Home

Service members are required to be absent from home for extended periods of time. This absence fades the warrior's perception of home as the length of deployment grows. The warrior may feel that he does not know a child born at the beginning of a deployment, and having a parent absent for long periods of time during critical periods in a child's development can result in a degree of estrangement when the warrior returns. In many children there will be a great deal of resentment when the long-absent parent returns and attempts to resume the parental role vacated pre-deployment. These issues can exacerbate tensions that are already running high and if not addressed will result in even greater strain on the family relationship and destroy intimacy between partners.

Infidelity and Suspicion

Infidelity is a realistic concern for both service members and spouses during deployment. One can help to avoid infidelity by maintaining a line of communication during deployment that remains loving, devoted, and supportive in nature. Fighting is inevitable, however, and suspicion of infidelity will only increase the stress of an already extremely stressful situation. The human imagination is one the most pleasant, powerful, and scary tools with which our bodies are equipped. When no infidelity has occurred, it may be best to talk about the feelings of suspicion, using "I" statements rather than being accusatory—saying, for example, "When you are gone, I worry that you will find someone else to replace me," instead of saying, "You must have been unfaithful to me." In the event that infidelity does occur on the part of either the service member or their significant other, each individual couple must decide how it will be handled. Regardless of the circumstances that precipitated the betrayal, the act of infidelity is undeniably a betrayal that may or may not be forgivable, but will certainly require attention.

If the non-betraying partner does not know about the infidelity, and is not likely to find out, should the betrayer tell? Confession may be "good for the soul," but it is usually in the service of alleviating the guilt of the betrayer, and may cause far more pain than gain in the betrayed party. Again, how a couple handles infidelity is very individualized, and may be more effectively achieved with the assistance of professional advice. Many couples will insist on full disclosure of infidelities, and others will relate more to the words of an old song that recirculates from time to time: "How many arms have held you and hated to let you go? I wonder, I wonder, I wonder, but I really don't want to know."

Near-Death Experiences

Near-death experiences may cause the service member to face mortality at a premature stage of development. Some warriors who have these experiences will be forever changed by them, sometimes for the better, sometimes for the worse. Many warriors react to these experiences by feeling that they are invincible, and may engage in risky behavior because of these feelings that nothing can harm them. Others may react with a certain peacefulness and certainty that when death actually does come, they have no fear. Probably a minority of warriors will become more fearful of their surroundings and of the possibility of death.

Exposure to Violence Involving Women and Children

Many warriors report incidents in which they witnessed or caused violence in which women and children were killed or seriously injured. Consequently, when they come home and are confronted with the normal crying of children, they are often unable to tolerate this reminder of war zone experiences. In a similar way, witnessing or causing violence to women may cause the warrior to have difficulty with sexual activity with his partners because of the negative images attached to female contact. Recent studies have indicated that the feedback loops in the brain that make sex pleasurably rewarding are the same as for aggression and food, so it is understandable that sex and aggression may become inextricably paired, so that the presence of one may enhance or substitute for the other.

Sexual Victimization

The incidences of military-related sexual trauma can be at least as debilitating as the exposure to combat violence. The survivor of sexual assault, whether male or female, may or may not have been able to report the assault while in theater, but it is almost certain that the experience will induce an enormous amount of shame in the victim, such that some victims never are able to share even the fact that this happened with family members or anyone else. Military-related sexual trauma issues generally merit working with counselors who are well trained in the effects of sexual trauma. Because it is perpetrated in the context of the military environment, military-related sexual trauma compounds the sense of betrayal and powerlessness of the victim. Again, it is best if friends and family members respect the service member's choices of when, whether, and how much to disclose of the experience.

Other Barriers to Intimacy

Reintegration Time

Reintegration from the battlefront is a daunting task for warriors. Many things have changed for you, your service member, and your family. Reintegration will not happen overnight, as adjustment is a somewhat slow process, which has several steps that cannot be rushed. Keep in mind that your warrior is adjusting to many things at once and will require compassion and patience during the initial adjustment period. A few simple words will lend a tremendous amount of perspective: "Small steps bring big changes."

Understanding the Roles of Warrior and Partner

Understanding the differences and changes in your family's roles is crucial to making reintegration go as smoothly as possible. For the most part, spouses take on the responsibilities associated with the traditional roles of the service member while he or she was deployed. After the warrior returns home, barriers to intimacy will persist if the differences in roles are not understood and respected. Drawing a parallel to World War II, most of America's women worked in factories and plants, and even played baseball. After the war was concluded, most of the men returned to their jobs and respected the role that women played to keep the war effort and country afloat. Similarly, reintegration upon returning from a combat deployment will require mutual respect and an understanding of how roles have shifted.

Disclosing Details about OPSEC

OPSEC (Operations Security) plays an integral role in every warrior's life when returning home. Bonds are built, and information is shared that can never be repeated outside of inner military circles. This can affect romantic relationships. As a spouse or family member you must be able to accept this code that will exist after deployment. Virtually every returning service member will have to keep some secrets (some more than others) after returning from a forward area. Confidentiality is the primary source of trust within the ranks and thrives at the core of the returning warrior. He will be instructed to maintain OPSEC after returning home. As prominent couples' researcher John Gottman suggests, one strong predictor of success in romantic relationships is being fully known to one another. This is very difficult for the returning service member who may not be able to be fully known due to OPSEC. In order to fill the gaps that OPSEC creates, you may need to accept that some things will have to remain unknown. Rather than knowing details, which are restricted, focusing on how the warrior actually felt during traumatic or classified experiences will let him or her be better known.

Combat Stress Reactions

Learning how the brain reacts to threats as a basic biological process will help you better understand what might be going on with your warrior. At the center of combat stress reactions is the *Limbic System*, which has the following functions:

- Acts as an alarm signal, sending messages to other parts of the brain that control physiological responses to threat, ensuring that the body responds rapidly.
- Triggers the release of adrenaline to tense muscles, increases alertness, attention, heart rate, and blood pressure, and also changes the way one scans the environment for threats.
- Causes the release of stress hormones that increase endurance, as well as chemicals that dull the awareness of pain.
- During times of stress it directs or "hijacks" the conscious, rational frontal part of the brain, so that one's entire attention and focus is directed toward survival.

The primary emotion of the Limbic System is anger, which helps to control fear. During times of extreme stress, emotions other than anger shut down. The speed of information processing increases, but the ability to be self-reflective or to consider things in rational sequence diminishes. Military training and combat hones one's reflexes (so that the warrior feels as if she is operating on "automatic pilot") and emphasizes dominance of the Limbic System.

The Medial Prefrontal Cortex connects to the deeper limbic neurons involved in the fight-or-flight reflex, dampens or controls the fight-or-flight reflex, and tries to keep it from indiscriminately firing when there is no threat. It also governs planning, decision-making, thinking through actions, and anticipating sequences. Under normal circumstances, the fight-or-flight response, which is basic to survival in all animals, provides an automatic response to a perceived threat. It activates processes needed for survival (heart rate speeds up to increase blood flow to extremities, respiration increases, and stress hormones are released). All processes not vital for immediate survival shut down. When the perceived threat is over, the arousal terminates.

Pleasure and Combat Stress

Pleasure is directly linked to the chemistry of the brain. When a neurotransmitter called dopamine is released in the brain, it binds to receptors, signaling pleasure. High amounts of dopamine generate greater feelings of reward, pleasure, and feeling good about life. High amounts of stress deteriorate the receptor sites, limiting the net amount of pleasure that can be felt. This biological shift limits the warrior's ability to feel a sense of reward, pleasure, and well-being. A common misperception is that the warrior chooses to not engage in feelings of pleasure, but the inability to feel pleasure is a consequence of high amounts of stress.

The Limbic System ensures that one reacts immediately to threat, and the Medial Prefrontal Cortex helps to keep reactions in balance. But in the presence of sleep deprivation, high intensity combat, or other very stressful conditions, the Medial Prefrontal Cortex may not be able to help balance out protective reflexes, thus keeping the arousal high long after the threat is terminated. If the stress response is allowed to stay "on," such as is common in a combat arena, continued sympathetic nervous system activation ("chronic stress") can interfere with natural immune system function and damage health. Prolonged activation of the sympathetic nervous system leads to a chronic state of hyperarousal, alternating with numbness, and depletion in the availability of natural biochemicals that help us calm down and return the nervous system to homeostasis.

As depicted in Figure 14.1 below, as level of arousal increases, the ability to think and process information also increases to a point (the "zone"). If arousal continues to rise, the ability to think declines, so that at the highest levels of arousal, thinking and problem solving become increasingly less efficient, and exerting self-control becomes increasingly difficult. Memories may be stored in fragmented fashion. Primary cues for retrieval may then become sensory, with no verbal retrieval cues or coherent narrative of the event. Thus, warriors may get memories triggered simply by smells, sounds, sights, or feelings that may have been present at the time of a traumatic event, without having any idea why they are feeling threatened.

Table 14.1 depicts the impact of trauma on the information-processing system, using the acronym "STARTLE" to compare and contrast Normal Processing in someone with no significant traumatic stress history, what is "normal" processing in the aftermath of a single traumatic incident, and the devastating effects of trauma on information processing in someone who is inundated with trauma, as is frequently the case with combat veterans.

Figure 14.1   The Impact of Arousal and Anxiety on Information Processing Efficiency and Memory

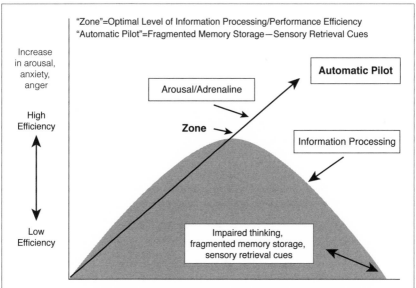

As level of arousal increases, the ability to think and process information also increases to a point (the "Zone"). If arousal continues to rise beyond the Zone, the ability to process information declines, so that at the highest levels of arousal, thinking, problem solving, and decision-making become increasingly less efficient. Exerting self-control becomes increasingly difficult, and memories may be stored in fragmented fashion. Primary cues for retrieval may then become sensory, with no verbal retrieval cues or coherent narrative of the event.

Table 14.1 Continuum of STARTLE Responses: The Effects of Traumatic Disruption on Information Processing

Stage of Information Processing	ADAPTIVE (Normal Response)	ENABLING (Post-trauma Survival Response)	DISABLING (Inundated by Trauma)
Sensory Activation	Reacts normally to signals	Hyper-alert to danger signals	Unable to differentiate between signals of danger/not danger
Thought/ Movement Activation	Appropriate to environmental signal	Hypersensitive to Danger	Makes catastrophic attributions; assumes all = danger
Arousal Activation	Appropriate to signal	Hyper-activation of arousal	Chronic over-activation of arousal
Regulation of Emotional Arousal	Regulates arousal with accurate threat evaluation	Hyper-arousal in proportion to threat; danger over-evaluated	Dysregulated arousal All-or-nothing evaluation of threat; ALL arousal = danger
Termination of Arousal	Terminates arousal when threat is over	Partial/ delayed arousal termination; reenactments of trauma to facilitate termination	Ineffective termination; leads to maladaptive re-enactments, living in a trauma world
Learning	Makes sense of the experience; integrates learning	Initial errors in interpretation with delayed integration, growth	Misinterpretation leads to helplessness, arrested development, no growth
Encoding & Storage Information	Labels & stores experience w/ related cues, narrative	Some fragmentation, delayed connection of cues & narrative	Total fragmentation, no connection of cues, disrupted narrative, amnesia

Source: Sharon Wills, PhD

In the Adaptive or Normal trauma response, disruptions to intimacy will likely be temporary, if at all, in a person who has previously attained that level of psychological development. As the individual makes sense of the experience and integrates learning, the underlying needs of safety and trust (mentioned above) will be restored and the frame of reference will be positively altered in order to integrate the experience. For example, a crime victim may learn that although certain situations may increase the possibility that one will be a crime victim, these situations do not increase the probability of being a victim. She will be able to weigh the possibilities versus probabilities and continue to take calculated risks based on the probabilities of the situation. The spouse of an individual who is having an adaptive response to a traumatic situation can best help by being supportive, listening if the individual wants to talk about the experience, and giving her room to reflect and process the experience.

In an enabling post-trauma survival response, the individual's processing time may be longer and may result in greater disruptions to intimacy as he makes sense of the experience. The sense of safety will be disrupted for a longer period of time, and the restoration of other basic psychological needs will proceed at a slower pace, with some initial errors in interpretation (for example, telling oneself initially that all threat signals mean something is wrong, then realizing as processing proceeds that some threat signals are false alarms). The restoration of the psychological needs underlying intimacy will eventually occur, with some delay in learning and growth. In this case, the spouse can best help by being patient and encouraging, but not intrusive, listening when the combat veteran wants to talk, but not demanding what he may not yet be ready to discuss.

Some individuals who are biologically, environmentally, and psychologically more predisposed to be overwhelmed in traumatic situations may become inundated by trauma and suffer a disabling response. They may be individuals who pre-trauma had not attained the higher levels of psychological development that form the basis for intimacy, and are thus more vulnerable to becoming re-traumatized by even sensory activation of the flight-or-fight response. Their arousal levels are chronically dysregulated, and they make all-or-nothing attributions to all threat signals, leading to helplessness and arrests in normal development. Any arousal is interpreted as a danger signal, and the individual is highly unlikely to be able to alter his frame of reference in order to accommodate learning or to restore a basic sense of safety. This individual's capacity for Intimacy is likely to remain, at best, severely impaired. He may be avoidant, isolated, asocial, and reluctant to try new things. Spouses of such individuals should educate themselves as to what is realistic to expect from their warrior, and try to be patient and supportive within those parameters. Having a life of your own may help you to avoid being resentful of something your warrior is unable to change. Invite him to go out with you, but if he does not want to, go without him. Do not walk on eggshells around him, but try to refrain from intrusive questions, criticism of his behavior, or trying to "fix" him. Remember that you are not the cause of his problems, and it is highly unlikely that you can fix them, but if you maintain a life, you will be better able to provide love and comfort, even when it seems you are getting little in return.

Pornography

Pornography is inescapable for the deployed service member. Sexual tension can overwhelm a warrior, especially one who is newly deployed, often leading to increased aggression and frustration. Generally there is limited availability of live sexual partners, such as is the case in deployments to Iraq and Afghanistan, so to cope with this tension, most service members masturbate on a somewhat regular basis. The use of pornography can both aid and enhance this experience. As a spouse or romantic partner of a service member, pornography may be viewed as a form of cheating. Ironically, pornography is often a substitute for infidelity for the deployed service member.

"Currency" among Warriors

In the combat theater pornography is considered a form of currency, and those who have it tend to trade it in mass quantities. A warrior on his first deployment may be unprepared for the sexual tensions that the presence in a war zone brings, and arriving in theater with no pornography may render the service member as "different." However, that person is likely to be quickly ushered into the realm of sexual objectification that is pornography. Then, that warrior may become completely immersed in pornography, either through magazines, DVDs, or the most accessible: downloadable content. Being bombarded with such an influx of sexually explicit material may lead to a reliance on pornography as a means of releasing tension that is built up. The warrior will (more than likely) begin exchanging pornography like a prepubescent boy trading baseball cards. Some countries do not allow pornography at all, which makes the risk and reward much greater for service members deployed to those countries.

Distortion of Sexual Perception

Pornography, especially after repeated usage, has a detrimental impact on the user's sexual perception, often resulting in objectification of sexual partners, and unrealistic expectations of the performance of one's sexual partner.

Continuing Use of Pornography Post-Deployment

A vast majority of warriors will have a very difficult time refraining from using pornography after returning from deployment. In the mind of the warrior, pornography is quick, to the point, and can be controlled. Sexual intimacy with a spousal partner, which may be viewed as more threatening, lacks these key ingredients for an objectified sexual experience. Accessing emotion is difficult for the warrior, and continuing use of pornography after deployment may feel safer than to risk the emotions involved in sexual contact with another person. A frequently used form of making contact at a safe distance is known as "sexting," or using text messaging as a means of transmitting pornographic images and sexually explicit dialogue, with the ultimate goal of sexual release. Among combat veterans this likely began in theater between soldiers and their significant others at home as a slightly more connected way of dealing with sexual tension. When the warrior returns home and finds that traditional face-to-face contact feels threatening, he may revert to more tolerable means, which create emotional distance.

Many warriors also use "sexting" (sexual texting) during combat and when they return. Variations of sexting include using e-mail as the medium rather than text messaging, and meeting willing partners in online chat rooms, all with the goal of obtaining sexual release without having to risk emotional intimacy with another person. Counseling, which addresses the addictive and compulsive nature of whatever form of pornography is being used, may be helpful.

Another complicating factor in post-deployment sexual adjustment is the effects of many of the medications used to treat the typical psychological issues that are related to Combat Stress Reactions (including post-traumatic stress disorder or PTSD), such as anti-depressants, anti-psychotics, or anti-convulsants. These medications, in some persons, may cause loss of libido, erectile dysfunction, ejaculation latency, and priapism (an erection lasting more than four hours). Often, if a warrior works closely with the prescriber, the latter will be able to make adjustments in the medications that minimize the sexual side effects.

It would be a mistake to underestimate the challenges that warriors returning home from combat and their families face. It will often take every ounce of patience the parties can muster to keep any degree of peace in the family, even though on the surface it may seem that everyone should be happy. The family and loved ones want the warrior to be the same person they sent to war, but the warrior knows that person died on the sands of Iraq or Afghanistan as surely as if she had been shot, and is forever gone. It is a long road back to finding a new life with new meaning, and the situation will surely get worse before it gets better. But with a lot of patience, tolerance, and hard work, things can change, and although no one concerned will have the life they thought they wanted, they can, with help, find a life of purpose. And purpose, after all, is what gives meaning to any life.

Where to Get Help

The Department of Veterans' Affairs' facilities throughout the country specialize in the treatment of specific symptoms of Combat Stress Reactions. These facilities have highly trained professionals who can offer individual and group counseling, family and couples therapy, and medication management of psychiatric issues. Also, each VA medical center has a Military Sexual Trauma coordinator who sees to it that counseling is made available to all veterans who report military sexual trauma during their military service, at no cost to the veteran. All OEF/OIF/OND (Operation Enduring Freedom/Operation Iraqi Freedom/Operation New Dawn) veterans are entitled to treatment at no cost to them by the VA for a five-year period following their discharge from active duty in the military. Vet centers are also available in many communities and offer individual and group counseling to combat veterans. Many communities also have a number of non-profit agencies that provide treatment to veterans on a sliding scale. The National Center for PTSD Web site also has a number of resources available at no charge for combat veterans and their families at http://www.pstd.va.gov. Another valuable online resource is managed by Patience Mason, author of *Recovering from the War*, at http://www.patiencepress.com. For veterans who do not wish to avail themselves of any of these resources, and who are judged to be at risk for harming themselves or others, call 911 and request Mental Health Transport to a hospital emergency room of your choice. Private hospitals will require a co-pay for admission.

References

Herman, J. L. *Trauma and Recovery.* New York: Basic Books, 1992.

Hoge, C. W. *Once a Warrior, Always a Warrior.* Guilford, CT: GPP Life, 2010.

McCann, I. L., and L. A. Pearlman. *Psychological Trauma and the Adult Survivor.* New York: Bruner/Mazel, 1990.

Female Warriors

15

Lisa Teegarden

Since 2001, approximately 200,000 women have served in wartime Iraq or Afghanistan. Approximately 134 have been killed in addition to 721 wounded in action, with these figures growing almost daily. While women are increasingly casualties of war, the Military Leadership Diversity Commission—a commission tasked with addressing diversity in our military—recommended that the Department of Defense (DoD) and the services eliminate the "combat exclusion policies" for women, including the removal of barriers and inconsistencies, to create a level playing field for all qualified service members, finally removing the ban on women serving in ground combat units including those in the infantry, armor, and special forces. Given this and other trends, it is increasingly likely we will see greater numbers of female warriors filling formerly non-traditional roles within the military and returning from deployments having served in ground combat units. With increasing numbers of female warriors fighting and dying, we need to recognize the unique needs and experiences of female warriors, and the impact on their spouses and families.

Women currently serve in combat support and combat service support roles; but they also are warriors serving as gunners, combat pilots, military police, and a whole host of military professionals that are in the direct line of fire. This is not an anomaly. Since the beginning of civilization, female warriors have existed although certainly not in numbers commensurate with male warriors. Historical well-known examples of female warriors are Saint Joan of Arc and the Amazons, an entire army of female warriors. Even in our own historical record, women have served as warriors in our military since the American Revolution, increasingly fighting and dying in service of our nation. The consequences of serving in combat are no different for females than they are for males. Female warriors suffer from post-traumatic stress disorder (PTSD), depression, suicide, traumatic brain injuries (TBI), amputations, and death. While the relative numbers appear to be low, the growing impact to our society and our military is increasing. Most of the research regarding the mental, physical, familial, and social consequences of combat has focused on men and their families. This chapter is an initial attempt to correct this imbalance.

As the roles of women in the military expand and evolve, so will their role within their family and society at large. What is presented in this chapter is a general understanding of experiences, challenges, and stressors experienced by female warriors and their families in the military and upon return from deployment. While it strives to be thorough while addressing a wide range of experiences, challenges, and stressors specific to female warriors, it is important to understand that each female warrior's experiences are unique. Thus, it is not possible to offer a highly detailed analysis addressing every unique situation, family variation, or cultural nuance. Further, to date there are relatively few research studies that adequately address or offer a broad, comprehensive understanding of the female warrior's day-to-day experience(s) as well as experiences returning from deployment and the impact upon her family. A paucity of research information exists related to the unique needs of female warriors and their families. Understanding the female warrior's perspective and the impact of deployment upon her and her family is a new and burgeoning area of interest. As our society accepts females in ground combat units, and the longer our military continues to engage in war, the greater the need to understand the unique challenges women face and the impact of those experiences on their children, their partners, and their families, as well as our society as a whole.

Please note that the author of this chapter acknowledges that this chapter likely represents a predominately Army perspective. This is not intentional. Rather, it is a by-product of personal and professional experiences as an Army psychologist. Additionally, the Army accounts for a disproportionate number of deployed service members to combat zones and thus has a disproportionate number of female service members.

Background

An examination of female warriors is necessary given their unique challenges that are quite different from those of their male counterparts. Approximately 15–20 percent of the military are females and that percent varies as a function of type of military service: the Air Force has the highest percent of females (20 percent), the Marine Corps the fewest (6 percent), and the Army and Navy are fairly equal (13 percent and 15 percent respectively). Across the military, approximately 53 percent of enlisted military men are married and 45 percent of enlisted military females are married. For officers the rates of marriage are 72 percent for men and 52 percent for women. Approximately half of all married women in the military are married to other service members. This compares to less than 10 percent of all married men in the military who are married to other service members. Of all spouses in the military, only 6 percent are male. Husbands of female service members are less likely to be employed outside the home than military wives.

In terms of family, 38 percent of active-duty females have children, compared to 44 percent of active-duty males with children. Further, 11 percent of female warriors in the military are single parents, as compared to just 4 percent of male warriors. Divorce for enlisted females in the military is nearly three times as common as compared to their male enlisted counterparts; in 2010, nearly 9 percent of enlisted females divorced as compared to 3 percent of enlisted men. In general, the divorce rate in 2010 for females in the military was 7.8 percent and 3 percent for military men. Women in the military also divorce at higher rates than their civilian counterparts. Military men, however, divorce at rates significantly lower than their civilian counterparts.

Perhaps not surprisingly, the military continues to be a traditional organization in terms of gender roles. The overwhelming majority of the military are men. Within the military the established responsibilities and duty standards are comparatively equal between women and men. Men and women in the military receive equal pay for the same rank and time in service and they are rated against the same position description. Despite this progress in equality within the military, society as a whole still continues to expect that men and women will fulfill their traditional family role(s) and obligations and this places additional burdens on the female warrior. Some of this burden is self-imposed as many women in the military may also continue to expect that they will fulfill a predominately traditional female role outside the military. For them, navigating the contrasting expectations between military and civilian life can be challenging to manage, especially when the roles are reversed for the female warrior and her spouse since she works outside the home while he stays at home to raise the children.

The professional female warrior—like any professional individual—strives to receive the appropriate recognition for her work performance. While there is equality between men and women for their rank and pay, it may be the case that she feels as if she needs to work harder and smarter and do more than her male counterparts in order to overcome the fact that she is a female. Unfortunately, stereotypes remain about women in general as well as women in the military, and their ability to be successful and progress in rank based solely on their abilities. The female warrior may struggle with a host of double-binds: Should she be too direct and assertive as a leader, she may be perceived by her superiors, peers, and subordinates as a "bitch." If she lacks too much assertiveness or fails in her ability to communicate directly, she may be perceived as a "typical female." Regarding her appearance, she may try and disregard or downplay her feminine side, or conversely she may wear makeup and appear more feminine.

There are real physical differences between men and women. One primary difference between men and women is a woman's ability to sustain life and give birth. Again, given the socially conservative attitudes that prevail within the military culture, this can present the female warrior with additional double-binds. She is biologically driven to nurture and care for her children. If the female warrior remains true to her biological drive and remains with her children in their time of need (e.g., illness), she can be perceived by her male counterparts as a slacker. However, if she overrides her biological drive and remains at work, then she feels as if she is abandoning her children. For many female warriors, this is a no-win situation. In the end, she may be left feeling that she can never be truly successful in either environment because she can never fully commit to either the military or her family.

The ease with which a non-traditional female warrior and her family navigate the waters within a traditional military environment may depend on several factors. How did she and her partner come to choose such an arrangement? Were they forced into the non-traditional family roles because of hard economic times or was it a pre-planned transition? Are they non-traditional in their thinking and approach to life in general? Did they meet when they were both in the military? Or, was the female warrior already in the military? Does the spouse have any prior affiliation with the military? In the military it is very challenging for both individuals to work outside the home and gain equal career success. The demands of the military are such that typically the husband and wife choose which career will be the priority. If the choice is that the priority will be the military member, the duties of this job demand frequent absences from the family, long work hours, deployments, and frequent moves from duty station to duty station.

Within a traditional organization such as the military, life can be lonely for men who are stay-at-home dads responsible for the day-to-day care of the children, cleaning, shopping, and managing the home, because they have no peer group with whom they can share experiences or from whom they can draw support. Moreover, the existing family support groups cater to military wives, thereby inadvertently disregarding and ostracizing the unique needs of the male stay-at-home spouse. Thus the stay-at-home dad may lack support from the military as well as from the local community. Other men he comes into contact with are likely to be in the military and these males may find it difficult to establish common ground with which to connect. Further, the stay-at-home dad may receive little recognition for his efforts—even from his own family and wife. This may especially be the case if the stay-at-home spouse is used to being in the work force and receiving recognition in the form of awards, reviews, promotions, and the like.

Female Warriors and Deployment

Deployment does not occur in a vacuum. It occurs within the broad and complicated context of the female warrior, her and her spouse's immediate and extended family, the military unit, and the broader context of society. Additionally, there is a cycle to the deployment process consisting of four phases: pre-deployment, deployment, re-deployment, and reintegration. It is important to recognize that there are experiences and situations that may occur within this broad and complicated context at any point in the deployment cycle. These may seem relatively insignificant in and of themselves. Yet taken together, these factors have the potential to subsequently prove of importance and influence the female warrior's return home, and can greatly impact the adjustment of her family.

Pre-Deployment

Just as it is vital for units to prepare tactically for deployment, it is paramount that the female warrior and her family prepare personally for the deployment. The female warrior's family begins to prepare for deployment as soon as she receives the warning order from her unit. The more stressors the individuals within the family possess, the more challenging or stressful the deployment may be for the warrior and the family. Some considerations are the pre-deployment health and stability of the female warrior's marital relationships, as well as her and her family's own individual psychological and physical health. Weaknesses here may negatively impact the return home, and any slit in the fabric of the family is likely to become increasingly unraveled, worn, or torn.

Some aspects or factors to consider that can positively or negatively impact the family throughout the deployment cycle are: the family's ability to communicate effectively; the level of intimacy (which often directly relates to communication) and trust within the marriage; the sharing of responsibility within the family; and any unresolved issues of the family such as financial stressors. Other factors include how well adjusted the children are; their overall level of adjustment in school; developmental concerns; as well as medical or psychological conditions or issues experienced by the child or the partner. While these factors are also likely to affect and impact the male warrior who deploys, the female warrior may feel greater responsibility for the family given her maternal expectations. This may especially be true if she is the primary nurturer of the family or she maintains a traditional female role.

Additional pre-deployment factors to consider are how well the family plans for the deployment. Was there a long lead time that allowed them to prepare? Or did the deployment suddenly arise leaving little time for preparation? Did the family set realistic expectations prior to deployment? For example, did the family consider or factor in long periods of no communication with each other? Or did they plan for the female warrior to have the ability to communicate with the family daily in the form of e-mail, Skype, and other social media means? While today's ability to communicate in real time can lessen the anxiety for the family, it can work at cross purposes. More specifically, the family may find it lessens their anxiety but it may leave the female warrior to continue to feel responsible for them at a time when she cannot possibly assume such responsibilities. Assumptions here can be misleading. Perhaps the family assumed that life would change little with the female warrior deployed. Given their accessibility to her via instant messaging and video chat, the family may continue to look to her for direction on a daily basis despite her inability to adequately provide it from a battlefield halfway around the world. The tyranny of time and distance can increase frustration and resentment on behalf of both parties if the family member is not getting their needs met and the female warrior is not be able to rise to her own expectations.

Factors such as how well integrated the female warrior and her family were in the unit and community prior to deployment are also worthy of consideration. Traditionally, Family Readiness Groups and installations support services cater to female family members or spouses. Depending on how much experience the male spouse has with the military, he may be left feeling disregarded, or outright excluded. Or the male spouse may not feel comfortable with attending family readiness groups, which have historically been oriented to the female spouse. The male spouse may not recognize his need for external support. How much support the family had or has from in-laws and their extended family will impact the female warrior as well. Sometimes it is the case that in-laws and extended family members who pledged their help and support to the family during the deployment experience unforeseen circumstances that ultimately render their prior pledge of help and support null and void. This may leave the female warrior's family in crisis or responding to a crisis that was unexpected. Another important consideration is how willing the spouse or husband is to accept help or ask for help. If, during deployment, the female warrior's family needs help, but her spouse proves too proud to ask, she may feel stress and resentment.

Deployment

A number of family factors and issues back home can impact female warriors' resiliency during deployment. Such factors to consider are those stressors experienced by the female warrior, her family, and the unit. Life does not stop once the warrior deploys. No matter how well planned the deployment was by the female warrior and her family, the female warrior may find herself struggling with feeling as if she has abandoned her family. While it may not sound reasonable, she may find herself feeling guilty for having left the family—for not "being there" for her children. This guilt may be somewhat related to the age of the children: the younger the children, the greater the guilt may be. This may not always be the case. She may feel resentful, jealous, or suspicious that her children are being nurtured by someone other than herself. She may find herself feeling "replaced" and unimportant. Family issues may arise that she feels helpless to have any positive impact on.

There are factors regarding her deployment surroundings that may impact her return home. The boundaries separating combat from combat support roles are virtually nonexistent in today's active theaters. Female warriors find themselves engaging with the enemy and in the direct line of fire. The enemy does not adhere to conventional rules of warfare and both women and men face uncertainty. That uncertainty can be amplified if the unit suffers from poor leadership, low morale, and lack of cohesion. Her unit may experience a high number of causalities, a greater than expected number of in-theater suicides, or other mental health issues.

A lack of positive leadership and the character of war can have the negative effect of manifesting itself in individual doubt and insecurity. The term "fog of war" is used to describe the general uncertainty over situational awareness experienced by individuals in military operations. This "fog" can lead some individuals to make decisions they would not otherwise make, leading to infidelity or behavioral misconduct. If the female warrior is the only female in her unit, or one of very few, she may feel she has no one to talk to. The unit may not have the resources to help her with her stressors. She may find herself feeling alone, depressed, or otherwise abandoned. During times of increased stress, the female warrior may develop emotionally or physically intimate relationships with someone in her unit. As a result of any or all of these experiences, she may distance herself from her family—decreasing letters home, e-mailing less often, and decreasing her instant messaging and video calls. She may find security elsewhere.

During deployment, the female warrior is also living in closer confines to men. This can have unintended consequences such as sexual assault. Both men and women report being sexually assaulted in the military. Overall, the rates of sexual assault for women are far greater in the military than for the civilian population (approximately 23–33 percent in the military compared to 17 percent for civilians). The rate of sexual assault for men is approximately 3 percent regardless of military or civilian. In addition, rates of re-victimization are higher in the military than for the civilian world. Notably, the most common psychiatric reaction to rape is PTSD. Approximately 65 percent of men and 46 percent of women who are sexually assaulted report symptoms consistent with PTSD. Increasingly there are reports of sexual assault during deployment by fellow service members. When sexual assault occurs during military service, it results in twice the risk for PTSD. The reasons for this are not clear. These experiences can lead the female warrior to feel vulnerable physically and emotionally, and unprotected. While she has the ability to report sexual assault, a recent DoD study found that 71 percent of women and 85 percent of men do not report unwanted sexual contact. Among many reasons cited were fears of retaliation or retribution.

The female's expectation, beliefs, and attitudes about engaging in combat will largely affect her coping or resiliency upon her return home. Despite the military providing uniform training for all of its service members, different people have different expectations, sense of purpose, and meaning with regard to their experiences/service in the military. Some individuals may have joined because of the need for money for college, to receive an enlistment bonus, or to serve their country. Nonetheless, females are vital in the roles that they serve in. If a female has had difficult or traumatic experiences, one factor that may help her cope is how consistent her experience was with her sense of self and purpose in the military.

Post-Deployment

During deployment, the female warrior and her family will think about her return home. Everyone in the family will have a fantasy about the female warrior's return home. These fantasies or ideals are important in helping to shape the reunion of the family. However, it is critical that each person shares these fantasies and expectations for the reunion so that clear expectations can develop. The less realistic the expectations are, the more likely it is that difficulties will arise. Other factors that may impact the post-deployment and reintegration period are related to how well or poorly pre-deployment and deployment were implemented. The more challenging pre-deployment and deployment were for the female warrior, the more challenging reintegration will be for the family. Conversely, the opposite may be true.

Reintegration

Factors Affecting Reintegration

Upon returning home there continue to be factors that can affect reintegration. These factors are not unique to the female warrior but what is unique is her role in the family. Issues and factors such as unit stability and predictability back at her home station are likely to affect reintegration. Many times the family longs to have the female warrior home, sharing responsibilities and re-establishing contact with the spouse and children. Expectations are high that she will attend important family events such as holidays, birthdays, school and teacher conferences, helping with homework, attending ball games, swim meets, recitals, graduations, and so forth. The daily routine is vital for re-establishing connection with the family. However, it is often the case that once the unit returns from deployment, there is less predictability. This is because the unit is getting ready to deploy again. There is training that needs to be completed and a whole host of mini-deployments ensue at a rapid pace. Time at home is whittled away and eaten up by unit activity. Gradually the family once again reverts to attending events without the female warrior. Given the predictability (so to speak) of deployment, there is a lack of predictability back home that is frustrating for everyone. Thus, the female warrior may miss the routine of deployment. With lack of predictability, the impact on the family can be great—kids act out, frustration, anger, or resentment build, and the female warrior has little to no control over her schedule.

Family and marital stability are important to successful reintegration. While any family experiences stressors associated with military members returning from deployment, there are stressors unique to the family with female military members. Depending on the roles within the family, the family may have unrealistic expectations of roles or how life may return to "normal" once their female warrior returns. Life may never return to "normal." Following deployment, there is likely a permanent change to the family equilibrium. While it is nearly impossible for any family to return to pre-deployment dynamics, the disruption of familial equilibrium may be especially strained if the marital dynamics had been fairly traditional as well. With a mother/wife returning in a more traditionally male role, the family's ability to adjust may not support such change. The female warrior may return less empathic, more outspoken, direct, and used to communicating within a military framework. This may be surprising for family members that are not used to the military. As with any system where change occurs, change is stressful. The tendency is to restore the status quo. This return to status quo may or may not be possible. The healthier a family system is, the easier it is to accommodate change. For families who have a female warrior, changes in family dynamics may have an impact. How well integrated/supported the male spouse felt during the deployment may have an impact. As previously mentioned, the more the male spouse may have felt alienated, the greater his expectations of his spouse may be upon her return. Increased expectations upon the female warrior may increase her stress reintegrating into the family. In turn, the warrior may miss deployment because of camaraderie and similar shared experiences among the peers in her unit.

Aspects that may affect reintegration with the family are the experiences the female warrior had during deployment. As mentioned earlier, sexual assault does occur during deployment. If this occurred, the victim may not have reported such an incident for fear of retribution of either her chain of command or that of her spouse and family. Such a life-changing experience may be largely unknown to the family for any number of reasons. For example, she may feel responsible, may not want to worry her family, she may not want to share because she feels ashamed or guilty, or she may have previously been raped and believes that there is no use in reporting.

However, certain aspects may play a larger-than-expected role in the deployment experience and present unanticipated secondary effects/post-deployment challenges regarding integration back into the family. Such experiences may be related to her role in combat. Females are by and large closer to combat than in the past. More now than ever, women find themselves engaged in direct combat. How well integrated or accepted into the unit was the female? Did she possess a sense of mastery over her role and the gear that was provided to her? Additionally, unit cohesion and unit morale may play a role in her coping. More specifically, the better unit morale, the better she may cope. Pride, in this instance, is of benefit.

For the benefit of those concerned, this chapter now turns its attention to practical considerations germane to improving resiliency among female warriors post-deployment.

Helping with the Reintegration

Be supportive—recognize that some of what your female warrior says may not make sense to you. Feelings are feelings and there is no need to make excuses for why one feels the way one does. Each individual within the family has a right to their feelings. Give the female warrior space. Be respectful. Increase communication about feelings and experiences, or expectations. The female warrior may not feel welcomed back or as if she belongs back in your family. This may especially be the case if the female warrior perceives that the family is functioning better in her absence. The family may need to be conscious of welcoming the warrior back into the family and find ways or areas that the warrior can integrate back in. It is important to not "dump" all the responsibility back onto the female warrior. This may cause other challenges to all who are involved. Sensitivity and communication are key to helping with the reintegration. Lack of consistency or a routine may challenge her ability to integrate back into the family. Encourage her to take advantage of supportive services such as individual and family counseling, or talking to a chaplain, to help with coping and reintegration.

Aspects Indicating a Need for Support

There are several behaviors that may indicate the need for professional help. For more in-depth understanding, please refer to chapters 4, 8, and 9 in this book. If your warrior starts to display any of the following behaviors please encourage her to seek professional help. Both the DoD and VA have numerous resources and counselors who can provide this type of assistance.

- Increased alcohol use in the form of daily use or binge drinking.
- Symptoms or signs of post-traumatic stress disorder (PTSD) such as increased startle response or vigilance.

- Not wanting to talk about events during deployment.
- Displaying symptoms or signs of mild traumatic brain injury (known as concussion) including increased forgetfulness, decreased memory, poor balance, and mild depression.
- Displaying signs of depression including sleep difficulty, or difficulty initiating or maintaining intimacy with her spouse/partner.
- An inability to nurture her children. This is may be more common with PTSD and may be more pronounced with younger children.

Impact of the Male Spouse's Experience

A male spouse may feel isolated and unsupported by the military during his wife's deployment. He may have difficulty accepting his new role within the family as well as that of his wife. This may especially be the case if the spouse has no familiarity with the military prior to his wife's deployment. Upon returning from her deployment, the female warrior may be unable to validate her spouse's experience. The female warrior may not understand the challenges her spouse or children faced and dealt with.

Other Considerations

Multiple Deployments

It tends to be the rule that all military members will deploy multiple times. Typically, the more successful deployments the family experiences, the less problematic they are expected to be. Experience—especially successful experience—tends to bolster resiliency. However, this is not always the case. There is a point at which multiple deployments and repeated separations will stress the family. In situations of multiple deployments, increased vigilance to warning signs of stressors is necessary. As well, greater attention should be paid toward encouraging practices designed to increase the emotional health of the family and its members.

Wounded Female Warriors

More women are returning from deployment with severe wounds than at any other time in our nation's history. Upon return to a medical facility, the medical care required for recovery of such wounds can take months to years, thereby extending the time that the female warrior may be away from her family. This can be especially difficult for a family that has school-aged children. The need to maintain as much consistency and routine as possible is paramount for any family dealing with a wounded service member. It may not be possible for the female warrior's family to uproot and remain close to the military medical facility or civilian hospital where she is receiving care. Not only does this extend the separation between the female warrior and her family but it also affects her own self-image, how she views herself as a nurturer, caretaker, mother, wife, sister, aunt, and so on. And, if there are additional considerations such as PTSD, this can profoundly impact her ability to integrate back into the family and reconnect with her children and her spouse.

Summary

Supporting and promoting resiliency of the female warrior and her family requires a comprehensive approach tempered with care and understanding. At a minimum, friends and family should consider the following things to support their female warrior:

- Encourage healthy, practical, and realistic definitions of success as both a warrior and a matriarch. Promote a healthy self-image in all roles.
- Get a family "health" check-up. Be honest and take a dose of preventive "medicine" to avoid an acute crisis.
- Prepare for deployment and set realistic expectations regarding separation.
- Encourage help from your extended family. However, ask them to "under-promise, over-deliver" within established boundaries.
- Reinforce the female warrior's sense of involvement. Do not allow her to feel as if she has abandoned her family or that she has been "replaced."
- Help the female warrior define a positive sense of self and purpose in her roles as both warrior and family member.
- Prepare for re-deployment and set realistic expectations regarding reunion. Discourage fantasy.
- Encourage your female warrior and your family to define your own new "normal." Do not permit societal pressures to become a burden.
- If you suspect that the female warrior has been either the victim of a crime or witness to an atrocity, encourage her to report such events to authorities.
- Be supportive, respectful, and sensitive. Communicate openly and encourage the use of existing support services when appropriate.
- Do not neglect the male stay-at-home spouse. Acknowledge his sacrifices and help him recognize both his importance and contribution.

By acknowledging and actively supporting the above actions, our female warriors and their families will prove healthier, happier, and well positioned to withstand the demands of service in a time of war.

Conclusion

The factors affecting the female warrior are no different than those affecting the male warrior; both are in the military and undergo the same deployment cycle/process. What is unique is the role the female warrior plays within her family as well as in the military. While females comprise approximately 15 percent of the military and fill combat support roles, they find themselves in combat every day. Their fellow service members must rely on them for their survival and vice versa. They are at higher risk for divorce, sexual assault, and being a single parent than their male counterparts. They are expected to disregard their gender while serving in uniform. But when they come home, society—and perhaps they and their families—expect they will assume a traditional female, maternal role. While female warriors are as competent as their male counterparts, they and their families have unique challenges and stressors related to deployment and reintegration. The challenges outlined in this chapter need to be empirically validated because the existing information available on women and deployment tends to be anecdotal. What is certain is that female warriors will continue to exist and grow in numbers. We must ensure we take the time to understand more thoroughly their unique needs and to provide supportive programs for them and their family.

References

Bushatz, A. "Study: Male Spouses Need More Support." *Military.com*. 22 February 2011. http://www.military.com/news/article/study-male-spouses-need-more-support.html (accessed 18 June 2011).

Deal, P. "Darnall Professionals Help Restore Resiliency of Sexual Assault Victims." *Fort Hood Press Center*. 13 April 2011. http://forthoodpresscenter.com/go/doc/3439/1064823 (accessed 29 June 2011).

Leland, A., and M. J. Oboroceanu. *American War and Military Operations Casualties Lists and Statistics*. Washington, DC: Congressional Research Service, 2010.

Lutton, N. *Operation Family Support—Northwest Military*. 20 January 2011. http://www.north westmilitary.com/families/support/2011/01/northwest-military-ranger-airlifter-news paper-JBLM-military-divorce-rate-support-programs/print/ (accessed 26 June 2011).

Lyles, L. L. *Military Leadership Diversity Commission*. 11 March 2011. http://mldc.whs.mil/ (accessed 19 June 2011).

Office of the Assistant Secretary of Defense for Personnel and Readiness. *Population Representation in the Military Services, Fiscal Year 2008 Report*. Center for Naval Analyses, 2009. http://ngycp.cna.org/PopRep/2008/summary/poprepsummary2008.pdf.

Schultz, P. "Sexual Assault in the Military." The Center for Deployment Psychology. 2011. http://deploymentpsych.org/topics-disorders/sexual-assault-in-the-military (accessed 20 June 2011).

Science Daily. "Women Warriors Show Resilience Similar to Men, Psychological Study Shows." 7 June 2011. http://www.sciencedaily.com/releases/2011/06/110607105336.htm (accessed 16 June 2011).

16 | Families of National Guard and Reserve Service Members

Jaine Darwin

Since the beginning of the wars in Iraq and Afghanistan, 785,000 members of the National Guard and Reserve components of all the services have deployed. This is the first time in our nation's history that citizen-soldiers have served multiple deployments. Since there is no service member without a family, these deployments and returns have impacted many of you who never thought of yourselves as military families. *Time* magazine referred to you as "suddenly military families." What is different for Reserve and National Guard family members from family members of active-duty military? What challenges are unique to your families?

Families of active-duty military usually live on military bases or in towns located near military bases, where everyone is familiar with the rhythms of the military. Everyone knows when a unit readies for deployment and when the families prepare to welcome them home. You, as Reserve and National Guard families, reside in every community, identified only if you choose to place a blue star in the window or a yellow ribbon on a tree. Your warriors may drill with a unit close to home or a unit in another state. As long as your service members can make it to a weekend drill, they may live far away from the armory where they meet each month. Some warriors may be deployed with an outfit other than their own, in what is called cross-leveling. The warrior is sent to fill a vacancy on another unit, perhaps even one based in another region of the country, so even if your family knows other families in the original unit, you will not share the deployment. Your families rarely have other families of deployed warriors living close to you. The children and younger siblings of your deployed citizen-soldiers may be the only ones in their school coping with a deployment. While spouses and children become eligible for the benefits afforded other military families, like TRICARE health insurance, providers may not be close by. In states with few active-duty military bases, families will routinely be too far away to make use of benefits like a base exchange or PX. Families may also face new financial challenges if the military pay is less than the warrior's pay from a civilian job, or if the parents shared child-care responsibilities but now either need to pay someone else to help with those responsibilities or handle it by having the remaining spouse cut back on his or her work schedule.

Pre-deployment

Currently, most citizen-soldiers are notified about an upcoming deployment many months in advance. In the early years of OEF and OIF, sometimes units mobilized with only a few days' notice. Still, much has to be done literally and emotionally for a family to be ready to cope with the ups and downs of a deployment. The first phase, called alert, is the time between the citizen-soldier receiving notice of a deployment and the time the warrior reports for the next phase, mobilization, when the outfit departs for training in the United States to ready for the actual deployment to the combat zone.

Families preparing for a first deployment may not know what to expect and may be baffled or scared by the information they receive. The deploying family member will be required to draw up a will, name insurance beneficiaries, and arrange for who will receive paychecks and information from the military. This is a significant thing to keep track of because if your service member does not put your name on the form, the military will not release any information to you. The deploying family member will be spending time preparing his equipment, receiving vaccinations, acquiring combat gear, and gradually giving up a civilian identity to become an active-duty warrior. You as family members may begin to experience a growing feeling of separation even though no one has actually left home yet.

For those of you remaining at home, you must begin to figure out what new responsibilities may come with the departure of a family member. These may be specific duties like paying the bills, doing home maintenance, or dropping off the kids at daycare. They may also be jobs that have informally been taken on, like sending birthday cards, arranging the family's social engagements, or being the go-to person for a shoulder to lean on. Will you continue with your existing health insurance or transfer to TRICARE, the insurance provided by the military during the deployment and for six months after reunion? Will you need help shoveling snow, raking leaves, or fixing the water heater? Do you know the name of the plumber, the electrician, or the mechanic who repairs your car?

Family members will be invited to attend pre-deployment briefings conducted as part of the Yellow Ribbon program, a national program with centers in every state. You will be welcomed into the wonderful world of acronyms that abound in the military, where initials are used more often than words: the lawyers are

JAGs (members of the Judge Advocate General Corps), and your deploying family member may go to a FOB (a forward operating base). You may feel like a foreign language is being spoken. Feeling overwhelmed by information is par for the course. Luckily, the military rarely says something only once so you will have more chances to make sense of all you hear.

You will learn about services available to you, like help lines such as Military OneSource, and participation in phone and e-mail chains to receive information from your family member's unit during the deployment from the COM (chain of command). National Guard units that tend to be composed of people residing in the same state may run FRGs (Family Readiness Groups). These groups meet regularly during the deployment, supplying support and information to family members and allowing family members to meet with others who are sharing the stress of the deployment. For some this will be a second, third, or even fourth deployment so they may appear less dazed. We know that each deployment, whether it is the first or fourth, challenges family members in different ways.

Challenges for the Family

Concrete Tasks

- What duties performed by the deploying family member need to be delegated to someone else to do?
- How will the family deal with finances during the deployment? What if family income is reduced? What if the income is increased?
- How will the plans for childcare change if only one parent is now home?
- Who will care for the children if the family member deploying is a single parent?
- What contingency plans are in place for emergencies?
- Who needs to be informed of the impending deployment? One might notify the family doctor, the children's teachers, and the family's clergy person.
- What is the plan for communicating with the deployed family member? This might include installing Skype on computers, acquiring phone cards, learning how to text, or to use e-mail.

Emotional Tasks

- Does the family's current style of dealing with feelings allow for the expression of fear, worry, anger, excitement, and missing a family member?
- Are family members and the service member ready to deal with the fact that they may each have different kinds of feelings? Your service member may

be eager but family members may feel scared and even hurt by the service member's excitement at leaving.

- How does each child's developmental level affect the reaction to deployment? Younger children may not be able to understand anything except that daddy or mommy is going away. Adolescents may hide their worry and feel responsible for protecting the parent who remains at home. School-age children may have sleep problems or behavior problems in school. For more information on communicating with your children see chapter 12.
- Is the family ready for the feeling that the service member may have already withdrawn emotionally even if she is still at home?

Mobilization and Deployment

On the designated day, the service member and the family will attend a deployment ceremony, which ends with the service member marching off with comrades to go to a base within the United States for training and the family coping with the first hours and days of a deployment that will last from four months to one year, depending on the branch in which the service member belongs. At that moment, the separation becomes real. Family members may report feeling numb, feeling sad, or even feeling relieved that the painful anticipation is finally over. It takes time to get used to absence, especially when the service member is so present in everyone's thoughts. These first months of training stateside, when communication remains easy, is a good time to see which plans are working and which plans may need to be adapted. The service member may find it hard to let go of old roles and may try to run the house at a distance. At the end of these months of training, the service member will leave for the duty station, which may be in the war zone. Next, you will move into a new stage called sustainment.

Sustainment

Sustainment is the time when the service member is no longer training and has moved "in country" or gone overseas. Depending on your family member's duties, this may also be a time of great worry for the safety of your loved one. At the beginning of the sustainment phase, you may feel like you are facing an unbearable length of separation with less opportunity for communication because of the differences in time zones and the unpredictable nature of schedules in a combat zone. Taking it one day at a time is helpful; marking off each day on a calendar may help remind you that there is an end in sight.

Separation is hard for everyone and there is no right way to cope. Some may scour the news on television and on the Internet, searching for any bit of information relevant to their family member. Others may want to go on as if nothing is happening. Sometimes this causes friction when different people in the same household choose opposite styles of coping. Having someone who is physically absent, but still very much on everyone's mind, is very hard. Allowing yourself to experience a full range of feelings is helpful. You can feel worried and at the same time enjoy the sense of mastery you achieve by the new tasks you have assumed since the deployment. You may feel angry and burdened, which is okay too. Thoughts in the privacy of your mind will not hurt or endanger your family member. Similarly, feeling happy is not a betrayal.

Things that May Help during Deployment

- Seeking out others with a deployed family member and talking by phone or e-mail. The director of Family Readiness for your service member's group may be able to provide introductions.
- Sending care packages. Sometimes veterans' service organizations (VSOs), like the Veterans of Foreign Wars (VFW) or the American Legion, may assist in assembling and sending these packages. Grassroots support groups in your community may also welcome your participation.
- Asking for help when you need it. For emotional help, seek out your clergy person, your physician, or a mental health professional. The VSOs are eager to help with mowing the lawn, raking the leaves, shoveling the snow, or helping get estimates to fix the leaky roof.
- Talking to children's teachers to let them know they are dealing with a deployed relative. Kids may worry as much about an aunt or uncle who is deployed as they would about a parent or sibling.
- Cutting yourself some slack. When a service member deploys, the whole family serves. You are serving on the home front so they can serve on the battlefront.

The expanded modes of communication—text, e-mail, Skype, cell phones—serve to bring the war into your living room and your living room into the war. This is both good and bad news. What do you as a family member share with your service member and what do you want your service member to share with you? For families of active-duty military, living on bases or near bases, information from the service member or from the family may be part of a collection of stories gleaned from multiple conversations with multiple families and service members. Families of National Guard and Reserve members may only have one source, so the need to receive, share, or withhold information may appear more crucial. The military may recommend not telling your service member anything that may be upsetting or may distract them from doing the mission. Each person and each family has different norms about how much is shared at any time, at home or in country. If your family norm is to share most things, then not telling may worry your service member more than telling. The warrior might be more worried by imagining what is going wrong instead of having the option of hearing and deciding not to think about it until later. Service members at war may be sleep-deprived, hungry, revved up, or spaced out. You should try not to be alarmed when your service member sounds different than usual. Another challenge for families of National Guard and Reserve warriors is not always having a family member of another deployed warrior available who might confirm that the whole outfit sounded a certain way during a specific day or week.

The communication families fear most is being notified that your service member has been wounded or killed. Luckily, many will never have to cope with this possibility. Still, most families describe feeling panicky whenever the doorbell rings unexpectedly throughout the whole sustainment phase. With the help of satellite phones, a wounded warrior can sometimes call the family before the family is notified through official channels. Generally, no news is no news, neither a good nor a bad thing. Phone and e-mail chains help assure worried family members when something may have happened. To ask you not to worry would be to ask you to do the impossible. To ask you not to live in a constant state of worry is to give you a goal to work toward.

As the deployment continues, family members will be confronted by holidays, birthdays, and both joyous and sad events that will take place without their service member. Planning ways to celebrate that include acknowledging the missing family member may help. Thinking of Christmas coming in two parts, part one when you mail packages to your warrior and the second part on Christmas day is one way of managing the feelings of missing your service member. Reaching out to friends and family and accepting the same overtures from friends and family may also work. Each holiday or event is another milestone that can remind you that the deployment will end at some point.

Most service members receive two weeks of leave at some point in the deployment. Sometimes, this leave can be scheduled to coincide with a graduation, the birth of a child, or some other special event. Sometimes the timing is more random. This mini-homecoming can be confusing and disappointing if both family members and service members are not clear about expectations and plans. Friends and family may wish to spend time with the service member and to participate in shared activities. It is equally possible that a family, where routines are running smoothly, may worry about disruption and reopening painful longings that have been put away. The service member is usually sleep-deprived, fixed on the mission and on protecting comrades. This is not a person who wants to be placed in loud, boisterous groups in the middle of a crowd.

Family members and service members must discuss plans to avoid such situations. Family members also need to prepare themselves for feeling relief at seeing the service member safe followed immediately by feelings of loss and worry when the service member departs. Allowing each person to state needs and expectations and then looking for compromises can turn the leave into the rest and refueling that both the family and the service member need. Families of National Guard and Reserve do not always know other families who can tell them about their own experiences, both to help plan and to understand that their reactions are normal.

During this long separation, both spouses and service members, in reaction to their own anxiety, can become jealous and distrustful of their partners. Yes, we have a coed military, and yes, for some couples this is the first time they are living apart. That does not mean that most people are unfaithful. Yet the worry can cast a shadow that interferes with optimal coping. Hopefully you can understand that amid the stress of combat and of single parenthood at home, you and your service member will share things with other people whom the other does not know. Service members like to talk with other service members. We say that service members have two families: the family they fight alongside and the family to which they come home. While in combat, the service member's energy and interest may be more focused on comrades than on family. Hard as this might be, you may want to work on tolerating feeling slighted or rejected.

The service member has to cope with the fact that life at home goes on without her. Again, these perspectives may be new for National Guard and Reserve families, while families of active-duty military already understand that the mission always comes first.

During the sustainment phase of the deployment, you may have discovered new abilities, strengths, and resilience of which you were previously unaware. That is a good thing about challenges. Families of active-duty military always expected deployments. For family members of National Guard and Reserve members, you had a sharp learning curve. Feel proud of your accomplishments and learn from the things that were hard. The rigors of a deployment change everyone; hopefully much of the change will be for the better. At the same time, there is no shame in having a hard time; seek out support and learn how to deal with these hard tasks and feelings.

Redeployment

To most of us, redeployment means leaving home to serve. For the military, redeployment means the troops preparing to return home after the completion of a deployment. This marks the beginning of a process of reunion and reintegration that heralds the return home of your service member and the reconstituting of your family group to include the returning service member. This is a transition for most family members from missing to anticipating. This is a time of both excitement and worry for the family and the service member. The idea of having your service member home and no longer in harm's way is wonderful. Thinking of the family being whole again and returning to sharing responsibilities is eagerly awaited. Families also have concerns. So much is heard about post-traumatic stress disorder (PTSD) that they may worry whether their family member will come back emotionally or physically wounded. For those who have learned new skills and taken on new responsibilities in running the household, they may wonder if the returning service member will be okay with these changes. The same is true for the service member: "Will the family have changed? Will the kids still recognize me? Will I be able to readjust to civilian life?"

Yellow Ribbon reintegration, a national program that has a component in every state, will invite you for a pre-return briefing. They will tell you about available benefits. National Guard and Reserve service members keep TRICARE health insurance for the first six months they are home. At the end of the six months, the service member can choose to continue to use TRICARE, but has to pay a higher premium. The service member, if they served in a combat zone, is eligible for free care at the VA for five years, or for their lifetime if they received service-connected injuries. Every returning service person is entitled to a free screening for traumatic brain injury (TBI) from the VA. This is something family members should encourage them to utilize. To maintain operational security (OPSEC), you will not know the exact date of return until several days before your service member's actual arrival in the United States. Your service member will be sent to a military base, usually the one at which he trained prior to deploying, where he will be screened for health problems, return equipment, and begin to return to civilian life. You will not be able to visit him at this base, but he will usually return home within five days of being processed.

The same guiding principles that applied to planning the two-week periods of leave apply to planning for the service member's return. Communicate about what you would like (perhaps a big party) and what your service member would like (perhaps just a hot shower and a home-cooked meal for the nuclear family). Planning large parties or meals in restaurants with noisy crowds tend to be bad ideas. When a family has been separated for up to a year for any reason, good or bad, coming back together is a process. As you plan for the return, you might want to catalogue for yourself all the changes that took place in the family during the deployment. You will be surprised at the length of the list. The list may include new babies, children who have grown several inches, relatives who became ill or died, new hobbies, new furniture, new hairdos, and new distribution of household duties. Mom may have learned to fix the leaking sink and dad may have learned to make French braids for his daughter. Similarly, the nineteen-year-old who was a screw-up may return from deployment having been responsible for a job that protected the lives of his comrades.

Reunion and Reintegration

The actual reunion will take place in a short ceremony, followed in a month or so by a more formal ceremony replete with politicians and commanding officers. While at that moment your citizen-soldier returns to civilian status, reintegrating is a long road. As one wise family member, a pro after three deployments, said, "You get your soldier home first and your husband six months later." Your service member has been in a high-stress environment for a long time, so it takes time to switch gears. You may see many behaviors that were appropriate in the combat zone but just seem weird at home.

Some of the new behaviors may include:

- Startling easily and ducking when she hears any loud noises like cars backfiring.
- Feeling edgy in open spaces when he cannot have his back to the walls. Thus going to restaurants and supermarkets can be hard.
- Wanting to keep track of everyone at all times and wishing that family members would all stay in one place.
- Driving in a zigzag pattern on the highway to try to avoid explosives.
- Getting panicky or rageful in traffic.
- Expecting everyone to do what is asked immediately.

The Army's resilience training program (http://www.resilience.army.mil) has a presentation that elaborates on some of these points. Also see chapter 7 on how you can build resiliency. Hopefully, these combat stress responses will lessen over time.

Returning service members frequently have sleep problems. In a combat zone, troops are sleep-deprived or used to sleeping only a few hours at a time. Some will avoid sleep because of nightmares. Don't be surprised to find your family member coming back from a walk at 3 a.m. She may smoke or drink too much. Younger returning family members may just want to party. Try to be patient, but also firm when behaviors are too disruptive for the rest of the family. Here again is the challenge of being a National Guard or Reserve family member. You are not surrounded by families all sharing the same experience at the same time. You are left having to guess about what is average and expectable and what is problematic.

Your service member, now a civilian, is home. What does that mean?

This period of readjustment is for getting to know each other again: How are you the same? How are you different? How do you come back together as a couple or as a family? Be as clear as you can with yourself about your expectations and then ask if your expectations are realistic. See if your returned family member can do the same and then talk with each other. Often family members want to hear about the time in combat. Returned service members may not want to talk about it or to talk only to battle buddies who shared the experience. The returned family member is surprised to find her side of the bed occupied by the children in the family who took to coming into their parent's bed during the deployment. Younger children may be hesitant to interact with the returned service person or be demanding to the point of being annoying. Returned service members often describe feeling like strangers in their own homes, and family members sometime feel that the person who came back is too different. Remember, reintegration is a process, not a discrete event.

If your service member remains in the National Guard or Reserves, he will return to monthly drilling after thirty days. Try not to feel hurt if he is so eager to be reunited with his comrades. Within the first three drill weekends, families will be included in one of them. You will be invited to participate in seminars as part of the Yellow Ribbon program. The military will pay for a hotel room and encourage you to learn more about benefits and about coping. One of my personal favorites is a class taught by a chaplain for unmarried soldiers in Massachusetts called "How Not to Marry a Jerk." This is aimed at younger soldiers with accrued money from combat pay and high spirits about being home again. Make sure to let your service member know you want to be included. For couples, the chaplaincy runs weekend programs for couples to facilitate communications after deployment. The National Guard program is called "Strong Bonds" and has been helpful to couples who have attended. They are also starting to run programs for unmarried soldiers and their family members for the same purpose.

Only in the National Guard and Reserve can someone expect to make the transition from soldier to civilian overnight. The returned civilian will have to return to work or find a job after the deployment. If the ex–service member returns to an old job, she will have to readjust to a place where life went on without her for a whole year. She may be baffled by new policies and procedures and feel as if she no longer fits in. Under the Uniformed Services Employment and Reemployment Act (USERRA), by law her place of work is required to hold the job or to give her a comparable job upon return. In this economy, coming back to no job is also difficult. Networking with veterans' service organizations and finding work sites that support vets may help. The GI Bill provides tuition and living subsidies for vets who want to return to school. Seeking out schools that have programs to support returning veterans or have veterans' clubs may make reentry easier. Many veterans find it hard to cope with what they see as the frivolous attitudes of other college students. They may have trouble concentrating or have their combat stress triggered by sounds and crowds on campus. Family members can help by being supportive and encouraging them to make use of support networks. (See chapter 13 about how you can help your service member look for a job or go to school after military service.)

For many returning service members, the transition from soldier to citizen will have a few bumps in the road, but generally proceed smoothly. For others, the transition is problematic. As family members, you will probably be the first to spot trouble. These troubles may include drinking too much, overuse of prescription drugs, angry outbursts, moodiness, social isolation, symptoms of PTSD and/or TBI, and, most seriously, suicidal behavior. Urge or insist that your family member seek help at the VA, the Vet Center, online sites, their primary care provider, a clergy person, or from anyone they trust. See chapter 4 about injuries and chapter 8 about suicide.

Members of the National Guard and the Reserves go back and forth from service member to veteran and, if they redeploy, back to being a service member. Each deployment allows family members to apply what they learned during the earlier deployment(s) and to face new hurdles. Each return allows family members to grow, learn, and face new challenges. You and your service member are important participants in our new volunteer military. Thank you and your family member for your service to our country.

Unmarried Partners and Blended Families

17

Jaine Darwin

The new military is just catching up with the concept of the modern family. The military family is no longer just a stay-at-home mother and several children who pack up and move to a new base every three years. Our volunteer military is co-ed, so we now have fathers who stay home with the kids and single mothers who are serving. With the large influx of activated National Guard and Reserve component troops, we have older people serving so grandma or grandpa might deploy. More people are living in domestic relationships without formally marrying, and many in our military are divorced and remarried so they have blended families. The sub-heading of this chapter could be: "If it's not in writing, you don't exist." When a warrior deploys, informal or de facto arrangements have no standing with the military.

When a warrior deploys, he will write a will, designate someone to have power of attorney, assign beneficiaries for insurance benefits, and indicate with whom the military may share information. Some family members (i.e., parents of younger soldiers, ex-spouses, fiancées, or life partners) may not even know that they need to step in before the service members deploys to make sure they will have rights during and after the deployment.

Divorced, blended, and merged families may become disrupted because informal arrangements that allowed for easy co-parenting do not work when the other parent is in combat. Very young spouses may not understand the wish by the parents of the service member to stay actively involved in raising the kids. Single parents, who normally juggle to keep the family running smoothly while based at home and living with the family, may be swamped by how to arrange child care during a deployment.

Problems anticipated are problems that usually can be averted. This chapter will describe some of the problems that may arise when a service member transitions home to her unmarried, blended, and other "unwritten" family and how these types of families can try to avert these problems.

Parents

Let us start with the role of parents with whom a younger warrior might have lived up until enlistment or deployment. While as parents you have emotional ties, when your warrior deploys you have only the legal ties your child allows. When parents and service members have good relationships, the service member will easily include parents in pre-deployment briefings, allowing you to receive all relevant information. You may be very helpful to your adult child as he makes plans to depart and figures out what responsibilities need to be met during the deployment. Who will pay the car insurance or the cell phone bill? Who may ride the motorcycle in the warrior's absence? Who does he want to name to make medical decisions if he becomes disabled? Who will be the beneficiary of death benefits? The last two are of major importance and may be hard for young adults to imagine, but they must do this in order to make good decisions.

The thought of the loss of your child in combat is unbearable for most parents to consider. These worries may cause stress in the marriage of the parents as each of you copes in your own way with this painful possibility. Young service members may be fairly intolerant of a crying mother—a frequent sight at a deployment ceremony, or on the phone during a deployment. However you may feel about your service member's current girlfriend or boyfriend, you will do better if you have good relationships with him or her. Girlfriends and boyfriends are more likely to hear from your service member during deployment than you. Feeling resentful of these relationships is understandable. The most important thing is to make sure your offspring has listed you as one of the people to be contacted with any information coming from this command. Without this permission, you have no standing in the eyes of the military and will not be informed about good things like leaves and homecomings or bad things like injuries. You may want to look for local chapters of Blue Star Mothers and Blue Star Fathers, which are national organizations of people with children who are serving or who have served. Group members can offer many helpful tips and provide emotional support and validation for what you are feeling.

As a parent of a warrior you struggle with reconciling the wish to protect your child and the understanding that your child is going off to war to protect all of us. Younger siblings of deploying service members may still be living at home with the parents. They too may be profoundly impacted by the deployment, yet ineligible for services from the military. Parents of service members may want to inform the schools and pediatricians of the siblings of the service member that they have an older sibling in combat.

Parents and siblings may have a hard time when a young service member returns from deployment. Often the service member wants to seek out friends and party as a way of decompressing, leaving the parents and siblings standing at the door. Service members may have accrued large amounts of combat pay and be behaving in ways that upset the family. Tact is required to find the line between understanding and not tolerating behavior that goes against family values. Negotiating issues of moving into adulthood are hard when done against the backdrop of going to and returning from war. Parents also serve as good monitors of how a young service member is readjusting. You will know if your service member's drinking has increased or if she has become more withdrawn. You may still be the person who encourages your service member to make use of the GI Bill benefits and attend or return to school (see chapter 13 in this book about educational benefits).

Unmarried Partners

How much you love your service member is irrelevant in the eyes of the military, as is the distinction about whether you are a fiancée, part of a serious couple, or even a domestic partner. You do not have any legal standing. Your access to any information and any interaction with the support services depends on your partner granting permission for you to be on the contact list. You are ineligible for any benefits that go to spouses. Your partner can grant you power of attorney so you can manage his finances while he serves or he could name you as a beneficiary. Some couples choose to marry before the service member's deployment to end this ambiguity but we do not recommend marrying just for this purpose. Many partners find deployment a lonely time because they may not know other friends with deployed partners and they may feel they have little in common with spouses with children. Still, partners will benefit from reaching out to spouses in their partner's unit. These spouses can be an excellent source of information, formal and informal, about what is happening. They will also be a good conduit to help include you in meetings and unit-related events. Were your service member to be hurt, it is unclear whether the military would transport you to your loved one's bedside as they would a spouse or parent. Just as I urged parents to be friendly to their children's partners, I urge you to be friendly to your partner's family members. They are probably the people who understand best what you are enduring.

If you and your service member have children together, your children are eligible for services like medical insurance, but you will not be covered. If you are the partner of a member of the National Guard or Reserve component service member, this may be very confusing. You may have been covered as a domestic partner by private health insurance, but this is not possible with military insurance. This may necessitate buying your own health insurance for the eighteen months your partner and your children are covered by TRICARE. If you live together with children that are biologically yours but not your partner's, these children deal with the emotional hardships of deployment and return without necessarily receiving any help from the military.

Blended or Merged Families

Managing blended or merged families is a skill at any time. Deployment and return can highlight the harmony or act like a laser pointer to show unresolved areas of discord within your family. The disparity between what is in the divorce agreement and what has happened in practice may cause problems. Issues of custody and visitation come first. Usually, if a parent who has primary custody deploys, the child goes to live with the other biological parent, even if the child is currently living with the primary-custody parent and a step-parent. While this disrupts the child's routine and may necessitate changing schools, the step-parent is not the guardian of the child. The ex-spouses have the option of choosing a different course, but must consider what would happen if the deploying parent becomes disabled or dies during or as a result of service. Usually the other biological parent would assume full custody. In a family with both step and biological children, the biological child of the service member may be eligible for different benefits than her siblings.

What happens to visitation? One problem that appears is when a parent who had weekend visitation deploys. Will the step-parent continue to see the child on weekends? How will visits be maintained with half-siblings who live with the step-parent? Will the child-support arrangement change if the child's place of residence changes? Certainly in families with cordial relationships with ex-spouses, things may run smoothly. When friction already exists, a deployment can cause real tensions that are not helpful to anyone. If the divorce and custody agreements do not offer sufficient guidance or protection for the emotional stability of the children, then this is the time to consult an attorney to update the custody agreement. You might also consult an attorney to see if the divorce agreement requires that an ex-spouse remain as the beneficiary of a life insurance policy. The current spouse should be aware and prepared for this.

Again, we face questions of who gets notified of what when things happen during deployment. A deploying parent who may be remarried but does not have primary custody of children from the first marriage needs to make it possible for both his current spouse and his ex-spouse to obtain information during the deployment. This is a time when we hope everyone can behave maturely, even if stress elicits someone's worst behavior. Keep in mind that step-children may care deeply for a deployed step-parent. This may be hard for the biological father to acknowledge if the step-father deploys, or for the biological children who want to think this is only their loss.

Grandparents and Extended Family

My most surprising moment came at a deployment ceremony when I asked a little girl who she was saying good-bye to that day and she replied, "Grandma." We see grandparents going to war today mainly because of the multiple deployments of National Guard and Reserve where older service members may continue to serve in uniform. Aunts, uncles, and cousins are also going on deployments. Any deployment may affect multiple generations. Families may have to figure out how each child is dealing at each stage of life. Kids may be surprised by how preoccupied a parent becomes with a sister, brother, or parent in combat.

Parents may not realize how attached a child is to a favorite aunt or uncle. Everyone may be astounded at how unprepared they are to have grandpa back in uniform. Some family members may feel resentful when an older relative deploys multiple times. They may have "put up" with drill weekends and summer camps, but are unwilling to cope with the upset of waiting for them to return from war. Sometimes young service members are able to rely on grandparents who serve as important role models and confidants.

When an extended family member returns on leave or comes home at the end of the deployment, it is hard to resist the urge to immediately go and see them. The service member may need some time to adjust before seeing groups of well-meaning but boisterous relatives.

Conclusion

The essence of being a member of a group without a category when a service member deploys is that you matter, but you do not count. You will have to work harder to be included in activities traditionally attended by spouses and children. You will do well to seek out support groups in the community. Many communities have a number of groups that meet monthly that both support our troops by sending care packages and phone cards and support family members of those who serve. Veterans' service organizations (VSOs) like the Veterans of Foreign Wars (VFW) and the American Legion may also provide support and understanding. Siblings and step-children may want to check out an organization called Speak Out for Military Kids, which trains kids to do outreach to raise awareness about the challenges of being a military family (http://www.operationmilitarykids.org/public/somk.aspx). This is a group made up of military and non-military kids who are empathic to the challenges you are facing.

The military is trying to catch up to the new modern family. Until they do, you have to make sure you get heard.

Appendix: Resources for Your Family

Hundreds of books, Web pages, and other sources of information can provide you and your family with information, guidance, and suggestions. Scores of veterans' service organizations (VSOs) can also help you. All of the authors of this book were asked to recommend the resources (including Web pages, books, videos, VSOs and other organizations) that they thought would be the most useful for you and your family. This appendix is a compilation of their recommendations.

While the information you can gain from these resources will be helpful, your family and service member must make the effort to reach out to them, continue to follow up with them, take action with their recommendations, and seek out additional resources. The information presented in this appendix can also become outdated as things change over time—Web pages may change, organizations may disband, new organizations may form, laws may change, and new materials may be released—so you will need to keep yourself up to date. And as we mentioned in the introduction to this book, many of the organizations and Web pages listed in this appendix have been overwhelmed by the sheer number of service members in the transition process and the demands that they have placed on the system. Many families have expressed frustration or disappointment with these organizations and Web pages. We thus remind you to consider this appendix as a list of some tools—and a partial one at that—that you can draw from to use, but remember that they will not address all your needs or answer all of your questions. Use this list as a starting point and continue to reach out to other places and learn about more sources through your own contacts and research. The only one who has your family's best interest at heart is you, so you will need to become your family's main advocate.

We also offer this caution: A number of unscrupulous individuals have used our nation's desire to help service members and their families to create online scams that give money to themselves rather than to veteran families, or that make promises to veteran families (for educational programs, credit relief, etc.) and then fail to deliver. All of the resources listed in this section have been vetted by this book's authors as legitimate and helpful. Nevertheless, you should always be careful; if something sounds too good to be true, it probably is. Before you give your money or support to any group, be sure to check them out. Contact a reputable VSO (like one of the ones listed in this appendix) or ask other military families about their experiences with the group.

We thank you for your family's service to this nation and wish you the best of luck with using these resources.

Suicide Prevention

As discussed in chapter 8, we have seen an increase in the number of suicides among returning service members. Here are some resources you can contact with questions about suicide (or if you or someone you know may be suicidal):

- *The Veterans Crisis Line* is run by the Suicide Prevention Action Network and provides free, confidential support for veterans and their families and friends twenty-four hours a day: (800) 273-TALK (8255), http://www.veteranscrisisline.net, or by sending a text message to 838255.
- *The VA's Resource Locater for Suicide Help*: http://www.veteranscrisisline.net/GetHelp/ResourceLocator.aspx.
- *The DoD/VA Suicide Outreach Center*: http://www.suicideoutreach.org.
- *The Army's Suicide Prevention Program* includes the Web site for suicide policy and programs: http://www.armyg1.army.mil/hr/suicide, and the Army's Public Health Command resources for suicide prevention: http://phc.amedd.army.mil/topics/healthyliving/bh/Pages/SuicidePreventionEducation.aspx.
- The Navy's Suicide Prevention Program: http://www.suicide.navy.mil.

Important Web Sites and Resources for Families

- *Military OneSource* is recommended by many of our authors as a virtual one-stop center for information for military families. If you have difficulty finding services or are overwhelmed by the number of services in your area, this is a useful resource: http://www.militaryonesource.mil or http://www.militaryonesource.com, and (800) 342-9647.
- *MilitaryHOMEFRONT* is the official DoD Web site for official Military Community and Family Policy (MC&FP) program information including family centers, financial management, child and youth programs, family advocacy, new parent support, relocation assistance, spouse employment, and general counseling. The site is designed to help troops and their families, leaders, and service providers: http://www.militaryhomefront.dod.mil.
- *TRICARE* provides health care to military members and their families. All active-duty families are eligible for TRICARE, and those in the Reserves or National Guard may be eligible if they have a service member either deployed or who recently returned home from a deployment: http://www.tricare.mil.

- *The Department of Veterans Affairs (VA)* maintains an extensive Web site. The main Web site is http://www.va.gov/. The General Benefits Information number is (800) 827-1000. Healthcare eligibility information is at (877) 222-VETS (8387).

- *VA Vet Centers:* The VA has three hundred vet centers around the country. Find the one closest to you at http://www.vetcenter.va.gov/, or through the call center at (877) WAR-VETS (927-8387).

- *The VA's Returning Service Members Site* for members of the recent conflicts: http://www.oefoif.va.gov/.

- *My HealtheVet* is the way to manage your VA health care needs online: http://www.myhealth.va.gov/.

- *State Departments of Veterans Affairs:* Locate your state's resources at: http://www.nasdva.net/.

- *The Defense Centers of Excellence for Psychological Health and Traumatic Brain Injury* (run by the DoD and VA) conduct research and disseminate information on military mental health and psychological injuries: http://www.dcoe.health.mil/.

- *The Yellow Ribbon Reintegration Program* has information for Reservists and members of the National Guard and their families: http://www.yellowribbon.mil/.

- *After Deployment* is a Web site with pages on mental wellness and other health issues for military families with common post-deployment problems, such as stress, anger, depression, and relationship issues: http://www.afterdeployment.org/.

- *Courage to Care* provides electronic fact sheets on health topics relevant to military life. They were developed by leading military health experts from the Uniformed Services University of the Health Sciences: http://www.usuhs.mil/psy/courage.html.

- *Support Your Vet* was created by Iraq and Afghanistan Veterans of America, with information for family and friends of OIF/OEF veterans about reintegration after deployment as well as personal stories and a place to post thoughts and experiences: http://www.supportyourvet.org/.

- *The National Caregiver Support Phone Line* has social workers who can answer your questions and connect you to the Caregiver Support Coordinator at your local VA Medical Center: http://www.caregiver.va.gov/, or (855) 260-3274.

- *The National Call Center for Homeless Veterans:* http://www.va.gov/HOMELESS/, or (877) 4AIDVET (424-3838).

- *Coaching into Care* provides free telephone-based coaching for families and friends to help them encourage veterans to seek care: (888) 823-7458.

- *The Substance Abuse and Mental Health Services Administration (SAMHSA)* has a comprehensive resource list for military members, veterans, and their families: http://www.samhsa.gov/vets.

- *The American Red Cross* runs its "Coming Home Series" throughout its local chapters and provides other resources and services for military families: http://www.redcross.org/.

- *The Real Warriors Campaign* has a Web page for families and also provides 24/7 help and a message board for family members: http://www.realwarriors.net/family/, and (866) 966-1020.

- *The National Alliance on Mental Illness (NAMI)* has a Web site dedicated to service members and their families: http://www.nami.org/veterans/.

Veterans' Service Organizations

VSOs perform many critical roles for service members and their families: In addition to helping you network with others in your situation, they also can provide you with resources and guidance while they lobby and advocate for your needs. We highly recommend contacting the groups that apply to your family's situation, joining them, attending their meetings, reading their publications, and contacting them regularly for their information and resources.

The list of all VSOs is at http://www.va.gov/ogc/apps/accreditation/index.asp. Some of the largest and most respected ones are:

- American Veterans (AMVETS): http://www.amvets.org/.
- American Veterans with Brain Injuries: http://www.avbi.org/.
- Association of the U.S. Army: http://www.ausa.org/.
- Brain Injury Association of America: http://www.biausa.org/.
- Disabled American Veterans: http://www.dav.org/.
- Family Caregiver Alliance: http://www.caregiver.org/caregiver/jsp/home.jsp/.
- Military Officers' Association of America: http://www.moaa.org/.
- National Family Caregivers Association: http://www.thefamilycaregiver.org/.
- National Military Family Association: http://www.nmfa.org/.
- United States Naval Institute: http://www.usni.org/.
- Veteran Caregiver: http://www.veterancaregiver.com/.
- The Wounded Warrior Project: http://www.woundedwarriorproject.org/.

Other Organizations and Resources for Military Families

- *The Coming Home Project* provides compassionate care, support, education, and stress management tools for Iraq and Afghanistan veterans, service members, their families, and their service providers: http://www.cominghomeproject.net/.
- *A Different Kind of Courage: Safeguarding and Enhancing Your Psychological Health* is an educational DVD depicting how service members and their families may be affected by combat and deployment stress: http://www.mentalhealthscreening.org/programs/military/resources/a-different-kind-of-courage.aspx.
- *Give an Hour* provides free psychotherapy to military families and returning service members: http://www.giveanhour.org/.
- *The Leader's Guide for Managing Marines in Distress* is designed to provide guidance and tools to leaders on what to look for, what to do, and specific resources for helping Marines who are in distress: http://www.usmc-mccs.org/LeadersGuide. The Navy has a similar book called *The Navy Leader's Guide for Managing Sailors in Distress*: http://www.nmcphc.med.navy.mil/lguide.
- *Medal of Honor Program*: Thirty of the ninety-one living Medal of Honor recipients have joined in a public service campaign in which they share their experiences and spread one simple message: "Don't let the enemy defeat you at home! Get help if you need it!" http://www.medalofhonorspeakout.org/.
- *Operation Comfort* provides free psychotherapy to military families and returning service members: http://www.operationcomfort.org/.

- *Operation Enduring Families* is a family education curriculum for OEF/OIF veterans and their families: http://www.ouhsc.edu/oef.
- *Operation Save Our Troops* provides services and resources to support the morale and the well-being of military families: http://www.osotamerica.org/.
- *A Reintegration Action Plan: A Guide for Returning Service Personnel* is published by the state of Alabama but useful for any service member in any state: http://www.alabama returningveterans.org/.
- *Strategic Outreach to Families of All Reservists*: http://www.sofarusa.org/.
- *Together We Served* is a Web site that helps you find and reconnect with other service members: http://www.togetherweserved.com/.
- *United Service Organization (USO)* works to lift the spirits of service members and their families: http://www.uso.org/.

Resources for Families of Injured Warriors

- *Courage to Care, Courage to Talk about War Injuries* was developed by the Center for the Study of Traumatic Stress. It has information for providers and families about TBI and war injury: http://www.couragetotalk.org/index.php.
- *Cover Me* is a DVD produced by the Injured Marine Semper Fi Fund, encouraging warriors to seek care for mental health problems. It does contain some graphic images of combat: http://semperfifund.org/resources.
- *The Defense and Veterans Brain Injury Center* is an information clearing house on TBI: http://www.dvbic.org/.
- *The Family of a Vet* is a Web site that provides information for families of service members with TBI or PTSD: http://www.familyofavet.org/.
- *InTransition* is a voluntary and confidential program to support service members and veterans that offers a personal coach, resources, and tools: http://www.health.mil/ intransition/.
- *Medicare Resources for Caregivers*: http://www.medicare.gov/caregivers/index.html.
- *Mental Health America* (formerly known as the National Mental Health Association) promotes mental health wellness: http://www.mentalhealthamerica.net/.
- *Military Pathways* has mental health information and a referral program offered to families and service members affected by deployment: http://www.MilitaryMentalHealth .org/.
- *The Military Severely Injured Support Hotline* is available twenty-four hours a day: (888) 774-1361.
- *The Military Veteran's PTSD Manual* is published by a disabled Vietnam veteran. Parts of the book are available online. The book contains a lot of practical information about how to work with the VA to obtain assistance, including the types of forms and documentation that will be required and how to navigate the system: http://www.ptsd manual.com/.
- *National Alliance on Mental Illness*: http://www.nami.org/veterans, and (800) 950-6264. Specific information on post-traumatic stress disorder (PTSD) treatment and recovery is available at: http://www.nami.org/PTSD.

- *The National Center for Post-Traumatic Stress Disorder*: http://www.ncptsd.va.gov/.
- *The National Resource Directory for Wounded Warriors* is an online tool for wounded, ill, and injured troops, veterans, and their families, and provides access to more than 11,000 services and resources at the national, state, and local levels: http://www .nationalresourcedirectory.org/.
- *The Navy Safe Harbor* was created to provide information and non-medical care for seriously wounded, ill, and injured sailors, coast guardsmen, and their families: http://www.public.navy.mil/bupers-npc/support/safe_harbor/Pages/default.aspx, (877) 746-8563, or safeharbor@navy.mil.
- *Picking up the Pieces after TBI: A Guide for Family Members*: http://www.la publishing.com/blog/wp-content/uploads/2009/08/TIRR-Picking-up-the-pieces.pdf.
- *REACH (Reaching Out to Educate and Assist Caring, Healthy Families) Program* is a multifamily group psycho-educational program for service members and veterans living with PTSD and their families. The entire curriculum is available for free download: http://www.ouhsc.edu/REACHProgram.
- *Returning from the War Zone: A Guide for Families* is a video created by the National Center for PTSD: http://www.ptsd.va.gov/public/reintegration/returning_from_the_ war_zone_guides.asp.
- *S.A.F.E. (Support and Family Education) Program: Mental Health Facts for Families* is a curriculum for people who care about someone who has a mental illness or PTSD: http://www.ouhsc.edu/safeprogram.
- *Team Up to Facilitate Functioning (TUFF)* is a series of interactive brochures for treatment of post-concussive symptoms in returning veterans with a history of traumatic brain injury: http://www.mirecc.va.gov/VISN16/providers/TUFF.asp.
- *Traumatic Brain Injury: The Journey Home* is a Web site filled with information that was created by the Defense and Veterans Brain Injury Center (DVBIC) and offers information to caregivers of veterans and service members who sustained a moderate, severe, or penetrating TBI: http://www.traumaticbraininjuryatoz.org/.
- *The Traumatic Brain Injury National Resource Center* has fact sheets and other information about TBI as well as books, DVDs, and assessment tools at http://www.neuro .pmr.vcu.edu/.
- *Traumatic Brain Injury: A Guide for Caregivers of Service Members and Veterans* can be downloaded or ordered at: http://www.traumaticbraininjuryatoz.org/Caregivers-Journey/Caregiver-Guides.aspx.
- *The VA Caregiver Support Program*: http://www.caregiver.va.gov/.
- *The VA TBI/Polytrauma System of Care* has information for those with TBI and other injuries: http://www.polytrauma.va.gov/.
- *The Warrior Care Blog*: http://www.warriorcare.dodlive.mil/.
- *The Wounded Warrior Resource Center*: http://www.woundedwarriorproject.org/pro grams/wwp-resource-center.aspx, or (800) 997-2586.

Resources for Families of Service Members with Children

Resources for Parents

- *The American Academy of Pediatrics* has a site of videos and documents to help military youth understand deployment and reintegration: http://www2 .aap.org/sections/uniformedservices/deployment/videos.html.
- *American Association of School Administrators Toolkit: Supporting the Military Child*: http://www.aasa.org/content.aspx?id=9008.
- *Courage to Care, Courage to Talk about War Injuries* was developed by the Center for the Study of Traumatic Stress and contains information about talking to children about war injuries: http://www.couragetotalk.org/index.php.
- *Defense Center of Excellence's Children of Military Service Members Resource Guide*: http://www.dcoe.health.mil/Content/Navigation/Documents/DCoE%20Children %20of%20Military%20Service%20Members%20Resource%20Guide.pdf.
- *Helping Children Cope with Deployments and Reunions*: http://www.realwarriors.net/ family/children.
- *Military K-12 Partners*: A collaboration between the DoD and the Department of Education to ease transitions of military youth: http://www.militaryk12 partners.dodea.edu/.
- *Military Kids' Bill of Rights*: http://www.nmfa.org/site/DocServer/Military_Child_Bill _of_Rights5-08.pdf?docID=13201.
- *National Child Traumatic Stress Network's* Military Children and Youth Resource Page: http://nctsn.org/nccts/nav.do?pid=ctr_top_military.
- *Operation Child Care* for National Guard and Reservists: http://www.childcareaware. org/en/operationchildcare.
- *Operation Purple* is a program of free summer camps run by the National Association of Military Families for military youth: http://www.militaryfamily.org/.
- *Operation Military Kids*: http://www.operationmilitarykids.org/.
- *Salute Our Services* sends a free personalized card to military children: http://www .saluteourservices.org/.
- *Students at the Center* is a resource for families, the military, and schools: http://www .militaryk12partners.dodea.edu/studentsAtTheCenter.
- *SOAR (Student Online Achievement Resources)*: http://www.soarathome.com/.
- *Tackling Tough Topics: An Educator's Guide to Working with Military Kids*: http://www .operationmilitarykids.org/resources/ToughTopics%20BookletFINAL.pdf.
- *Veteran Parenting Toolkits* was created by the Oklahoma City VA Family Mental Health Program: http://www.ouhsc.edu/VetParenting.
- *Young Children on the Homefront* is a place where military families share their unique deployment experiences, and where professionals offer tips and strategies for dealing with difficult issues such as grief and loss from deployment and the challenges that often arise upon reunification: http://www.zerotothree.org/about-us/funded-projects/ military-families/children-on-the-homefront.html.
- *Welcome Back Parenting: A Guide for Reconnecting Families after Military Deployment*: http://www.welcomebackparenting.org/.

- *We Serve, Too: A Toolkit about Military Teens*: http://www.militaryfamily.org/assets/2010-Teen-Toolkit-PDF.pdf.
- *Zero to Three* supports families with babies and toddlers affected by a military parent's deployment, injury, or death: http://www.zerotothree.org/.

Resources for Your Children
- *Army Reserve Child and Youth Service's Online Teen Deployment Class*: http://www.arfp.org/teenclasses.
- *The Military Child Education Coalition* is an organization that helps military families, schools, and communities with the challenges that school-age children of military families face: http://www.militarychild.org/.
- *Military Kids Connect*: http://www.militarykidsconnect.com/.
- *Military Teen Online*, an online community that offers support for teens: http://www.militaryteenonline.com/.
- *National Guard Family Program*: http://www.guardfamily.org/.
- *National Guard Youth Program*: http://www.guardfamilyyouth.org/.
- *The Price of Peace* is a song by two military teens about deployment: http://www.priceofpeace.org/ or http://www.nationalguard.com/priceofpeace.
- *Sesame Street* has videos and other resources for your children at: http://www.sesameworkshop.org/our-impact/our-stories/military-families.html.
- *Military Families Near and Far* is created by Sesame Street and the Electric Company: http://www.familiesnearandfar.org/login/.
- *Talk, Listen, Connect: Deployments, Homecomings, Changes* are Sesame Street DVDs for families with youth ages two to five, available at http://www.militaryonesource.org/ or at http://www.sesameworkshop.org/.
- *Youth Coping with Military Deployment: Promoting Resilience in Your Family* is a video from Operation Purple summer camp with interviews with military kids. *Mr. Poe and Friends* is a video about deployment for elementary-school children. Both were made by the American Academy of Pediatrics and are at: http://www2.aap.org/sections/uniformedservices/deployment/index.html.
- *Tutor.com* (free online tutoring): http://www.tutor.com/military-programs.
- *Young Heroes: Military Deployment through the Eyes of Youth* is a video created by teens of the New Jersey Operation Military Kids' Speak out for Military Kids Program explaining the deployment cycle: http://www.operationmilitarykids.org/public/somk.aspx.
- *VA Kids*: http://www.va.gov/kids.

Resources on Building Resilience in Your Family
- *Military Family Support Centers*: Each branch of the military has a community service or family support center.
  - *Army Community Service (ACS)*: (877) 811-ARMY or http://www.myarmyonesource.com/.
  - *Navy's Fleet and Family Support Center (FFSC)*: http://www.cnic.navy.mil/CNIC_HQ_Site/WhatWeDo/FleetAndFamilyReadiness/FamilyReadiness/FleetAndFamilySupportProgram/index.htm.

– *Marine Corps Community Services (MCCS)*: http://www.usmc-mccs.org/family.
– *Coast Guard Family Advocacy Program*: http://www.uscg.mil/worklife/family_advo cacy.asp.
* *Warrior Mind Training* is available to help your service member learn resilience at http://warriortraining.us/.
* *Comprehensive Soldier Fitness (CSF)* provides service members and family members with the physical and mental skills required for optimal performance and well-being. CSF is an integrated resilience-building program developed by the Army in collaboration with researchers in positive psychology and resilience-building. The CSF Resilience for Family Members has Family Resilience Training Modules online for spouses of service members to help prepare for deployment and the post-deployment transition. CSF offers Post-Deployment Resilience Training for Spouses/ Couples. Initially developed for the Army community, CSF has been adapted for use by the Air Force, Navy, and Marines: http://csf.army.mil/.
* *The Human Performance Resource Center* is a Web site that can help your family build resiliency. It is a Department of Defense initiative that translates and disseminates scientifically based information on physical fitness, nutrition/supplements, family and relationships, mind tactics, environmental factors, and total force fitness to commanders, service members, family members, medical personnel, and researchers for human performance optimization: http://www.hprc-online.org.
* *The Joint Family Support Assistance Program (JFSAP)* augments existing family programs to provide support and services with a primary focus on families who are geographically dispersed from military installations: http://www.militaryhomefront.dod .mil/.
* *After Deployment* is a Web site that has self-assessment tests on marital satisfaction, perceived social support, parenting confidence, and other areas. The results from the self-assessment may help you and your family identify areas where you are doing well, as well as areas for improvement: http://www.afterdeployment.org/.
* *The Military Pathways Program*, available online or over the phone, provides free, anonymous mental health and alcoholism self-assessments for family members and service personnel in all branches including the National Guard and Reserves: http:// www.militarymentalhealth.org/welcome.aspx.
* *Building Resilient Kids* is a course for school personnel focused on building resilience among students from military families, and was created by the Johns Hopkins Bloomberg School of Public Health's Military Child Initiative: http://www.jhsph.edu/ mci/training_course.
* *Army Strong Bonds Couples Training* is a couples' training program provided by the Army to service members and their significant others. The program, led by a chaplain, aims to improve individual and family resilience by having couples go on a weekend retreat where they can receive relationship education and skills training: http://www.strongbonds.org/.
* *Families Overcoming Under Stress (FOCUS)* is a family-focused resilience initiative that was developed by the Navy and researchers at the Semel Institute at the University of California–Los Angeles. FOCUS is an evidenced-based program that helps military family members address military-specific stressors such as deployment, reintegration issues, and service members returning from deployments with mental health concerns: http://www.focusproject.org/.

Resources about Addictions

- *Alcoholics Anonymous*: To find meetings in your area: (212) 870-3400, or http://www
.aa.org/.
- *Al-Anon Family Groups*: (800) 344-2666, and http://www.al-anon.alateen.org/.
- *The Army's Substance Abuse Program*: http://pubssod1.acsap.hqda.pentagon.mil/sso/
pages/index.jsp.
- *Narcotics Anonymous*: (818) 773-9999, or http://www.na.org/.
- *Nar-Anon Family Group Headquarters*: (800) 477-6291, or http://www.nar-anon.org/.
A list of meetings can be found at: http://www.nar-anon.org/Nar-Anon/Nar-Anon_
Groups.html.
- *The U.S. Centers for Disease Control and Prevention* provides useful information on
alcohol use and abuse. Information on alcohol use can be found at http://www.cdc
.gov/alcohol/.

Resources on Education for Transitioning Service Members

- *The Student Veterans of America*: http://www.studentveterans.org/.
- *The Student Veteran Project* provides free supported education services for any veteran
in college or returning to college: http://www.uta.edu/ssw/research/veterans-project
.php.

The colleges listed below offer programs geared for service members transitioning into
college.

- *Cleveland State University Veteran Student Success Program*: http://www.csuohio.edu/
studentlife/vikingvets/services.html.
- *Virginia Commonwealth University VETS in College program* for service members with
spinal cord injury or traumatic brain injury: http://www.worksupport.com/VETS/
index.cf.
- *Arkansas State University Beck Pride Center for Wounded Veterans*: http://www2.astate
.edu/cpi/beckpride/.
- *The University of Kansas Consumers as Providers Project* for veteran mental health consumers: http://www.socwel.ku.edu/mentalhealth/projects/value/cap.shtml.

Resources on Employment for Transitioning Service Members

- *Corporate Gray* is the publisher of the *From Army Green/Navy Blue/Air Force Blue to
Corporate Gray* books and has a step-by-step transition guide online. They also sponsor career fairs for service members and have other information for service members
seeking employment: http://www.corporategray.com/.
- *Employment Incentives* lists information about incentives and accommodations for
organizations that hire employees with disabilities: http://www.employmentincen-
tives.com/.
- *FedsHireVets* is the Office of Personnel Management's Web site for information about
how service members and their family members can obtain federal employment:
http://www.fedshirevets.gov/index.aspx.

- *The Job Accommodation Network* can provide you with information about getting a job or going back to school with a disability. They also have an extensive database of accommodations of all types of disabilities and information that you can provide to a potential employer: http://www.askjan.org/.
- *Military-to-Civilian Crosswalk*: Enter in a Military Occupational Specialty (MOS) and the program will check the Department of Labor's O*NET to offer recommendations of civilian jobs that use these skills: http://www.onetonline.org/crosswalk.
- *One-Stop Centers* are local centers operated by the Department of Labor that will provide information, guidance, and leads for those seeking employment. Locate the closest one at http://www.careeronestop.org/ReEmployment/Veterans/. To locate a Disabled Veterans Outreach Program specialist (DVOP) or Local Veterans Employment Representative (LVER) at these centers, go to: http://www.taonline.com/VetReps/SearchVetRep.asp.
- *Patriot Express* is a small-business loan program (run by the U.S. Small Business Administration) for veterans: http://www.sba.gov/content/express-programs.
- *RecruitMilitary* works with employers to help them recruit veterans. Their Web site lists job openings at these companies: http://www.recruitmilitary.com.
- *The Transition Assistance Program* is organized by the Departments of Labor and Defense, and will walk you through all of the transition steps into civilian employment. It also has other links, guides, and manuals: The TurboTAP is at http://www.turbotap.org/, and the Centers for Transitioning Military Web site is at http://www.taonline.com/.
- *Verification of Military Experience and Training Web Site*: This is the online version of Form 2586, which will access documentation of your military experience to show to potential employers. Military credentials are needed to access it: http://www.dmdc.osd.mil/appj/vmet.
- *Veteran Success*—the Department of Veterans' Affairs Web site for transitioning into the private sector: http://www.vetsuccess.gov/.
- *What Color Is Your Parachute?* Web site to accompany the material in the book: http://www.jobhuntersbible.com/.

Resources for Female Service Members

- *The Women Warriors Project Blog*: http://womenwarriorsproject.posterous.com/.
- *Blog about stay-at-home dads and military husbands*: http://mylifeasamilitaryspouse.blogspot.com/2010/05/military-husbands-stay-at-home-dads.html.

Books and Publications

Books for Service Members

Cantrell, B. C., and C. Dean. *Down Range to Iraq and Back*. Seattle, WA: WordSmith Books, 2005.

Grossman, D. *On Combat: The Psychology and Physiology of Deadly Conflict in War and in Peace*. Milstadt, IL: *Warrior Science Publications*, 2004.

———. *On Killing: The Psychological Cost of Learning to Kill in War and Society.* New York: Back Bay Books, 1995.

Hoge, C. *Once a Warrior, Always a Warrior: Navigating the Transition from Combat to Home— Including Combat Stress, PTSD, and mTBI.* Guilford, CT: Globe Pequot Press, 2010.

Lewis, L., K. Kelly, and J. G. Allen. *Restoring Hope and Trust: An Illustrated Guide to Mastering Trauma.* Baltimore, MD: The Sidran Press, 2004.

Moore, B. A., and C. H. Kennedy. *Wheels Down: Adjusting to Life after Deployment.* Washington, DC: American Psychological Association, 2010.

Shay, J. *Achilles in Vietnam: Combat Trauma and the Undoing of Character.* New York: Simon & Schuster, 1995.

Books for Family Members

Armstrong, K., S. Best, and P. Domenici. *Courage After Fire: Coping Strategies for Troops Returning from Iraq and Afghanistan and Their Families.* Berkeley, CA: Ulysses Press, 2006.

Hay, M. T., L. H. Rorrer, J. R. Rivera, R. Krannich, and C. Krannich. *Military Transition to Civilian Success: The Complete Guide for Veterans and Their Families.* Manassas Park, VA: Impact Publications, 2006.

Henderson, K. *While They're at War: The True Story of American Families on the Homefront.* Boston, MA: Mariner Books, 2006.

Howell, T. *The Military Advantage: The Military.com Guide to Military and Veterans' Benefits.* Annapolis, MD: Naval Institute Press, 2012. (Updated every year.)

Matsakis, A. *Back from the Front: Combat Trauma, Love, and the Family.* Baltimore, MD: The Sidran Press, 2007.

The National Military Family Association. *Finding Common Ground: A Toolkit for Communities Supporting Military Families*: http://www.militaryfamily.org/publications/community-toolkit.

Slone, L., and M. Friedman. *After the War Zone: A Practical Guide For Returning Troop and Their Families.* Cambridge, MA: Da Capo Press, 2008.

Washington Family Policy. *Welcome Home: How to Make a Difference in the Lives of Returning War Zone Veterans* (includes Dr. James Munroe's "Eight Battlefield Skills that Make Life in the Civilian World Challenging"): http://www.fpc.wa.gov/publications/welcomehome.pdf.

Books for Families of Injured Service Members

Ainspan, N. D., and W. E. Penk, eds. *Returning Wars' Wounded, Injured, and Ill: A Reference Handbook.* Greenwood, CT: Praeger Security, Inc., 2008.

Cassidy, J. W., and L. Woodruff. *Mindstorms: Living with Traumatic Brain Injury.* Cambridge, MA: Da Capo Press, 2009.

Driscoll, P., and C. Strauss. *Hidden Battles on Unseen Fronts: Stories of American Soldiers with Traumatic Brain Injury and PTSD.* Drexel Hill, PA: Casemate, 2009.

Freeman, S. M., B. A. Moore, and A. Freeman, eds. *Living and Surviving in Harm's Way: A Psychological Treatment Handbook for Pre- and Post-Deployment.* New York: Routledge, 2009.

Marrella, D. *Everything about ME for Military Personnel and Families: A Guide to My Future Caregivers.* Washington, DC: DC Press, LLC, 2011.

Matsakis, A. *Back from the Front: Combat Trauma, Love, and the Family.* Baltimore, MD: The Sidran Press, 2007.

Orange, C. *Shock Waves: A Practical Guide to Living with a Loved One's PTSD.* Center City, MN: Hazeldon, Inc., 2010.

Philpott, D., J. Hill, and B. McCaffrey. *The Wounded Warrior Handbook: A Resource Guide for Returning Veterans.* Lanham, MD: Scarecrow Press, 2009.

The RAND Corporation. *Post-Deployment Stress: What Families Should Know, What Families Can Do.* (2008) Available at: http://rand.org/pubs/corporate_pubs/CP535-2008-03 .pdf.

Seahorn, J. J., and E. A. Seahorn. *Tears of a Warrior: A Family's Story of Combat and Living with PTSD.* Fort Collins, CO: Team Pursuits, Inc., 2008.

Wizelman, L. *When the War Never Ends: The Voices of Military Members with PTSD and Their Families.* Lanham, MD: Rowman & Littlefield Publishers, Inc., 2011.

Books for Your Children

BOOKS FOR YOUNG CHILDREN

Andrews, B. *I Miss You: A Military Kid's Book about Deployment.* Amherst, NY: Prometheus Books, 2007. (For elementary-school kids whose parent is deployed.)

Brisson, P. *Sometimes We Were Brave.* Honesdale, PA: Boyds Mills Press, 2010. (For elementary-school kids whose parent is deployed.)

Brown, M. W. *The Fathers Are Coming Home.* New York: Margaret K. McElderry Books, 2010. (For kids ages six to twelve, about homecoming.)

Bunting, E. *My Red Balloon.* Honesdale, PA: Boyds Mills Press, 2005. (For kids ages four to eight, this is a picture book focused on homecoming.)

Ehrmantraut, B. *Night Catch.* Aberdeen, SD: Bubble Gum Press, 2005. (For kids ages four to eight about dealing with parental separation.)

Ferguson-Cohen, M. *Daddy, You're My Hero!* and *Mommy, You're My Hero!* New York: Little Redhaired Girl Publishing, Inc., 2005. (For kids ages four to eight.)

Jensen-Fritz, S., P. Jones-Johnson, and T. L. Zitzow. *You and Your Military Hero: Building Positive Thinking Skills during Your Hero's Deployment.* Minneapolis, MN: Beaver's Pond Press, 2009. (For kids ages five to twelve, focusing on parental deployment.)

Lowry, L. *Crow Call.* New York: Scholastic Press, 2009. (For kids ages nine to fourteen, about homecoming and reconnecting.)

Madison, A. *100 Days and 99 Nights.* New York: Little, Brown Books for Young Readers, 2008. (For kids ages eight to twelve, about parental deployment.)

Sportelli-Rehak, A. *Uncle Sam's Kids: When Duty Calls.* Island Heights, NJ: Abidenme Books Publishing, 2003. (For kids ages five to eleven.)

BOOKS FOR TEENAGERS

Sherman, M. D., and D. M. Sherman. *Finding My Way: A Teen's Guide to Living with a Parent Who Has Experienced Trauma.* Edina, MN: Seeds of Hope Books, 2009.

———. *I'm Not Alone: A Teen's Guide to Living with a Parent Who Has a Mental Illness.* Edina, MN: Beaver's Pond Press, Inc., 2006.

———. *My Story: Blogs by Four Military Teens.* Edina, MN: Seeds of Hope Books, 2009. (For kids ages ten to eighteen.)

Contributors

Chapter 1

Lt. Col. David Cabrera, PhD, professor of Family Medicine and director of Social Work, Uniformed Services University of Health Sciences, Bethesda, MD.

Charles Figley, PhD, Paul Henry Kurzweg, MD, Distinguished Chair in Disaster Mental Health and professor and associate dean for research at Tulane University and Graduate School of Social Work, New Orleans, LA.

Lt. Col. Jeffrey Yarvis, PhD, LCSW, DCSW, deputy commander for Behavioral Health, Fort Belvoir Community Hospital, Fairfax, VA.

Col. Anthony Cox, LCSW, DCSW, deputy chief, Behavioral Health Division, U.S. Army Medical Command, Fort Sam Houston, TX.

Chapter 2

Shirley M. Glynn, PhD, clinical research psychologist, VA Greater Los Angeles Healthcare System at West Los Angeles, and research psychologist at the Semel Institute of Neuroscience and Human Behavior at University of California–Los Angeles.

Chapter 3

Michelle D. Sherman, PhD, director of the Family Mental Health Program, Oklahoma City VA; affiliate research investigator, South Central Mental Illness Research, Education, and Clinical Center (MIRECC); and clinical professor, University of Oklahoma Health Sciences Center.

Col. Alan Doerman, PsyD, ABPP, USAF (Ret.), Family Mental Health Program, Oklahoma City VA; and clinical professor, University of Oklahoma Health Sciences Center.

Col. James A. Martin, PhD, BCD, USA (Ret.), professor of Social Work and Social Research, Bryn Mawr College, Bryn Mawr, PA.

Chapter 4

Charles E. Drebing, PhD, manager, Mental Health Service Line, Edith Nourse Rogers Memorial VA Medical Center, Bedford, MA.

Chapter 5

Kristy Straits-Troster, PhD, ABPP, Clinical Health Psychologist, Department of Veterans Affairs, Phoenix VA Health Care System, Phoenix, AZ; and Department of Psychiatry and Behavioral Sciences, Duke University.

Monica Mann-Wrobel, PhD, Department of Veterans Affairs Mid-Atlantic Network Mental Illness Research, Education, and Clinical Center (MIRECC), Durham, NC.

Lt. Cdr. Erin M. Simmons, PhD, MSC/USN, Naval Health Clinic, Cherry Point, NC.

Chapter 6

Maj. C. Alan Hopewell, PhD, USA (Ret.), psychologist, Psychiatric Consultants of Fort Worth, TX.

Denise Horton, PhD, psychologist, alcohol/drug control officer, and employee assistance professional, Army Support Activity Dix, United States Army, Fort Dix, NJ.

Chapter 7

Col. Stephen V. Bowles, PhD, MSW, ABPP, associate professor of Behavioral Science, Industrial College of the Armed Forces, National Defense University, Washington, DC; and Uniformed Services University of the Health Sciences, Department of Medical and Clinical Psychology, Bethesda, MD.

Liz Davenport Pollock, PhD, LCMFT, Senior Family Fitness Scientist, Human Performance Resource Center, Department of Military and Emergency Medicine, Uniformed Services University of the Health Sciences, Bethesda, MD.

Colanda Cato, PhD, Licensed Clinical Psychologist, Deputy Chief, Resilience and Prevention Directorate, Defense Centers of Excellence for Psychological Health and Traumatic Brain Injury, Arlington, VA.

Monique Moore, PhD, psychologist, Resilience and Prevention Directorate, Defense Centers of Excellence for Psychological Health and Traumatic Brain Injury, Silver Spring, MD.

Shelley M. MacDermid Wadsworth, director, Military Family Research Institute at Purdue University, West Lafayette, IN.

Vasiliki Anagnostopoulos, research assistant, Department of Medical and Clinical Psychology, Uniformed Services University of the Health Sciences, Bethesda, MD; and Department of Psychology, American University, Washington, DC.

Kathleen K. Sun, Deloitte Consulting LLP, Washington, DC.

Mary Campise, Department of Defense, Office of the Assistant Secretary of Defense, Military Community and Family Policy's Family Advocacy Program, Washington, DC.

Col. William P. Mueller, MD, DABFM, MAJCOM, pilot-physician, Air Education and Training Command, United States Air Force.

HM1 (FMF) Daniel Freeland, USN, Brigade Adjutant, Uniformed Services University of the Health Sciences, Bethesda, MD.

Capt. Malvis Tarney, Uniformed Services University of the Health Sciences, Brigade, Bethesda, MD.

Maj. Katalin Brogdon, United States Marine Corps Headquarters, Combat and Operational Stress Control, Quantico, VA.

Maj. John Brogdon, United States Marine Corps, Operational Test and Evaluation Activity, Quantico, VA.

HMC (FMF/CAC) Alexis A. Alvarado, USN, enlisted advisor, General Education Office, Uniformed Services University of the Health Sciences, Brigade, Bethesda, MD.

Lt. Col. Mark J. Bates, PhD, USAF (Ret.), director of Resilience and Prevention Directorate, Defense Centers of Excellence for Psychological Health and Traumatic Brain Injury, Silver Spring, MD.

Chapter 8

Michael Russell, PhD, Licensed Clinical Neuropsychologist and Brain Injury Specialist, Headquarters, U.S. Army Medical Command (MEDCOM), San Antonio, TX.

Chapter 9

David S. Greenawalt, PhD, OAA Advanced Fellow in Mental Health Research and Treatment, Veterans Integrated Service Network (VISN) 17 Center of Excellence for Research on Returning War Veterans, Arlington, TX; and assistant professor, research, Texas A&M Health Science Center, College of Medicine, College Station, TX.

Sandra B. Morissette, PhD, Assessment Core Leader, Veterans Affairs VISN 17 Center of Excellence for Research on Returning War Veterans, Waco, TX, and associate professor, Texas A&M Health Science Center, College of Medicine, College Station, TX.

Suzy Bird Gulliver, PhD, director, Veterans Affairs VISN 17 Center of Excellence for Research on Returning War Veterans, Waco, TX; and professor, Texas A&M Health Science Center, College of Medicine, College Station, TX.

Chapter 10

Michelle D. Sherman, PhD, director of the Family Mental Health Program, Oklahoma City VA; affiliate research investigator, South Central Mental Illness Research, Education, and Clinical Center (MIRECC); and clinical professor, University of Oklahoma Health Sciences Center.

Jeffrey E. Barnett, PsyD, ABPP, professor, Department of Psychology, Loyola University Maryland.

Chapter 11

Rebecca Tews, PhD, licensed clinical psychologist, and professor of Clinical Psychology at The Illinois School of Professional Psychology at Argosy University, Schaumburg, IL.

Alaina Grover, LPC, doctoral candidate, The Illinois School of Professional Psychology at Argosy University, Schaumburg, IL.

Carol Getkin, TLLP, doctoral candidate, The Illinois School of Professional Psychology at Argosy University, Schaumburg, IL.

Desiree King, LPC, doctoral candidate, The Illinois School of Professional Psychology at Argosy University, Schaumburg, IL.

Angela Schroedle, doctoral candidate, The Illinois School of Professional Psychology at Argosy University, Schaumburg, IL.

Chapter 12 (listed alphabetically)

Jeffrey E. Barnett, PsyD, ABPP, professor, Department of Psychology, Loyola University, MD.

Carol Getkin, TLLP, doctoral candidate, The Illinois School of Professional Psychology at Argosy University, Schaumburg, IL.

Alaina Grover, LPC, doctoral candidate, The Illinois School of Professional Psychology at Argosy University, Schaumburg, IL.

Desiree King, LPC, doctoral candidate, The Illinois School of Professional Psychology at Argosy University, Schaumburg, IL.

Angela Schroedle, doctoral candidate, The Illinois School of Professional Psychology at Argosy University, Schaumburg, IL.

Michelle D. Sherman, PhD, director, Family Mental Health Program, Oklahoma City VA, and professor, University of Oklahoma Health Sciences Center.

Rebecca Tews, PhD, licensed clinical psychologist, and professor of Clinical Psychology at The Illinois School of Professional Psychology at Argosy University, Schaumburg, IL.

Chapter 13

Nathan D. Ainspan, PhD, Senior Personnel Psychologist, United States Army, Assistant G-1 for Civilian Personnel, Fairfax, VA.

Walter E. Penk, PhD, ABPP, consultant to the Department of Veterans' Affairs VISN 17 Center of Excellence for Research on Returning War Veterans, and professor in Psychiatry and Behavioral Sciences, Texas A&M Health Sciences Center College of Medicine, College Station, TX.

Alexa Smith-Osborne, PhD, assistant professor, School of Social Work, University of Texas at Arlington; and principal investigator, The Student Veteran Project, Arlington, TX.

Chapter 14

Sharon Wills, PhD, team leader and senior psychologist, Post-Traumatic Stress Disorder Clinical Team, Austin VA Outpatient Clinic, Austin, Texas; and assistant professor, Texas A&M Health Sciences Center School of Medicine, College Station, TX.

Matthew King, Collider Media Account Executive and AWV2(AW/NAC), U.S. Navy.

Chapter 15

Lt. Col. Lisa Teegarden, PsyD, clinical psychologist, Head Quarters, United States Special Operations Command, MacDill Air Force Base, FL.

Chapter 16

Jaine Darwin, PsyD, ABPP, co-director and co-founder of SOFAR: Strategic Outreach to Families of All Reservists, Cambridge, MA.

Chapter 17

Jaine Darwin, PsyD, ABPP, co-director and co-founder of SOFAR: Strategic Outreach to Families of All Reservists, Cambridge, MA.

Index

addictions: enabling behaviors, 118, 120, 128; as illness, 119–120; interventions, 119–127; lapses and relapses, 127–128; resources about, 268; suicide and, 112–113; weapons and, 27, 113

aggression, 55–56, 89

Air Force, U.S.: female service members, 230; FOCUS interventions, 55; military operations other than war, 67–68; size of and force strength, 65

Al-Anon, 119–120, 121, 122–123, 128, 268

alcohol use and abuse: addictions, resources about, 268; binge drinking, 114, 124; brain injury and, 113, 128, 142; controlled drinking, 124; detachment coping strategy, 119–120; genetics and family backgrounds and, 113–114, 119; impact of on families, 118–119, 128; interventions, 119–127; lapses and relapses, 127–128; normal drinking, 114; post-deployment period, 26, 252; PTSD and, 112, 113, 128, 142; risk factors, 113–114, 128; screening for alcohol problems, 114–115; stress and, 89, 112; suicide and, 101, 112–113; talking with loved ones about, 124–127; weapons and, 113; when to intervene, 114

Alcohol Use Disorders Identification Test—Consumption (AUDIT-C), 114–115

Alcoholics Anonymous (AA), 119, 120, 122–123, 127, 268

ambiguous loss, 145, 153–158

ambivalence, normalization of, 156–157

Americans with Disabilities Act, 203, 207, 210

amputations, 8, 140

anger: depression and, 56; grief stage, 151–152; impact of, 56; Limbic System and, 222; management strategies, 56–57; PTSD and, 56; range of, 55–56; usefulness of, 55; weapons and, 56

Army, U.S.: Comprehensive Soldier Fitness program, 2, 75, 91; deployment and resources for families, 74; female service members, 230; FOCUS interventions, 55; military operations other than war, 67–68; resilience training program, 250; size of and force strength, 65

Army Community Service Centers, 74

Ask, Care, Escort (ACE) program, 103–104, 105, 111

attachment, revising, 157

Back on Track program, 62

balance, work-life, 86

Battlemind Training, 55

benefits, xxi–xxiii, 242–243, 259. See also GI Bill education benefits

blended families, 2, 253, 256

Blue Star Mothers and Blue Star Fathers, 254

boyfriends and girlfriends, 254

brain injury/traumatic brain injury (TBI): alcohol and substance use and abuse

23–24; preparations for, 249; resources for successful, 27–28, 54; stress and, 22–23, 112

homes and home ownership, 30, 34, 35

hope and hopefulness, 157–158

hostility, 56

hotline (Veterans Crisis Line), 111, 192, 260

hypervigilance and hyperarousal: cognitive reframing strategy for perceptions, 95; combat stress reactions, 221–225; during deployments, 54; PTSD and, 56, 144, 159; STARTLE responses, 223–225

identity, identity diffusion, and identity consolidation, 215

infants and toddlers, tips for helping, 166–170

infidelity and suspicion, 219, 226, 235, 248

injured and wounded service members: ambiguous loss, 153–158; care providers for, family and friends as, 37–51; changes associated with, support for, 8; children affected by, 139–140; children of, tips for helping, 179–180; children's reactions to, 85, 139, 147–149; communication and notification of families, 5–6; concerns of families about, xix–xx; education programs for, 198–199, 203–204, 209–211; employment of, 203–209; family response to, 139; female service members, 239–240; financial problems, 142; health care visits for, preparations for, 150; homecomings and reunions, 149; impact of injuries on families, xiv–xv, 7–8, 143–149; independence of, 43–44, 50; marriages, effects of injuries on, 142–143; number of, 140; obligation to provide care and support for, 38, 51; physical limitations, 143; reintegration of, 139; relocating and continuity of care, 88; remaining in uniform, options for, xiv; resilience and, 87–91; resources for families, 263–264, 270–271; risk factors that could inten-

sify injuries, 141–143; stress and, 87–88; substance use and abuse, 112, 113, 128, 142; support systems, 143, 145–146, 147, 148; symptoms and behavioral changes, 47, 48, 49, 50, 88, 89–90, 143–144; types of, 143; types of injuries, 140. *See also* brain injury/traumatic brain injury (TBI); post-traumatic stress disorder (PTSD)

instrumental support, 23

insurance: beneficiaries of, 253, 254, 256; health insurance, 30, 87, 195, 243, 249, 255, 260; life insurance, 87; TRICARE, 30, 243, 249, 255, 260

internet and Web pages: resources for families, 259–269; scams, caution about, 259–260

intimacy and sex: barriers to intimacy, 220–228; combat and, 214; combat stress reactions and, 221–226; counseling and resources, 228; emotional intimacy, 214, 215; identity, identity diffusion, identity consolidation, and, 215, 216, 217–218; impact of war zone deployment on, 218–220; pleasure and brain chemistry, 222; pornography and, 226–227; prescription drugs and painkillers and, 227; redevelopment of postdeployment, 83; sexual intimacy, 214; trauma and impact on spouse, 217

isolation: avoidance of emotional experiences, 58; cognitive reframing strategy for perceptions, 94; injuries of service member and, 146–147, 156–157; moves and relocations and, 8; stress, coping strategies for, 81; stress response/stress injury, 88–89

Job Accommodation Network (JAN), 205, 207, 210, 296

Johnson Institute Intervention Approach, 121–122

leave, 247–248

legal services: custody and visitation arrangements, 256; guardians for chil-

vice members, 239; morale and, 108; National Guard and Reserve service members, 66–67, 242, 252, 257; organizational culture and, 66–67; prevalence and frequency of, 66; reasons for, 65–66; resources for families, 73–75, 76; TBIs and, 69–70

nagging, 186
Nar-Anon, 119–120, 128, 268
Narcotics Anonymous (NA), 120, 122–123, 127, 268
National Guard: assistance programs, access to, 73; benefits available to, 242–243; challenges for families of, 242–252; changes during deployments, 249–252; counseling support, 251; deployments and multiple deployments, 66–67, 242, 252, 257; family assistance programs, 74, 75; health insurance and health care, 243, 249, 255; number deployed to Afghanistan and Iraq, 242; pre-deployment, 243–245; redeployment, 248–250; resilience of families, 248
Navy, U.S.: female service members, 230; FOCUS interventions, 55; size of and force strength, 65; suicide prevention strategies, 107
near-death experiences, 219
networking, 193–194, 206–207
New Dawn operations, 228
numb feelings and emotional numbness, 16, 58, 94

operations security (OPSEC) and confidentiality, 221, 249
optimism, 3, 7, 32, 75

parents and siblings of service members, 254–255
"partner-aware" family structure, 19, 21
peer support groups, 145–146, 161, 211
perfection, 54
Persian Gulf War, 6
play therapy, 8

pornography, 226–227
positive attitudes and perspectives, 19, 20
post-deployment period: adjustments during, 17–18, 24–28, 72, 83, 85, 131, 220–221, 227–228, 236–238, 250–252; alcohol and substance use and abuse, 26, 252; children, tips for helping during, 176–178; communication during, 27, 54; conflict and irritability, 26, 27; depression and, 59; emotions and, 54–59, 72; female service members, 236–239; immediate post-deployment period, 22–28; preparations for, 131; resources for, 27–28; sleep patterns and difficulties, 25, 26, 59, 250; spouses, self-care and psychological wellness of, 134–136; stress, 27; time management, 25–26; weapons, possession of during, 27. *See also* homecomings and reunions
post-traumatic stress disorder (PTSD): alcohol and substance use and abuse and, 112, 113, 128, 142; ambiguous loss, 153–158; anger and, 56; assistance programs and self-help aids, 61, 75–76; brain injuries and, 70; caregivers and behavioral assistance, 40; caregiving for relative with, 47–48; children used in combat situations and, 72; cognitive reframing strategy, 93, 94; cost of care for, 140; counseling support for, 35–36, 40, 228; education and, 199, 210; employment and, 186, 191, 203; female service members, 238, 239; impact of injuries on families, 8; impact of on partners and families, 47; marriages and, 73; mindfulness meditation and, 61; prescription drug and painkiller abuse risks, 113; prevalence of, 47, 140, 144; resilience and, 87–91; resources for families, 263–264; sexual assault reaction, 235; sleep patterns and difficulties and, 59, 158–159; strategies and therapies to assist, 8; stress and, 87–88; support groups for people with, 48; symptoms of, 47, 48, 56, 89, 144; treat-

The Naval Institute Press is the book-publishing arm of the U.S. Naval Institute, a private, nonprofit, membership society for sea service professionals and others who share an interest in naval and maritime affairs. Established in 1873 at the U.S. Naval Academy in Annapolis, Maryland, where its offices remain today, the Naval Institute has members worldwide.

Members of the Naval Institute support the education programs of the society and receive the influential monthly magazine *Proceedings* or the colorful bimonthly magazine *Naval History* and discounts on fine nautical prints and on ship and aircraft photos. They also have access to the transcripts of the Institute's Oral History Program and get discounted admission to any of the Institute-sponsored seminars offered around the country.

The Naval Institute's book-publishing program, begun in 1898 with basic guides to naval practices, has broadened its scope to include books of more general interest. Now the Naval Institute Press publishes about seventy titles each year, ranging from how-to books on boating and navigation to battle histories, biographies, ship and aircraft guides, and novels. Institute members receive significant discounts on the Press's more than eight hundred books in print.

Full-time students are eligible for special half-price membership rates. Life memberships are also available.

For a free catalog describing Naval Institute Press books currently available, and for further information about joining the U.S. Naval Institute, please write to:

Member Services
U.S. Naval Institute
291 Wood Road
Annapolis, MD 21402-5034
Telephone: (800) 233-8764
Fax: (410) 571-1703
Web address: www.usni.org